TIME
LIFE ®
BOOKS

Other Publications:

*This volume is one of a series that explains and demonstrates
how to prepare various types of food, and that offers in each
book an international anthology of great recipes.*

Vegetables

BY
THE EDITORS OF TIME-LIFE BOOKS

Cover: Bundled together with a string for easy handling, asparagus stalks are lifted from the pot after 8 minutes of vigorous boiling. The stalks have been peeled *(page 21)* to ensure that they cook to tenderness in the same amount of time as their more fragile tips.

Time-Life Books Inc.
is a wholly owned subsidiary of
TIME INCORPORATED

Founder: Henry R. Luce 1898-1967

Editor-in-Chief: Henry Anatole Grunwald
President: J. Richard Munro
Chairman of the Board: Ralph P. Davidson
Executive Vice President: Clifford J. Grum
Chairman, Executive Committee: James R. Shepley
Editorial Director: Ralph Graves
Group Vice President, Books: Joan D. Manley
Vice Chairman: Arthur Temple

TIME-LIFE BOOKS INC.

Managing Editor: Jerry Korn. *Text Director:* George Constable. *Board of Editors:* Dale M. Brown, George G. Daniels, Thomas H. Flaherty Jr., Martin Mann, Philip W. Payne, Gerry Schremp, Gerald Simons. *Planning Director:* Edward Brash. *Art Director:* Tom Suzuki; *Assistant:* Arnold C. Holeywell. *Director of Administration:* David L. Harrison. *Director of Operations:* Gennaro C. Esposito. *Director of Research:* Carolyn L. Sackett; *Assistant:* Phyllis K. Wise. *Director of Photography:* Dolores A. Littles. *Production Director:* Feliciano Madrid; *Assistants:* Peter A. Inchauteguiz, Karen A. Meyerson. *Copy Processing:* Gordon E. Buck. *Quality Control Director:* Robert L. Young; *Assistant:* James J. Cox; *Associates:* Daniel J. McSweeney, Michael G. Wight. *Art Coordinator:* Anne B. Landry. *Copy Room Director:* Susan B. Galloway; *Assistants:* Celia Beattie, Ricki Tarlow

Chairman: John D. McSweeney. *President:* Carl G. Jaeger. *Executive Vice Presidents:* John Steven Maxwell, David J. Walsh. *Vice Presidents:* George Artandi, Stephen L. Bair, Peter G. Barnes, Nicholas Benton, John L. Canova, Beatrice T. Dobie, Carol Flaumenhaft, James L. Mercer, Herbert Sorkin, Paul R. Stewart

THE GOOD COOK

The original version of this book was created in London for Time-Life International (Nederland) B.V.
European Editor: Kit van Tulleken; *Design Director:* Louis Klein; *Photography Director:* Pamela Marke; *Planning Director:* Alan Lothian; *Chief of Research:* Vanessa Kramer; *Chief Sub-Editor:* Ilse Gray; *Production Editor:* Ellen Brush; *Quality Control:* Douglas Whitworth

Staff for *Vegetables: Series Editor:* Windsor Chorlton; *Anthology Editor:* Liz Clasen; *Staff Writers:* Gillian Boucher, Norman Kolpas, Anthony Masters; *Researchers:* Eleanor Lines, Suad McCoy; *Sub-Editors:* Katie Eason, Jay Ferguson, Nicoletta Flessati; *Permissions Researcher:* Mary-Claire Hailey; *Design Assistant:* Martin Gregory; *Editorial Department:* Anetha Bessidone, Pat Boag, Debra Dick, Margaret Hall, Joanne Holland, Molly Sutherland, Julia West

U.S. Staff for *Vegetables: Series Editor:* Gerry Schremp; *Text Editor:* Ellen Phillips; *Designer:* Peg Schreiber; *Staff Writer:* Susan Bryan; *Chief Researcher:* Lois Gilman; *Researchers:* Christina Bowie Dove, Eleanor Kask, Robin Shuster; *Copy Coordinators:* Allan Fallow, Tonna Gibert; *Art Assistant:* Cynthia Richardson; *Picture Coordinator:* Alvin Ferrell; *Editorial Assistant:* Audrey Keir

CHIEF SERIES CONSULTANT

Richard Olney is an American who has lived and worked since 1951 in France, where he is a highly regarded authority on food and wine. A regular contributor to such influential journals as *La Revue du Vin de France* and *Cuisine et Vins de France*, he also has written numerous articles for other gastronomic magazines in France and the United States, and is the author of *The French Menu Cookbook* and the award-winning *Simple French Food*. He has directed cooking courses in France and the United States, and is a member of several distinguished gastronomic societies, including La Confrérie des Chevaliers du Tastevin, La Commanderie du Bontemps de Médoc et des Graves and Les Amitiés Gastronomiques Internationales. Working in London with the series editorial staff, he has been basically responsible for the step-by-step photographic sequences in the techniques section of this volume and has supervised the final selection of recipes submitted by other consultants. The United States edition of The Good Cook has been revised by the Editors of Time-Life Books to bring it into complete accord with American customs and usage.

CHIEF AMERICAN CONSULTANT
Carol Cutler is the author of a number of cookbooks, including the award-winning *The Six-Minute Soufflé and Other Culinary Delights*. During the 12 years she lived in France, she studied at the Cordon Bleu and the École des Trois Gourmandes, and with private chefs. She is a member of the Cercle des Gourmettes, a long-established French food society limited to just 50 members, and is also a charter member of Les Dames d'Escoffier, Washington Chapter.

PHOTOGRAPHERS
Alan Duns was born in 1943 in the north of England and studied at the Ealing School of Photography. He specializes in food, and has contributed to major British publications.
Aldo Tutino, a native of Italy, has worked in Milan, New York City and Washington, D.C. He has won awards from the New York Advertising Club.

INTERNATIONAL CONSULTANTS
GREAT BRITAIN: *Jane Grigson* has written a number of books about food and has been a cookery correspondent for the London *Observer* since 1968. *Alan Davidson* is the author of several cookbooks and the founder of Prospect Books, which specializes in scholarly publications about food and cookery.
FRANCE: *Michel Lemonnier,* the cofounder and vice president of Les Amitiés Gastronomiques Internationales, is a frequent lecturer on wine and vineyards. GERMANY: *Jochen Kuchenbecker* trained as a chef, but worked for 10 years as a food photographer in several European countries before opening his own restaurant in Hamburg. *Anne Brakemeier* is the co-author of a number of cookbooks. ITALY: *Massimo Alberini* is a well-known food writer and journalist, with a particular interest in culinary history. His many books include *Storia del Pranzo all'Italiana, 4000 Anni a Tavola* and *100 Ricette Storiche.* THE NETHERLANDS: *Hugh Jans* has published cookbooks and his recipes appear in several Dutch magazines. THE UNITED STATES: *François Dionot,* a graduate of L'École des Hôteliers de Lausanne in Switzerland, has worked as chief hotel general manager and restaurant manager in France and the U.S. He now conducts his own cooking school. *Shirley Sarvis,* a freelance food writer and consultant, is the author and co-author of a dozen cookbooks. *José Wilson* wrote many books on food and interior decoration.

Correspondents: Elisabeth Kraemer (Bonn); Margot Hapgood, Dorothy Bacon, Lesley Coleman (London); Susan Jonas, Lucy T. Voulgaris (New York); Maria Vincenza Aloisi, Josephine du Brusle (Paris); Ann Natanson (Rome).
Valuable assistance was also provided by: Jeanne Buys (Amsterdam); Nina Lindley (Buenos Aires); Hans-Heinrich Wellmann, Gertraud Bellon (Hamburg); Judy Aspinall, Karin B. Pearce (London); Diane Asselin (Los Angeles); Bona Schmid, Maria Teresa Marenco (Milan); Carolyn T. Chubet, Miriam Hsia, Christina Lieberman (New York); Michèle le Baube (Paris); Mimi Murphy (Rome). The editors are indebted to Juliana Goldberg, Margaret C. MacDonald, and Patricia McNees, writers, for their help with this book.

For information about any Time-Life book, please write:
Reader Information, Time-Life Books
541 North Fairbanks Court, Chicago, Illinois 60611

Library of Congress CIP data, page 176.

CONTENTS

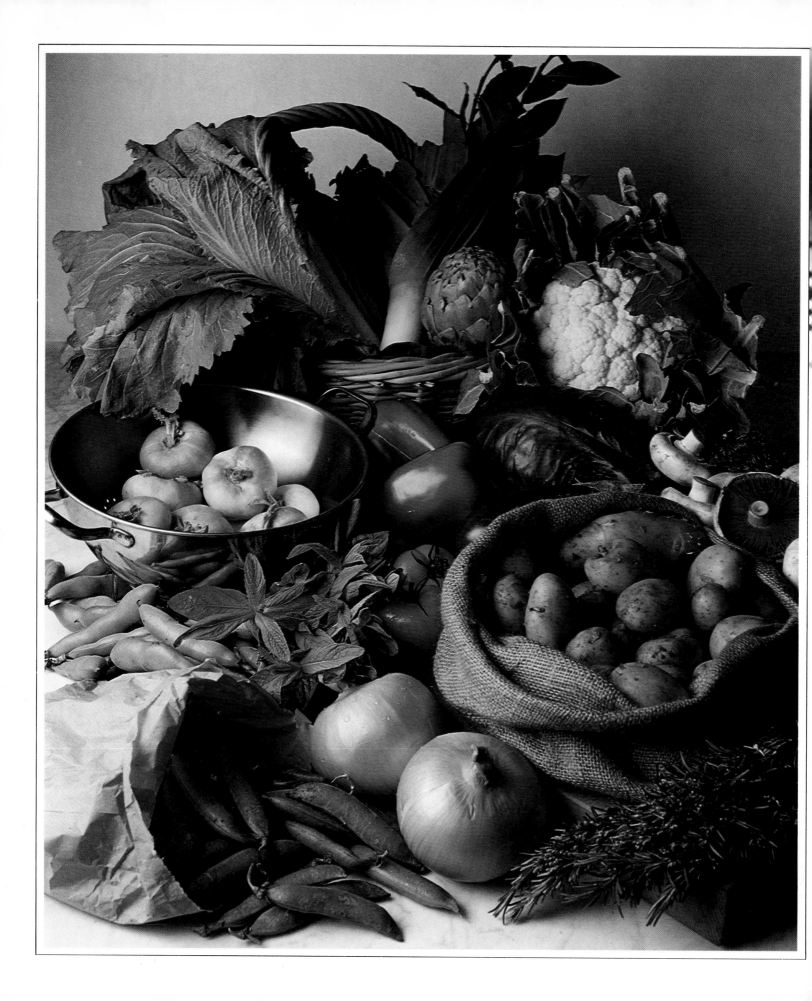

The Bounty of Fields and Gardens

This is a book of discovery, a guide to the wonderfully rich—yet too frequently neglected—world of vegetable cookery. Of all foods, the produce of fields and gardens contributes by far the most varied and abundant source of nourishment. In Asian and Middle Eastern cooking, vegetables are prized as highly as meats, and treated as carefully. In most of the Western world, however, they are often literally pushed aside and served as mere accompaniments to meat. On far too many tables, vegetables appear as boiled potatoes and overboiled greens—sodden offerings that hold little appeal for the palate.

More often than not, such uninspired treatment stems from lack of knowledge, both of the different vegetables themselves and of the many cooking methods that can be applied to them. How to deal with unfamiliar vegetables, therefore, is one aspect of this book; how to prepare all vegetables in exciting and imaginative ways is another. Step-by-step photographs in the chapters that follow teach these lessons in dozens of demonstrations: eggplant, tomatoes, peppers and zucchini are transformed into a fragrant *ratatouille;* potatoes become a rich gratin; broccoli, cauliflower, mushrooms and artichoke bottoms are coated with batter and deep fried to make crisp fritters.

Taming and tailoring nature

More than any other food, vegetables challenge cooks with their prodigal variety—a variety that reflects many centuries of experimentation with plant species. Prehistoric farmers domesticated edible wild plants as early as 6000 B.C., and during the next several millennia, great agriculture-based civilizations developed and spread throughout the ancient world. Tomb paintings from early Egyptian dynasties are testimony that vegetable farming was well established in Egypt by 3000 B.C. When Rome reached its pinnacle of glory three millennia later, cabbage, leeks and lettuce from Asia Minor were growing in the city's gardens, as were cucumbers from India, peas from central Asia and such plants of Mediterranean origin as artichokes, asparagus, beets, celery, garlic, parsnips and turnips. The oldest surviving European cookbook, attributed to the Roman merchant Marcus Gavias Apicius, devotes great attention to vegetables. (The cookbook probably was the first to offer the unfortunate advice that green vegetables be boiled with baking soda; the soda fixes their color, but it also gives them a brackish taste, a fact Apicius—and his successors—did not record.)

The cornucopia now open to the vegetable cook has been at least partly produced as a side effect of war and conquest. Apicius' colonizing countrymen carried seeds and roots from Rome to northern Europe, civilizing with the plowshare as well as the broadsword. In the Middle Ages, the Moorish occupation of Spain and the Crusades to the Holy Land introduced to Europe such Middle Eastern vegetables as eggplant and spinach.

The vegetable larder we know today was not completely stocked, however, until Europeans reached the New World in the 15th and 16th Centuries. Like their Old World counterparts, Indian farmers had been cultivating native plants for thousands of years. The conquering Spanish brought home from the Americas the seeds and roots of green beans, lima beans, peppers, tomatoes, potatoes and that greatest of the Indian staples, corn. Several of these vegetables were only slowly accepted (for example, the tomato, being a fruit from plants of the deadly nightshade family, was considered poisonous); yet it is hard to imagine modern cookery without them.

By Columbus' time generations of careful breeding by selection had greatly changed these vegetables from their wildling ancestors. By choosing the seeds of the best plants for reproduction, the Indians had developed in their crops such useful characteristics as large size and hardiness. When the Indians began to cultivate corn around 5000 B.C., the cobs were less than 1 inch [2½ cm.] long. By the time the Europeans arrived, careful breeding had yielded cobs that approached modern dimensions.

European farmers knew the technique well and already had employed selection to create many new varieties of vegetables, as well as bigger and better versions of existing plants. In some cases, a single plant had given rise to several varieties that now seem scarcely related at all. Starting with the scrawny wild cabbage, the Romans developed tender broccoli; centuries later in northern Europe, farmers used the very same plant to create today's cold-tolerant, tightly headed white and green cabbages, as well as Brussels sprouts and kohlrabi.

Despite such achievements, early plant breeding and improvement was a haphazard affair that left much to chance and to the mysterious green thumbs of a skillful few. In the 20th Century, however, plant genetics has replaced the traditional hit-and-miss methods with sophisticated breeding systems that give quick, reliable results. In turn, the geneticists' creation of disease-resistant, high-yielding plants has helped make American vegetable farming into an industry whose output would have been unimaginable not too many decades ago.

From farm to market

Only a small proportion of today's vegetable harvest is supplied by the small family farms so dear to American tradition. Vegetables are grown in every state of the union and every province of Canada, of course, and on small farms as well as large ones. But three quarters of the vegetables in American markets come from the states where climate and labor costs make large-scale farming profitable: California (which produces almost half of the United States vegetable crop), Florida and Texas. In these states, farming is big business indeed. Vegetable growing/shipping companies control huge amounts of farmland—as much as 10,000 acres, in a few cases. The companies also buy crops from independent farmers, and they often own packing, grading and storage facilities for the vegetables. Total annual sales by any one of these giants may exceed $40 million a year.

Inevitably, farming and marketing operations like these require varieties of vegetables developed less for flavor than for the uniform size and sturdy structure that make mechanization and long-distance shipping possible. To ensure a maximum yield, the land is intensively cultivated—one crop is scarcely out of the ground before another is planted—and almost every part of the farming process, from plowing to harvesting, is aided by machine. The highly mechanized, multiple-crop system means that California can harvest as many as five crops of potatoes—1.5 billion pounds—each year. Other vegetables are grown on a similar scale and they are harvested all year round.

After harvest, some vegetables—potatoes and onions, for example—are cured by chilling or drying so that they can be stored for several months. Most other vegetables, however, must be moved quickly to market to minimize deterioration. Just after they leave the field, many vegetables are put in a bath of cold water to reduce their temperatures; asparagus, for example, is reduced from 85° F. [30° C.] to 33° F. [0° C.]. Cooling the vegetables slows down their life processes, in much the way an animal's breathing slows during hibernation, and helps them survive the days or weeks it takes to get them to market. Before packing, the vegetables are graded according to appearance and size. Finally, they are packed and shipped to wholesalers and food brokers in fleets of refrigerated trucks.

Large-scale, multiple-crop production ensures that most vegetables are readily available throughout the year; however, some vegetables, raised in smaller crops, may be harder to find. The annual artichoke crop, for example, amounts to only 70 million pounds, compared to the two billion pounds of cabbages sold each year, so artichokes will always be rarer than cabbages. One reason for their scarcity is that artichokes are such sensitive plants; almost all American artichokes are grown in the 18 square miles around Castroville, California, a locale with a climate perfect for them.

Sometimes tradition rather than climate determines where specialty crops are grown: mushrooms, which are raised in windowless sheds, could be farmed anywhere, but more than half of the mushrooms sold in the United States still are grown in Pennsylvania, where Quaker settlers founded the industry in the 19th Century. Most shallots, the aristocrats of the onion family, are grown in the bayou country near New Orleans, where French settlers began raising them before the American Revolution. Some vegetables that require laborious cultivation by hand are not grown commercially at all in the United States.

A case in point is Belgian endive: each plant must be kept carefully packed in sand as it grows to ensure that it stays white and smooth; almost all the Belgian endive in American markets is imported from Europe. Other imports—tomatoes and cucumbers from Mexico, for example—supplement mass-produced American vegetables during seasons of low output.

Freshness: The basis of good eating

The cook pays a price for the logistical marvels that make so many vegetables available all year round—and the cost is measured in quality as well as money. When it comes to vegetables, it is impossible to overstate the virtue of freshness. "Vegetables," wrote the 19th Century London gourmet Dr. William Kitchiner in *The Cook's Oracle,* ". . . are more tender, juicy and full of flavour just before they are quite full grown: freshness is their chief value and excellence, and I should as soon think of roasting an Animal alive—as of boiling a Vegetable after it is dead."

A vegetable remains alive for some time after harvest—a few days in the case of leaves, a few months in the case of potatoes. But the plants begin to lose nutrients and flavor the moment they leave the ground. Clearly, then, the closer you are to the farm where the vegetable has been grown, the better the vegetable will be. As Ecclesiastes reminds us, "To every thing there is a season," and it is a foolish cook who ignores the dictum. Try to buy local vegetables during their natural seasons, and purchase them at farmers' markets or roadside stands or from small greengrocers with nearby suppliers. Local vegetables will be incomparably better in flavor and quality than the ones you see wrapped in plastic at the supermarket. No clearer example can be found than the mass-produced winter tomato. Bred for hardiness, picked when green, then artificially ripened with the aid of ethylene gas, it bears little similarity to the juicy red globes picked in high summer.

Many people, disenchanted with supermarket vegetables, grow their own. A plot of land only 1,500 square feet [139.5 sq. m.] can supply more than enough summer vegetables for a family of four, and a home garden is the best possible assurance of quality: the vegetable varieties can be chosen for flavor rather than hardiness. Best of all, the vegetables can be picked at the instant they are ripe and ready for cooking.

For other people, frozen or canned vegetables are the solution to problems of seasonal quality—and a way to save preparation time. But these are stand-ins at best. Before freezing, most vegetables are blanched—parboiled briefly to stop enzyme activity that might alter flavor or cause discoloration. But blanching can damage vegetables' texture. As part of the canning process, vegetables are cooked—frequently overcooked—in their containers.

You can avoid some of these liabilities, of course, by freezing or canning vegetables yourself when they are in season. Even so, some vegetables simply cannot be preserved without damaging their texture, taste and color. The structure of vegetable fruits such as tomatoes and eggplant breaks down during freezing, resulting in an unappetizing mush. Green beans and peas change color in canning. Even with the most suitable candidates, there is still a world of difference between fresh and preserved vegetables. Although canned tomatoes provide color and flavor for stews and braises, the appearance of vine-ripened tomatoes in seasonal abundance reminds all cooks that no substitute, however useful, can compare with the real thing. By using vegetables in their season, you can make your cooking taste better and be better for you—and nature will ensure that your menus have the virtue of variety.

The pages that follow provide a complete course in vegetable cookery. The volume begins with a series of illustrated guides to different types of vegetables, from leaves and roots to artichokes and mushrooms. Besides explaining the qualities and uses of individual vegetables, these guides offer information about how to shop for, store and prepare each type. In addition, the guides show how to prepare vegetables for cooking, demonstrating techniques as simple as peeling garlic and as complex as turning artichoke bottoms. The chart on pages 34-35 summarizes the seasonal availability of each vegetable as well as appropriate cooking methods, and a guide on pages 26-28 describes the use of different herbs.

The range of vegetables discussed is immense, but it is not comprehensive. Vegetables that are rarely, if ever, cooked —radishes, for example—are omitted from the illustrated guides, as are such preserved forms of vegetables as sauerkraut. Because of the ceaseless development of varieties, you may find—or may grow yourself—a vegetable slightly different from the ones described here; nevertheless, the guides' information about its relatives will almost certainly apply.

Immediately following the guides are chapters that explain such basic methods of vegetable cookery as boiling and steaming, frying, braising and baking. These chapters also demonstrate a host of more specialized techniques, from stuffing an artichoke to creating sauces that may accompany vegetables to the table. Finally, the second half of the book offers an international anthology of vegetable recipes, chosen from the best ever published. In combination, the two halves of this volume invite you to make more of your vegetables, to bring them from the edge of the plate to the center of the meal.

This is not a vegetarian cookbook, although vegetarians will find it useful. Where meat is used, it appears as an important flavoring element, but not as the main part of the dish. If you are cooking a formal dinner, you will find many vegetable dishes here that deserve to be served as separate courses, from simple fresh green beans boiled perfectly and buttered, to more elaborate gratins that boast layers of vegetables beneath a crisp golden crust made with bread crumbs, cream or a sauce. Less traditionally, you will be able to make up a main course from several different vegetable dishes, perhaps serving a purée with a braise or a stew, or combining a pudding with a mixed sauté.

The demonstrations and the recipes in this book do not, of course, cover every possible method of cooking a vegetable or every vegetable you might encounter, but they will teach you the rules—and the reasons behind the rules—that govern the cooking of all vegetable dishes. After that, the way is clear to your own improvisation and invention.

Storehouses of Nutrition

The importance of vegetables as guardians of good health has always been recognized by folklore and primitive medicine. Early on, doctors advised patients that vegetables would help to keep a balance between the "humours" of the body, and mothers nagged children to eat up their greens long before anyone had heard of the science of nutrition.

Modern biochemists have found that in addition to supplying energy-giving carbohydrates, vegetables provide almost all of the specialized vitamins and minerals needed to keep human beings in good health. Green leaves—whether from cabbages or such leaf vegetables as spinach—are rich sources of vitamins A and C; vitamin A is essential for eyes and skin, while vitamin C is necessary to maintain connective tissue. Calcium, important for the bone structure of growing children, and iron, a necessary component of blood, are also provided by these plants.

Other green vegetables—like kale, peas and beans—include some B vita-

mins, a large group needed to extract energy from carbohydrates. The only vitamin not found in any vegetable is B12; it must come from such animal foods as meats, fish and milk.

Roots and tubers, often considered mere carbohydrate fillers, are also rich in vitamins. One medium-sized baked potato can supply a third or more of the body's daily requirement of vitamin C, as well as some of the B vitamins. Sweet potatoes are similarly nourishing and provide vitamin A. Carrots are another good source of vitamin A: the compound carotene, a basis of the vitamin, was named after this vegetable.

Many vegetables are also important sources of proteins: peas and beans contain the highest proportion, but potatoes also have a significant amount, as do green leaves and some members of the cabbage family, especially Brussels sprouts. All proteins consist of long, intricately folded chains of lesser molecules called amino acids. The human body can make most of the amino acids

it needs for its growth and repair; eight or nine, however, must come from the proteins we eat.

No single vegetable contains all of these critical acids, as meat, fish and eggs do, but most vegetable proteins include at least some of them, and if you eat several vegetables together, certain combinations—green beans and corn, for example—can provide the complete complement of amino acids. Combining a variety of vegetables with even small quantities of meat, eggs, milk or cheese is another way to obtain these vital molecular building blocks.

To get the best from your vegetables, there is no need to turn your kitchen into a laboratory. When it comes to combinations of ingredients, food science has taken a long time to catch up with what good cooks have always known. Green beans in egg sauce *(recipe, page 129)* and baked cauliflower and tomato purée *(recipe, page 112)* are only two of many traditional dishes that anticipated the modern nutritionist.

Leaves: Unsung Candidates for Cooking

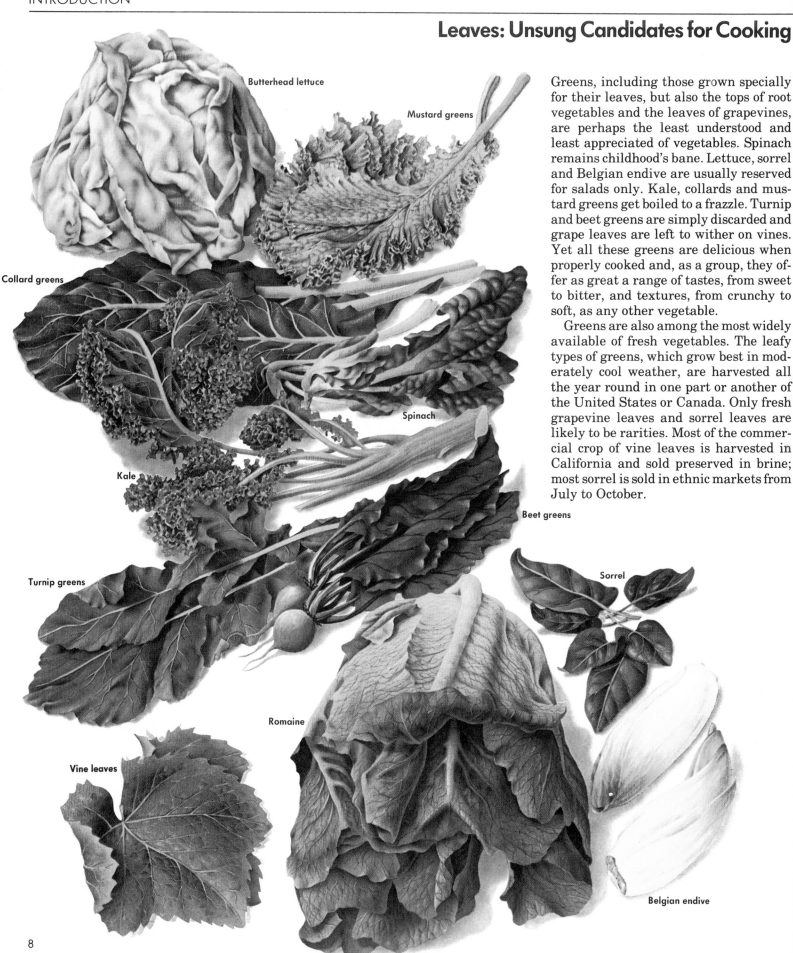

Butterhead lettuce

Mustard greens

Collard greens

Spinach

Kale

Beet greens

Turnip greens

Sorrel

Romaine

Vine leaves

Belgian endive

Greens, including those grown specially for their leaves, but also the tops of root vegetables and the leaves of grapevines, are perhaps the least understood and least appreciated of vegetables. Spinach remains childhood's bane. Lettuce, sorrel and Belgian endive are usually reserved for salads only. Kale, collards and mustard greens get boiled to a frazzle. Turnip and beet greens are simply discarded and grape leaves are left to wither on vines. Yet all these greens are delicious when properly cooked and, as a group, they offer as great a range of tastes, from sweet to bitter, and textures, from crunchy to soft, as any other vegetable.

Greens are also among the most widely available of fresh vegetables. The leafy types of greens, which grow best in moderately cool weather, are harvested all the year round in one part or another of the United States or Canada. Only fresh grapevine leaves and sorrel leaves are likely to be rarities. Most of the commercial crop of vine leaves is harvested in California and sold preserved in brine; most sorrel is sold in ethnic markets from July to October.

□ *How to shop:* Choose brightly colored and crisp leaves; they are the young and tender ones. Avoid plants with bruised or excessively dirty leaves; they have been improperly handled. And spotted, yellow or wilting plants are old ones. Their leaves turn yellow because they are too weak to produce the green pigment chlorophyll. (The exception is beet greens, which turn red at the tips when they age.) Kale, mustard greens and collard greens show other signs of having been left in the field too long: woody stems and leaves that are webbed with thick, coarse veins. Coarse-stemmed, straggly spinach plants should also be avoided; they will be tough and bitter.

If possible, buy leaf vegetables that are displayed on refrigerated racks, where low temperatures discourage the growth of decay bacteria. And, of course, buy unpackaged leaves so that you can examine them when you buy.

□ *Storing:* Because all leaves are short-lived, they are best when grown locally and cooked as soon as possible after they are picked. If you must store greens, keep them for no longer than two days; after that, flavor and texture suffer and much

of the vegetables' rich supplies of vitamins and minerals have disappeared.

Store leaves in a way that preserves their moisture and nutrients. Keep them in the coldest part of your refrigerator—usually one of the lower shelves. Do not cleanse them before storage: too much moisture encourages bacteria. If you enclose the leaves in a plastic bag, their own moisture will create a humid environment that will help to preserve crispness. But punch holes in the bag with a dinner fork so that air can circulate.

□ *Preparation:* Wash leaves thoroughly in cold water immediately before cooking. These vegetables tend to retain grit from the ground they were grown in, and some, such as spinach, may require two or three washings *(below, center)*. Trim off any bruised section, but remove as little of the leaf as possible; the outer leaves of lettuce and Belgian endive contain much of the flavor of the plants and almost all the nutrients. Lettuce stems should be trimmed and the bitter cores of Belgian endive should be removed *(below, right)*. The tough stems of spinach,

sorrel, kale, collards and mustard greens should be removed *(below, left)*. Turnip and beet greens should be cut off 2 or 3 inches [5 or 8 cm.] above the top of the root and any tough stems discarded.

Washing and trimming are almost the only preparation leafy greens require. The exception is pickled or fresh (if you can get them) grapevine leaves, used for enveloping meat or vegetable fillings. These must be rinsed with boiling water, to make fresh leaves supple and to remove the brine from preserved leaves.

Lettuce may also be used to enclose various fillings for braising or baking, but both lettuce and Belgian endive are delicious when cooked by themselves. Like all leafy greens, they should be boiled, steamed or sautéed quickly and gently to bring out their subtle flavors without ruining their delicate textures. Never add baking soda to the cooking water to keep leaves bright colored; this will give them a brackish taste and make them mushy. The way to preserve color, flavor and texture is to keep cooking time at a minimum. Then your leafy vegetables will not only stay bright, but also will taste as fresh as they look.

Stemming and Washing Spinach

Rinsing off grit. Fold each leaf in half so that its glossy upper surfaces touch. Grasp the stem firmly and pull it toward the leaf tip *(left)* so that it peels off the leaf. Plunge the stripped leaves into a bowl of cold water and pump them up and down to wash them *(right)*, changing the water twice. Then shake off the excess water. Do not use a colander: the grit will resettle onto the leaves.

Coring Belgian Endive

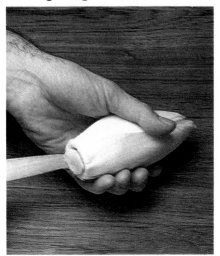

Cutting out bitterness. Remove the base of Belgian endive's bitter, conical core by inserting the point of a small knife about 1 inch [2½ cm.] into the plant's base and cutting around the core with a circular motion.

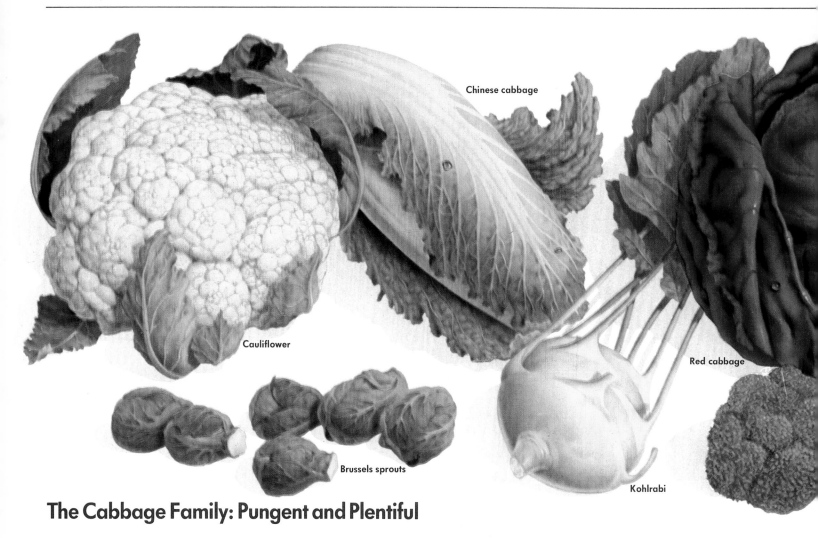

Chinese cabbage

Cauliflower

Red cabbage

Brussels sprouts

Kohlrabi

The Cabbage Family: Pungent and Plentiful

Cabbage plants produce crisp, pungent vegetables, but the vegetables come from different parts of the plants. Head cabbages—the red, green and Savoy varieties as well as their miniature version, Brussels sprouts—are the tightly rolled leaves of the plant; cylindrical Chinese cabbages are more loosely packed leaves. With kohlrabi (German for "cabbage-turnip"), the bulbous plant stem is the part used. Broccoli consists of green buds on a fleshy stalk; and a cauliflower head actually is a compressed flower.

Most cabbages are available the year round. Kohlrabi, however, is most plentiful in summer and fall.

□ *How to shop:* Good round-headed cabbages, including Brussels sprouts, appear tightly curled; they feel hard and weighty for their size. Their outer leaves are opaque and their cores white, not yellow. Chinese cabbages should be long and straight, pale green and very crisp.

Broccoli buds should be tightly closed; the tips may be tinged with blue or pur-

ple, but not with yellow—a sign of age. A cauliflower should be an unblemished, snow- or cream-white; its florets should be tightly pressed together. Kohlrabi is young and tender when the bulb diameter is less than 3 inches [8 cm.].

□ *Storing:* Do not wash cabbages before storage—extra moisture will hasten decay. If you wrap cabbages in perforated plastic bags for storage in the refrigerator, they will keep for as long as a week.

□ *Preparation:* All cabbages should be washed and trimmed just before cooking. Cut off the exposed stem of Chinese cabbage; slice head cabbage in half and cut out the tough, wedge-shaped inner stem. (Save the core to eat raw as a snack.) Then shred the leaves of both cabbage types *(page 30)* for boiling, steaming, braising or sautéing. If you want to stuff a head cabbage and cook it whole *(pages 46-47),* trim off any exposed stem; do not remove the core, which holds the leaves together. When trimming red cabbage, use a stainless-steel knife; the pigment

in red cabbage interacts chemically with carbon steel and turns the leaves an unappetizing blue.

For Brussels sprouts, remove the loose outer leaves and incise the stems *(opposite, far left).* Cauliflower may be kept whole if you remove its tough stem *(opposite, center),* but it will cook more quickly if you separate it into florets. Broccoli should be divided into florets and the stems peeled to ensure that they cook as quickly as the tender buds. Either slice the stems into 2-inch [5-cm.] pieces or make several shallow, lengthwise slits in whole, peeled stems. Kohlrabi needs only to be scrubbed or peeled; its leaves can be cooked with the bulb to itensify its flavor.

Only kohlrabi and Chinese cabbage, however, are mild tasting. The other cabbages are relatively strong flavored and become sulfurous in cooking. The rule is to keep the cooking time brief and, when boiling or steaming them, to use celery leaves, ribs or seeds in the pot to tone down their odor.

Savoy cabbage

Green cabbage

Broccoli

Trimming Brussels Sprouts

Slitting the stem. Peel off any wilted or yellowing leaves and shave off the stem end with a sharp knife. Then cut a shallow cross in the bottom of the stem *(above)* so that it will cook as quickly as the more tender leaves.

Preparing Whole Cauliflower

Cutting out the core. Tear off all green outer leaves except those clinging to the florets. Cut off the protruding stem end and remove the woody core by cutting around the stem with a small knife angled toward the center of the head *(above)*. Then pull off the leaves that were loosened by the coring.

Peeling Broccoli Stems

Removing tough skin. Trim off the woody base of the stalk. Then cut the tough skin away from the stalk by running a paring knife from the bottom up to the florets *(above)*. Keep your hand close to the tip of the knife and guide the blade with your thumb so that you do not cut too deeply.

Roots and Tubers: Dense-fleshed and Sturdy

Hardy vegetables that grow under the ground develop very dense flesh, which is sugar-filled in immature vegetables and starchy in older ones. The group includes such familiar roots as carrots, beets, turnips, rutabagas and parsnips, less common roots such as celeriac and salsify, and tubers such as potatoes, sweet potatoes and Jerusalem artichokes.

Potatoes, beets, turnips and carrots are routinely harvested when young and sweet. Most other roots and tubers are left in the field to mature so that their skins will toughen, making them easy to store and ship. Mature specimens are most plentiful in fall and winter.

□ *How to shop:* Choose potatoes according to the way you plan to cook them. New potatoes have waxy flesh best suited to boiling, steaming or frying; they do not have the dry, mealy texture successful baking requires. Among mature potatoes, long russets—cylindrical potatoes

with reddish-brown skins—are relatively dry-fleshed and are ideal for baking or frying; they tend to fall apart if boiled. Long white, round white and round red potatoes, on the other hand, should be boiled or steamed; they are very moist and acquire a sticky texture when baked.

Any potato you buy should be firm. It should not have sprouting eyes, a sign of a flabby interior; soft black spots, which indicate rot; or green areas, which taste bitter and may be slightly toxic.

Choose sweet potatoes according to the degree of sweetness and dryness you like. They range in skin color from light tan to brownish-red. In general, the darker the skin, the sweeter and moister the flesh. (Dark-skinned sweet potatoes often are erroneously labeled yams.) Any sweet potato should be firm and smooth.

Turnips and beets should be small— no larger than 2 inches [5 cm.] in diameter. Larger ones probably will be fibrous or tough. Carrots vary in size depending on their variety; older ones have a clearly

defined, woody core that should be removed before cooking.

Parsnips are broad-shouldered at any age, but young and tender only when about 8 inches [20 cm.] in length. They should be free of gashes and wet, soft spots. Look for smooth, heavy rutabagas without punctures from careless handling. (Size does not affect their quality.) Jerusalem artichokes come in many sizes, usually less than 5 inches [13 cm.] long, but are always gnarled and knobby. Buy only those that feel hard. Salsify should be smoothly tapered, firm and about 6 inches [15 cm.] long. Celeriac (also known as celery root) is globular and its white flesh is covered with a rough, brownish skin; if it is larger than a man's fist, it is old and woody.

□ *Storing:* Store roots and tubers unwashed; excess moisture encourages decay. Cut off beet, carrot, parsnip and turnip leaves so that they will not take

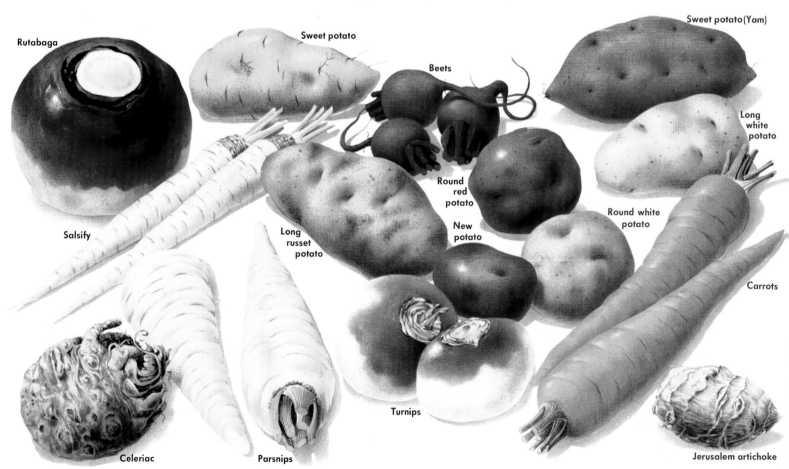

Rutabaga

Sweet potato

Beets

Sweet potato (Yam)

Long white potato

Round red potato

New potato

Round white potato

Salsify

Long russet potato

Carrots

Celeriac

Parsnips

Turnips

Jerusalem artichoke

moisture from the roots. Be sure to leave stems at least 2 inches [5 cm.] long on beets, lest color ooze out as they cook.

Jerusalem artichokes, refrigerated in perforated plastic bags, will keep for two days. Beets, carrots, celeriac, parsnips and turnips will last one week. Salsify will keep for three to four days, but its oyster-like flavor diminishes daily; try to cook it the day you buy it.

Potatoes, sweet potatoes and rutabagas should be stored outside the refrigerator. Under refrigeration, potatoes develop an unpleasant sweetness and sweet potatoes develop hard cores. White potatoes, rutabagas and sweet potatoes will keep for a week at room temperature, but all of them except new potatoes last up to two months if stored at 50° F. [10° C.]. Keep white potatoes in the dark; direct light develops chlorophyll, which turns them green and bitter.

□ *Preparation:* To preserve vitamins, all roots and tubers should be prepared immediately before cooking. They usually are left in their skins for baking and peeled for other types of cooking. But there are exceptions. Waxed rutabagas must be peeled; otherwise, the wax used to help preserve them will flake off during cooking. Delicate-skinned new potatoes and carrots should be scrubbed but left unpeeled. A beet should never be scrubbed hard or peeled; any break in the skin allows color to escape during cooking. Jerusalem artichokes are scrubbed *(bottom, right)* but left unpeeled; celeriac and salsify usually are peeled.

To keep peeled potatoes white before cooking, put them in cold water; put salsify, celeriac or Jerusalem artichokes in acidulated water *(bottom, right)*.

Other preparations include removing tough cores from carrots and parsnips *(bottom, left)*, cutting green spots from mature potatoes and removing belts of skin from new potatoes to keep them from bursting during cooking.

Three Basic Peeling Techniques

Removing thin skins. Use a vegetable peeler to pare strips ⅛ inch [3 mm.] deep from parsnips *(above)*, carrots, potatoes or salsify.

Removing thick skins. With a small, sharp knife, slice through the stem end of a rutabaga *(above)* or a turnip. Then cut off the skin in strips about ⅜ inch [½ cm.] deep.

Peeling celeriac. Use a medium-sized, sharp-bladed knife to pare off ⅛-inch [3-mm.] strips of the barklike skin. Cut out any places on the celeriac where the skin is deeply pitted.

Dealing with Older Carrots

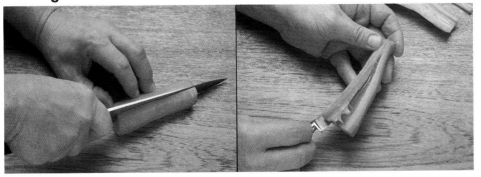

Cutting out the woody core. Trim off the ends and peel a carrot; then, with a sharp knife, slice it in half lengthwise *(left)*. The pale, fibrous core should be clearly visible. Insert a small knife beneath the core at the thicker end of the carrot and pry the core free along the entire length of the carrot *(right)*.

Cleaning Jerusalem Artichokes

Scrubbing the skins. Clean each artichoke with a stiff brush under running water *(above)*. Then plunge it into a solution of 1 teaspoon [5 ml.] of lemon juice to 1 quart [1 liter] of water.

Pods and Seeds: The Natural Sweetness of Youth

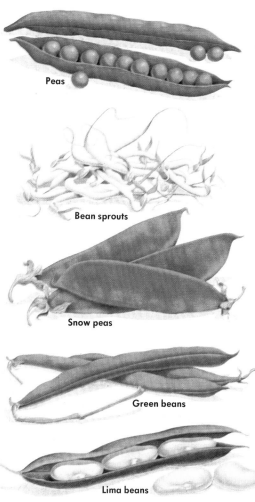

Peas

Bean sprouts

Snow peas

Green beans

Lima beans

Seeds, edible pods and young shoots—categories that encompass respectively lima and broad (or fava) beans, corn and peas; green and wax beans and snow peas; and bean sprouts—are sweet and tender only if they are harvested when they are immature and full of sugar. If they are to stay sweet, they must be cooked soon after they are picked—before their sugar turns to starch and their tastes and textures deteriorate.

Bean sprouts are sold all year long at health food stores and in some supermarkets, and broad beans appear primarily in specialty markets during the summer months. The other seeds and pods are more readily available. Peas, corn and beans will be at their best, however, when they are locally grown.

□ *How to shop:* Choose the smallest and brightest-colored seeds and pods you can find. Those that are wrinkled, dry, flabby or yellowed are overage; ones with thick, fibrous pods also are old.

The tenderest green beans and yellow wax beans are only ¼ inch [6 mm.] wide and 4 inches [10 cm.] long. Crisp, fresh ones will snap when bent.

Lima beans are available as the small, so-called "butter limas" or as the larger "potato"-type beans—plump, flat ovals with green or greenish-white skins. Good limas and broad beans are encased in velvety, dark green pods, which should be tightly closed and bulging.

Good peas are round, shiny and come in smooth, bright green pods. Snow peas are eaten for their pods. The best are a bright green and so thin that you can see the outline of the immature peas within.

For the best corn, buy ears that were picked that very morning—depend on a reliable grocer for this or buy corn at a farm stand. The cobs should be at least 6 inches [15 cm.] long under green husks; dry or yellowed husks indicate that the corn is old or damaged. The stem ends of the cobs should be moist and the hairlike silk a pale greenish-white. The silk tassel at the tip should be brown and brittle. Examine the kernels; they may range in color from white to bright yellow, according to variety, and should be plump and firm enough to offer some resistance to pressure. When you pierce a kernel, it should spurt thick white liquid.

Bean sprouts, whether they come from alfalfa or from mung beans, should be cream-colored or white, and crisp with moist tips. Alfalfa sprouts are best when they are approximately 1 inch [2½ cm.] long; mung bean sprouts ideally should

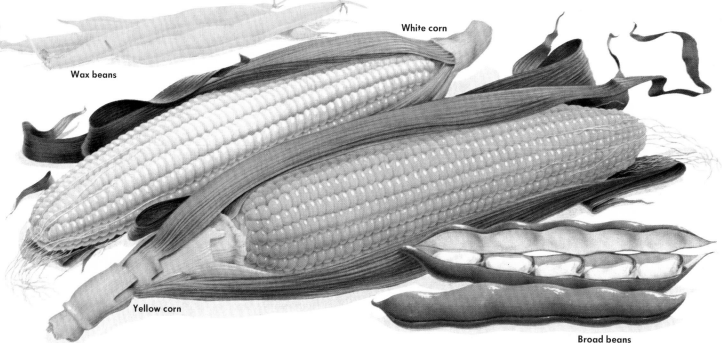

Wax beans

White corn

Yellow corn

Broad beans

be about 3 inches [8 cm.] in length.
□ *Storing:* Keep lima and broad beans, as well as peas, unwashed and in their pods. Refrigerated in perforated plastic bags, they will keep for one to two days. Stored similarly, green or wax beans, bean sprouts and snow peas keep for two days. Cook corn as soon as you buy it.
□ *Preparation:* Rinse both green beans and wax beans in cold water and cut their stem and tip ends off. If you buy green beans with strings, remove them the same way you would string snow peas *(below, left);* a green bean, however, has one string, not two. Snow peas and green or wax beans usually are left whole for cooking, but the beans may be cut diagonally into 2½-inch [6-cm.] lengths.

Peas as well as lima and broad beans are shelled as shown below at right; in addition, broad beans are covered by a protective membrane that must be removed. Bean sprouts need only rinsing.

Corn may be roasted in its husk *(page 94).* For all other cooking methods, cut off the stem end of the cob and any dried area on the tip, then pull off husk and silk. Corn may be boiled or roasted on the cob, or the kernels may be sliced off for frying, baking or stewing.

Mushrooms: Earthy Delicacies

The mushroom cultivated in this country is the *champignon de Paris;* its color is white, off-white or tan, and its cap size ranges from ¾ inch to 3 inches [2 to 8 cm.]. Its flavor is always subtle and reminiscent of freshly turned loam.

Mushrooms, cultivated indoors, are available all year. All are full of moisture and absorb it readily, a fact to be kept in mind during preparation and cooking. All contain protein and become tough if overcooked.
□ *How to shop:* Pick out mushrooms with smooth, unblemished skins. The caps should be closed so that no gills show around the stems.
□ *Storing:* Mushrooms should be refrigerated unwashed and loosely covered; they will last one to two days.
□ *Preparation:* Cut off the bottoms of mushroom stems. Then wipe off dirt with a damp cloth. Do not soak them—they will get soggy. Mushrooms are grown in sterilized soil and require little cleaning. Mushrooms cooked alone need no additional preparation. Those cooked with other foods must be prevented from releasing water. If a recipe calls for chopped mushrooms, wring the raw, chopped mushrooms in a towel to extract their liquid. If a recipe calls for whole mushrooms, sauté them beforehand to evaporate liquid.

Tan mushrooms

White mushrooms

Off-white mushrooms

Preparing Snow Peas

Removing strings. Slice through the stem end of each pod, but do not sever the string. Pull the stem end and attached string down the pod. Repeat on the opposite end for the other string.

Shelling and Peeling Broad Beans

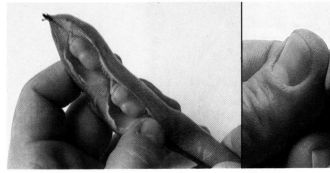

Freeing the beans. Pop open each pod by pressing the seam near the stem end; then run your thumbnail down the seam to split it and expose the beans. Then, again using your thumbnail, split the protective skin on each broad bean lengthwise so that you can pull away the skin in one piece. Discard the skins.

Vegetable Fruits: A Summer Potpourri

In botanical terms, a tomato, an eggplant or a pepper is a fruit; a cucumber is a squash and an okra is a pod. For shopping and cooking purposes, however, these vegetables form one group. All are warm-weather plants that reach their peak in flavor and availability during the summer. All except okra are available the year round, but they are more difficult to transport successfully than other vegetables: those that are shipped never taste as good as produce that has been locally grown and naturally ripened.

□ *How to shop:* Tomatoes, in particular, suffer in the course of a long haul. Because ripe fruit decays quickly, most tomatoes to be shipped are picked while green, then artificially ripened without sunlight; they tend to be tasteless and mealy, and usually are a lighter red than garden stock. Among them your best choice will be those labeled "greenhouse" or "hothouse"—they have been picked when almost ripe and thus have more taste than other out-of-season tomatoes. Buy those delicacies from a reliable gro-

cer since inferior tomatoes are occasionally mislabeled.

Choose tomato varieties according to the way you plan to cook them: unripened green tomatoes are suited to pan frying; tiny cherry tomatoes are a convenient size for broiling whole *(page 93);* pear-shaped plum tomatoes, which have thick, pulpy flesh, are best for sauces; and smooth, round, standard tomatoes are good for stuffing or broiling.

Buy hard, dark green cucumbers; yellow or flabby ones are old and may be bitter. Cucumbers range in size from varieties 3 inches [8 cm.] long—mainly for pickling—to large ones 10 to 12 inches [25 to 30 cm.] long, used mainly in salads. For cooking as a single serving, the best size is 6 to 7 inches [15 to 18 cm.].

The best eggplants are a glossy, uniform purple. When the eggplants grow old, their skins turn dull and tinged with brown, and the seeds inside become hard and the flesh flabby.

Peppers, including the frying variety, change from green to red as they ripen, and at the same time their sweetness increases. They taste good at either stage, but ripe ones deteriorate quickly. Any pepper should have a shiny skin, free from holes or punctures and from soft or black decaying spots.

Buy okra when it is so young and firm that a pod will snap when you bend it. The green pods should be 2 to 4 inches [5 to 10 cm.] long; larger ones can be woody.

□ *Storing:* All these vegetables deteriorate quickly in extreme cold and need humidity to prevent them from drying out. On the other hand, they will rapidly decay if kept too warm. The best storage temperature is about 50° F. [10° C.]. You may store most of these vegetables in the refrigerator, although its temperature is colder than desirable. Refrigerated okra and eggplants last only one or two days, peppers and cucumbers up to five days.

Ideally, tomatoes should not be kept in the refrigerator at all. Chilling diminishes their flavor. Ripe fruit can, however,

Eggplant

Plum tomato

Standard tomato

Cucumber

Pepper

Frying peppers

Okra

be refrigerated for up to five days, if necessary. Underripe tomatoes will ripen best when they are wrapped in newspaper or a brown bag and kept at a temperature of 65° F. [20° C.].

☐ *Preparation:* All of these vegetables require some preparation just prior to cooking, usually to remove their skin, seeds or excess moisture. Tomatoes for frying should be cored, then rinsed with cold water. If you plan to stuff and bake a tomato, hollow it as shown on page 78. If you plan to braise or stew a tomato, peel and seed it as shown below.

Most cucumbers are coated with wax to preserve them and to prevent the loss of moisture. For this reason, cucumbers should be skinned with a small knife or vegetable peeler before cooking. Many recipes require that cucumbers be seeded; to do so, slice them in half lengthwise and use a spoon to scoop out the seeds.

Before cooking, cucumbers and eggplants will benefit from a salt marinade that draws out excess moisture and bitter juices: salt the peeled pieces and let them drain in a colander for 30 minutes. Then pat them dry, rinsing them with water if a strong salt taste is evident.

Remove the seeds and pith of peppers as shown below. If the peppers have been waxed (they will feel extra slippery), they should also be peeled. To do so, char them over a gas flame or under a broiler. When the skins are blackened, place the peppers in a paper bag where humidity can soften their skins. You will then be able to peel them with your fingers.

An okra pod contains a liquid-filled sac. If it is pierced or cut, the sac releases a glutinous sap that is a natural thickener for soups or stews. If the okra is to be eaten alone, do not pierce the sac or overcook the pods; the freed sap inside would give the vegetable a slimy texture. Prepare okra for cooking as shown below.

Trimming Okra

Slicing the pods. Trim the tip of each okra pod and slice off the stem end. Do not pierce the sac inside the pod lest the liquid escape during cooking.

Halving and Seeding Peppers

1 **Splitting the pepper.** Slice through pepper crevices on opposite sides, from the base up to the stem. Pull the halves apart; the stem and the seed pod will cling to one side.

2 **Removing the seed pod.** Slide your finger under the pod clinging to one pepper half to snap it out in one piece. Use a knife to trim any ridges of membrane from each pepper half.

Peeling and Seeding Tomatoes

1 **Loosening the skin.** Cut conical plugs from the stem ends. Cut crosses at the base. Put the tomatoes in boiling water for 10 to 30 seconds *(above)*.

2 **Removing the skin.** Drain and cool the tomatoes. Slide the knife under one edge of the cross cut and strip off the skin in sections, working toward the stem end.

3 **Squeezing out seeds.** Halve each tomato, cutting perpendicular to the stem end. Gently squeeze each half to remove seeds and juice.

The Squashes: From Minuscule to Majestic

All squashes are gourds: fleshy vegetables with seeds on the inside and protective rinds outside. In summer varieties —such as zucchini, yellow crooknecks and the scalloped squash often called pattypan—the rinds and seeds are tender and edible because the squashes are harvested when they are immature. Winter varieties, however, are harvested when they are mature. These acorn, butternut, buttercup and Hubbard squashes, as well as pumpkins and the less well-known spaghetti squash have tough seeds and rinds. Chayote, or mirliton, is a pear-shaped squash with a thin, delicate, pale green skin, but a large, inedible seed.

The seasonal names give a clue to a squash's availability: winter ones are in plentiful supply from October through February, summer ones from April until August. Spaghetti squash is plentiful from August through February, chayote from October through April.

□ *How to shop:* Look for small summer squashes, which will prove sweet and tender. Zucchini and yellow squashes should be 3 to 6 inches [8 to 15 cm.] long, scalloped squash no more than 4 inches [10 cm.] in diameter. The rind should be easy to pierce and the squash should feel firm and heavy for its size.

Winter squashes should feel hard and have no cracks or blemishes. Color indicates ripeness: Hubbard or acorn squash should be blue-gray or green; buttercup squash should be dark green with lighter stripes or flecks. All three will develop orange patches as they ripen. Butternut squash should be entirely tan, and pumpkins bright orange. Chayote skins vary in color from white to green: some are covered with prickly hairs.

□ *Storing:* Refrigerated in plastic bags, summer squashes and chayotes will keep for three to four days. The thick rinds of winter squashes make it possible to store them for up to three months in net bags hung in a cool, dry place.

□ *Preparation:* Before cooking any summer squash, rinse, trim and slice or halve it; do not peel it unless a recipe requires peeling. Many recipes specify that you remove excess moisture. To do this, salt the exposed flesh and let it drain in a colander for 30 minutes. Then rinse, and dry it with paper towels; rinse again if its taste is too salty. Summer squashes usually are boiled, steamed or pan fried. A pattypan *(opposite)* makes an attractive container for stuffing.

To prepare any winter variety except spaghetti squash, halve it or cut off its stem end and remove its seeds and fibers *(opposite, far right)*. Then bake it in its skin or cut it into smaller pieces and peel them for boiling, steaming or pan frying.

To prepare a spaghetti squash, wipe it, pierce it to let steam escape, then bake, boil or steam it in its skin. Then halve it, remove the seeds and fibers, and use a fork to twist out its long strands of flesh.

Acorn squash

Pumpkin

Pattypan

Yellow crooknecks

Hollowing Scalloped Squash

Making a cavity. Place the squash, with its flat side down, on a work surface and use a paring knife to cut a small cone of rind and flesh from the top. With a melon baller, scoop out enough seeds and flesh *(above)* to make a cavity for stuffing.

Cleaning a Winter Squash

1 **Splitting the squash.** Snap off the stem and place the squash — here, an acorn — on a cutting board. Work the blade of a large chef's knife into the shell between two lengthwise ridges. With a mallet, strike the spine of the knife near the handle to force the blade into the squash. Strike until the squash splits.

2 **Seeding the squash.** With a large metal spoon, scoop the seeds and fibers from each squash half *(above)*. Then scrape the flesh to remove any clinging fibers. Discard the fibers, but dry the seeds on paper towels and sauté them in oil for 5 minutes to make a snack.

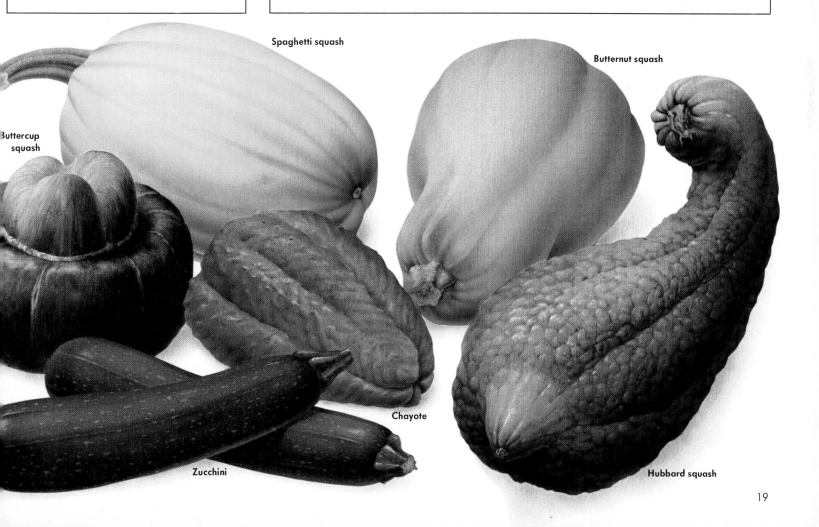

Spaghetti squash

Butternut squash

Buttercup squash

Chayote

Zucchini

Hubbard squash

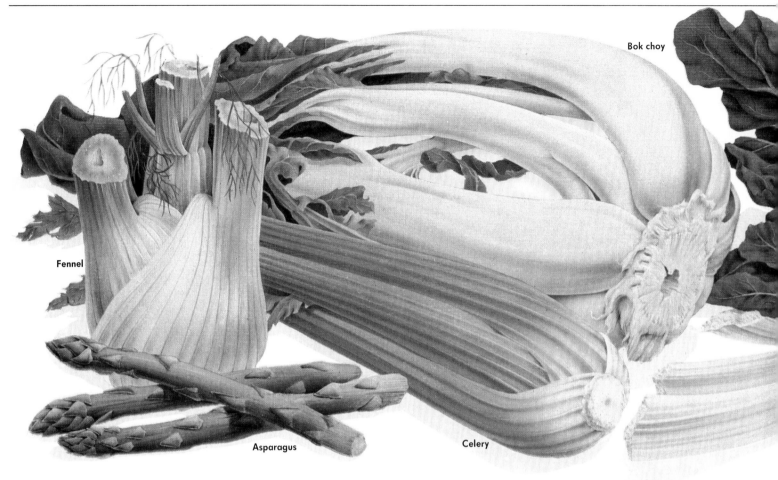

Bok choy

Fennel

Asparagus

Celery

Stalks: Texture plus Succulence

Stalk vegetables are plant stems that are high in cellulose fibers, the strings that are necessary to hold the stalks erect under the weight of their leaves and buds. For use as vegetables, all stalks should be young and almost all must be trimmed of their tough fibers, which cannot be softened by cooking.

Different stalk vegetables are available at different times of the year. Asparagus can be bought fresh from February through June and from September through December; celery is available all year round. Anise-flavored fennel is most obtainable in the fall and early winter. Delicate, spinach-like Swiss chard and sweet-tasting bok choy are both characterized by large leaves, often treated as separate vegetables. Swiss chard is plentiful from June through October, bok choy year round.

□ *How to shop:* In general, stalk vegetables should be firm, clean and free of signs of age or improper handling. Vegetables with coarsely striated stalks are old and pithy; those with limp, rubbery stalks and wilted, yellowed or browned leaves have dried out and lost flavor. Slippery brown spots on the leaves indicate that these vegetables have been overchilled and will be tasteless.

In particular, choose young asparagus with tightly closed buds, rejecting spears with open or seedy tips. The stalks should be round, not flattened or ridged. Size is not important except that all stalks being cooked together should be about the same size so that they will cook evenly.

Celery should always be green, with fresh leaves and brittle stalks that snap crisply. Fennel—in Italian, *finocchio*—should have a compact, greenish-white, bulbous base, green upper stalks and grass-green, ferny shoots. The color of Swiss chard varies widely, but the most popular variety possesses crinkled, dark green leaves and a firm white stalk. Bok choy—"white vegetable" in Chinese—should have very white stalks and shiny, dark green leaves.

□ *Storing:* Do not wash stalk vegetables before storing; doing so leaves water on them that hastens decay. Remove any limp outer leaves, wrap the stalks in a perforated plastic bag and refrigerate them. Celery and fennel will stay fresh for as long as a week kept this way, bok choy and asparagus for three days and chard for two days. If they are stored longer, too much water will evaporate from the stalks, taking the flavor with it.

□ *Preparation:* The first step in readying any of these vegetables is to wash it in cold water. Fennel, celery, bok choy and Swiss chard may collect grit in their folds. Asparagus tips often contain sand.

Cut off celery, fennel and chard leaves before cooking the stalks. The leaves of celery and fennel are useful only as flavorings for other dishes. Chard leaves, however, are excellent either served by themselves or with the stalks; but they cook so quickly that they must be prepared separately. If you choose to use the chard leaves, trim them by cutting out the tough middle rib from each one (*opposite, bottom left*). Then cook the leaves briefly: plunge them into boiling water,

Swiss chard

Trimming Asparagus

Peeling the stalk. After snapping or cutting off the tough end of an asparagus stalk, peel it with a small paring knife, cutting carefully toward yourself in order to control the depth of the peel; the layer of skin will be thick at the base of the stalk, but much thinner at the cluster of immature buds below the tip. The peelings will be tough and inedible, but they may be used to add flavor to soups.

Skinning Fennel

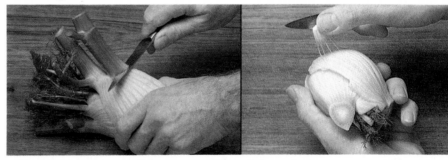

Stringing the base. Cut off the upper stalks and shoots from fennel *(left)*. Cut partway through the top of the fennel bulb at the inside edge of each stalk base, leaving the outer strings uncut. Then pull each half-cut piece away from you toward the bulb base; the strings will come with it *(right)*.

let the water return to a boil, then remove and drain the leaves immediately.

You may cook the leaves of bok choy in the same way as chard leaves, or leave them on and cook them with the stalks. Bok choy's tender stalks require no trimming before cooking. You can cook them whole or cut into bite-sized pieces. Fennel stalks, by contrast, are so tough they must be cut off near the base. Then the strings on the remaining stalks and base are removed *(center, right)*. Celery requires the same treatment. Swiss chard stalks have transparent membranes that need to be removed *(bottom, far right)*. Once this is done, Swiss chard may be cooked whole or cut into bite-sized pieces.

Asparagus stalks must be peeled so they will cook as quickly as the more tender tips. First hold each stalk near its bottom end and bend it; it will break at the point where the base becomes tough and inedible. (Or cut off the woody ends as shown on page 39.) Then use a small knife or vegetable scaler to peel the rest of the stalk *(top, right)*.

Stemming Swiss Chard

Removing leaves and skin. Cut the leaf away from the inner side of the stalk *(left)*. Cut through the top of the stalk without severing the skin on the outer side. Pull the piece of stalk with the skin attached toward the root end *(right)*. Repeat this procedure from the root end for the inside of the stalk.

The Onion Family: Food as well as Flavoring

The strongly flavored members of the allium family shown below—onions, garlic, shallots, leeks and scallions—usually are used as seasonings. But when cooked as vegetables in their own right, they offer a variety of interesting tastes of different intensities.

The bulbous Spanish, yellow and white boiling onions, along with shallots and garlic, are the most pungent. All are cured or dried after harvesting to develop the papery skins that protect their flesh during storage. Having been cured, all three are available year round.

The mild-flavored leeks and scallions are always sold fresh; scallions are available all the time and leeks reach their peak during the autumn months.

□ *How to shop:* When choosing cured alliums, look for ones that feel firm and dry. Those with green shoots growing from the root ends have been stored at too high a temperature with too much humidity, and sprouting will have spoiled their flavor and texture. Those that have soft or discolored spots are rotting.

Shallots, which are tiny and spherical with a subtle taste similar to that of onions, have brown, dry, papery skins. Garlic bulbs and their individual cloves should be tightly closed, with unwrinkled skins of white, pink to purple, or white with purple streaks.

Buy leeks and scallions with crisp, green, unwithered tops and clean white bottoms. Leeks, in addition, should be straight and cylindrical; those with bulbous ends probably will be tough and woody inside. The same is not true of scallions, however; some varieties develop bulbous ends naturally.

□ *Storing:* Do not keep dried onions, garlic or shallots in the refrigerator: the damp air encourages rot. Hang them in baskets or in net bags in a cool—preferably 50° F. [10° C.]—dark place. Direct light causes them to produce chlorophyll, which turns their flesh green and their flavor bitter. Shallots and bulb onions will keep several months stored this way;

Yellow onion

Garlic

Leeks

Spanish onion

Scallions

Shallots

Boiling onions

garlic will last approximately two weeks.

Fresh leeks and scallions are more perishable, because their flesh is not protected by papery skin. After cutting off any brown or limp tops, refrigerate leeks and scallions in perforated plastic bags and use them within three to five days.

□ *Preparation:* Both dried and fresh alliums must be trimmed before cooking, and the dried onions cause the cook the most trouble. Their clinging skins can be easily removed if you dip the vegetables quickly into boiling water *(bottom, right).* After peeling, dried onions usually are sliced or chopped, a process that releases eye-irritating vapors. The best

solution to this problem is to hold the onions under cold running water as you peel them; the water washes away the volatile sulfur compounds before they can vaporize and reach your eyes.

Peeling shallots requires only pulling off the skin and outer layer *(bottom, left);* they are the mildest members of this group and probably will not irritate your eyes. Garlic cloves can be simultaneously crushed and peeled *(below; top, right);* if you want whole, uncrushed cloves, use boiling water to loosen their skins.

Mild, fresh scallions and leeks do not

irritate the eyes. Cut off the root ends of scallions, pull off any damp, thin membrane covering the whites, and trim any dried or discolored sections. A leek root also should be trimmed and, since leeks trap quantities of grit, carefully washed *(below; top, left)* before cooking.

Dried onions benefit from long, slow cooking—baking, braising or boiling—that leaves them sweet tasting. Even garlic cloves, if cooked as shown on page 77, can be puréed and eaten. Their flavor becomes mild, their texture buttersmooth. Leeks may be braised, pan fried or boiled. Scallions may be pan fried or coated with batter and deep fried.

Freeing Leeks of Grit

Splitting and washing. Cut off the root base and the fibrous leaf tops. Pierce the leek where the white part joins the green and draw the knife through to the top end to split the leaves *(left).* Make a second lengthwise split at right angles to the first. Rinse the leek in a bowl of cold water *(right)* until no grit appears.

Splitting Garlic's Skin

Peeling a clove. Place a clove under the side of a knife blade. Thump the blade to split the garlic's clinging skin; it will then slip off easily.

Removing the Shallot's Shell

Peeling the skin. Cut off the tops and tails of the shallots. Peel them with your fingernails, pulling away the first layer of flesh with the skin that is usually firmly attached to it.

Peeling Onions without Tears

Parboiling the skins. Cut off the tops and tails of the onions. Put the onions in boiling water for about a minute to loosen their skins. Remove the onions and pull off the skins. Then peel off the thin, slippery membrane just beneath the skin.

The Artichoke: Prickly but Tender-hearted

The artichoke is actually an edible thistle. Its prickles consist of stiff, scalelike leaves that have delicate-flavored flesh at their bases. Inside the leaves is the choke, a mass of hairlike fibers that rests in the tender, cup-shaped part of the vegetable called the bottom.

Immature artichokes—those less than 2 inches [5 cm.] long—have leaves so soft that they may 'be eaten raw. However, fresh artichokes of this size are rare outside California, generally appearing only in ethnic markets. Larger, mature artichokes must be trimmed of prickles, and

cooked. They are plentiful throughout the country from March through June.

□ *How to shop:* The leaves of mature artichokes should be tightly packed. Artichokes with open, spreading leaves are tough. In spring, the leaves should be bright green; discoloration is a sign of age or damage. Between November and March, by contrast, the leaves may be bronzed—the result of frost. While they may look unattractive, bronzed leaves will have meaty, tasty flesh, since artichokes react to cold by putting on weight. To make sure an artichoke is moist and young, hold its tip up to your ear and squeeze the leaves together. A tender ar-

tichoke will produce a squeaky sound but an old, dry one will sound hollow.

□ *Storing:* Artichokes will keep for one week when refrigerated, unwashed and wrapped in perforated plastic bags.

□ *Preparation:* Artichokes will discolor during trimming and cooking unless you take certain precautions. Trim them only with stainless-steel knives and scissors; carbon steel darkens the vegetables' cut surfaces. As they are trimmed, rub artichokes with a cut lemon or drop them in acidulated water *(page 13)*. Similarly, cook artichokes in acidulated liquid or a

Preparing a Whole Artichoke

1 **Removing the stem.** Wash the artichoke in cold water. With a large, stainless-steel chef's knife, cut off the stem flush with the base *(above)* so that the artichoke will stand upright.

2 **Removing bottom leaves.** Hold the top of the artichoke in the palm of your hand and snap off any small or discolored leaves at the base.

3 **Trimming the top.** Place the artichoke on a cutting board. Cut off about 1 inch [2½ cm.] of the top *(above)*. Rub the cut edges with lemon juice or a freshly cut lemon, as here.

4 **Snipping the leaf tips.** With a pair of kitchen scissors, cut ½ inch [1 cm.] off the tip of each leaf *(above)*. Rub the cut edges with lemon. The artichoke may now be cooked, and its choke removed during eating.

5 **Exposing the choke.** To remove the choke before cooking, parboil the artichoke for 5 minutes. Plunge it into cold water and drain it. Spread the center leaves, work your fingers into the opening and twist out the inner leaves.

6 **Scraping out the choke.** Remove the exposed, hairy fibers of the choke by scraping them out with the tip of a sharp-edged metal spoon *(above)*. Squeeze lemon juice into the empty cavity to prevent discoloration.

blanc (page 41), using a stainless-steel, enameled cast-iron or tin-lined copper pot. Do not cook artichokes in aluminum or cast-iron pots.

Artichoke preparation is simply a matter of removing bristly, inedible parts to make the tender ones accessible. If you wish to serve the vegetable whole, cut off the stem, pull off the tough leaves at the base and cut off the thorny tips of the remaining leaves. To make the artichoke easier to dismember and eat, scoop out the hairy choke as shown opposite, bottom right. If you wish to use only the bottom, chop off the stem and cut away the leaves and choke *(below, right).*

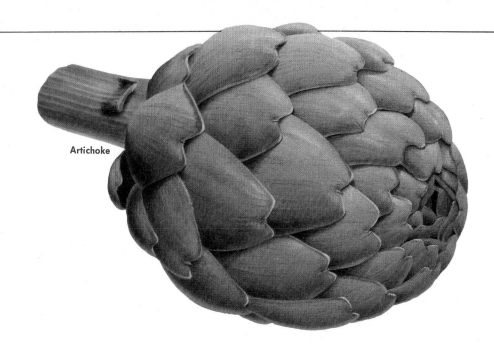

Artichoke

Turning an Artichoke Bottom

1 **Breaking the stem.** Hold the top of the artichoke firmly and bend the stem until it snaps from the base *(above)*. As it breaks, the stem will pull tough fibers out of the artichoke bottom.

2 **Removing the outer leaves.** Pull each leaf outward and down so that the top part snaps off the leaf's fleshy base *(above)*. Continue until you reach the tender, inner leaves, distinguished by their yellowish-green color.

3 **Topping the artichoke.** Slice across the tops of the inner leaves, removing the top one third to two thirds of each leaf, depending on how pale — and thus how tender — it is. Rub the cut surfaces with lemon juice.

4 **Paring the bottom.** Starting at the mark left by snapping off the stem, peel around the artichoke base in a spiral motion to pare away the dark bases of the leaves. Then moisten the cut surfaces with lemon or acidulated water.

5 **Trimming the top.** Slice off the remaining dark green parts of the leaves down to the point where they become almost white. This will expose the tightly packed central leaves that conceal the choke. Pull off these leaves so that the whole choke is visible.

6 **Removing the choke.** It is easiest to scrape the choke from a parboiled artichoke bottom. If a recipe calls for an uncooked bottom, scoop out the raw choke with a teaspoon. If you are not going to use the bottom immediately, rub its surface with lemon juice.

Chives

Basil

Chervil

Dill

Fennel

Tarragon

Curly-leafed parsley

Flat-leafed parsley

Sage

Herbs: A Basis for Kitchen Alchemy

Fresh vegetables, with their widely varying tastes, offer generous scope for the use of herbs. To some extent, tradition is a useful guide. Certain combinations of herbs, for example, are sanctioned by centuries of use: freshly chopped parsley, chives, chervil and tarragon are mixed to form the fines herbes of French cuisine; and a basic bouquet garni is invariably made by tying together parsley, thyme and a bay leaf or wrapping them in cheesecloth. Moreover, individual herbs may be traditionally associated with particular vegetables—mint with peas, for instance, or dill with cucumber.

However, there are no cast-iron rules dictating how herbs should be used. The following list offers suggestions and general guidance to spur the imagination:

Basil: This herb's clovelike aroma is perfect with tomatoes, but also complements squash, beans and potatoes.

Chervil: A cousin of parsley, chervil has a delicate anise taste that goes with any vegetable. Add it at the last minute; long cooking may kill its flavor.

Chives: Finely snipped, these mild relatives of onions can complement any vegetable. Add them during the last moments of cooking.

Coriander: Also called Chinese parsley and known in Spanish as *cilantro,* this herb has an acrid taste. Use coriander leaves sparingly with squash, eggplant, snow peas and onions.

Dill: In addition to its traditional alliance with cucumber, dill enhances potatoes, cabbages and peas.

Fennel: Anise-tasting fennel leaves go well with mild-flavored vegetables such as potatoes or carrots.

Hyssop: With its resinous, faintly bitter taste, hyssop should be used sparingly; try it on eggplant or in braises.

Lovage: Long cooking brings out the sweet, celery-like taste of this herb. It is good in braises and with potatoes.

Mint: For a cool, aromatic aftertaste, add mint to carrots, cucumbers and tomatoes as well as peas.

Parsley: Its taste is so mild that parsley may be used in quantity with any vegetable. Flat-leafed parsley is more pungent than curly-leafed.

Sage: The slightly musky taste of this plant can dominate; use it sparingly, with strong-tasting vegetables.

Tarragon: A strong herb with a sweet anise taste, tarragon should be used discreetly. Mix it with melted butter in a sauce for asparagus or artichokes.

Thyme: The several varieties of this herb include lemon thyme, whose faint citrus flavor is delicious with braised vegetables, and leaf thyme—a mild version of common thyme *(page 28)*—which is especially excellent in marinades.

All the herbs in this list may be used in their dried forms, of course, but once ▶

Hyssop

Leaf thyme

Lemon thyme

Coriander

Lovage

Mint

Preserving Herbs for Later Use

Herbs can be kept fresh in the refrigerator, frozen plain or with butter, or dried and stored in jars or bags.

A bunch of curly-leafed parsley or of coriander with its roots intact will last up to a week in the refrigerator in a glass partly filled with water. Depending on their fragility, other herbs—wrapped as shown at near right—will keep refrigerated for two to three days.

Herbs frozen in plastic bags last six months; they wilt and darken when thawed, but are still tasty in braises. To keep color and flavor fresh, beat chopped herbs into an equal measure of soft butter, and freeze the blend for use on boiled, steamed or baked vegetables.

Herbs dried at home will hold their flavor best if left on their stems, as shown at far right. After you use the leaves, the stems can be added to charcoal fires to perfume grilled vegetables.

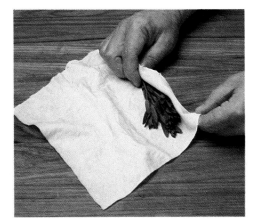

Keeping fresh herbs. Dampen a clean cloth (or a paper towel) with cold water. Put a few sprigs or leaves of the herb — in this case, hyssop — in the damp cloth as shown and roll it up loosely. Store the packet in the refrigerator until you are ready to use the herb.

Drying herbs. Loosely bunch the herb — in this case, thyme. Bind the stems together securely with raffia (above) or string. Hang the herb in a shaded, airy place to dry for two to three weeks. To protect herbs from dust and sun, hang them inside paper bags that have been punched with ventilating holes.

Dittany of Crete

Oregano

Winter savory

Common thyme

Rosemary

Sweet marjoram

Pot marjoram

Summer savory

Bay leaves

dried they never have the fine scents and flavors they do when fresh. Those pictured on this page, however, do lend themselves to drying *(page 27)* and two of them—dittany of Crete and its relative, oregano—are actually stronger tasting when they have been dried.

Stored in a cool, dry place away from the sunlight, dried herbs should keep their scents and flavors for at least six months. Should dried herbs develop a musty smell or change color—signs that they have lost their flavor—throw them away. Before using dried herbs, check the potency of their scent by crumbling at least a few of the leaves in your fingers.

Dried herbs should be used with greater discretion than fresh herbs, because drying tends to concentrate as well as alter their flavors. Once you have become familiar with their individual characteristics, however, you can be as adventurous with these dried herbs as you are with their fresh forms. Here are some particularly good combinations of dried herbs and vegetables:

Bay leaf: This aromatic herb is indispensable in a bouquet garni, and whole leaves often are threaded onto skewers to be used for broiling vegetables.

Dittany of Crete: A strong, pungent variety of oregano, dittany should be used sparingly on tomatoes and peppers.

Marjoram: Sweet marjoram and its stronger relative, pot marjoram, have a sweet, spicy flavor that blends with almost any vegetable.

Oregano: This pungent herb is an important component in many marinades and is a traditional herb for tomatoes.

Rosemary: Very intense and resinous, rosemary must be used with care. Sprinkle it on vegetables before grilling them or add it to the water for boiled ones.

Savory: Winter and summer savory both have a piquancy that makes them possible substitutes for salt; winter savory is stronger and should be used more discreetly. Often referred to as the bean herb, savory also complements cabbages, squash or onions.

Thyme: Common thyme, which has the strongest flavor of any member of the thyme family, appears most frequently in bouquets garnis and braises.

The Repertoire of Cutting Techniques

Most vegetables may be cooked whole, of course, but they are more frequently cut up for cooking. The techniques for cutting them vary not only with the type of vegetable, but also with the ways the vegetables are to be used. When vegetables serve as flavorings for other ingredients, they are finely chopped, as shown on page 31, so that they will release their essences readily. If root vegetables are used as garnishes, they are carved into attractive shapes *(page 32)*. Most vegetables, however, are usually cut up simply to reduce their cooking times.

Two factors determine how quickly a vegetable will cook. One is shape: greater surface area will expose more of the vegetable to heat; both the roll-cut and diagonal slicing techniques demonstrated on page 31 expose broad areas. The other factor is size: the smaller the piece, the more quickly heat will penetrate it.

The concentric layers of an onion can be chopped almost effortlessly as demonstrated below; techniques for slicing, julienning, dicing and shredding other vegetables appear on the following pages. No matter how they are produced, vegetable pieces should always be approximately uniform in size. That way, all will cook in the same amount of time.

1 **Grasping the knife.** For maximum control during chopping, hold the knife blade near the handle with your thumb and the middle joint of your index finger. Curl your other fingers around the handle in a firm but relaxed grip.

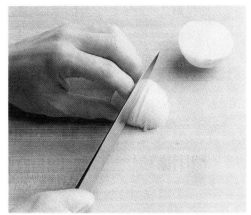

2 **Slicing vertically.** Halve the peeled onion through the root end. Place a half, cut side down, on a cutting board. Make lengthwise slices down through each half at regular intervals; cut to, but not through, the root end that holds the layers together.

3 **Slicing horizontally.** Turn a sliced onion half around and hold it by the root end. Cut horizontally through the onion — again going to, but not through, the root end. The more horizontal cuts you make, the smaller the pieces will be.

4 **Chopping.** Place your fingertips on top of one sliced onion half, and curl your fingers so that the side of the knife blade rests lightly against them at the onion's stem end. Holding the onion still and gradually moving your curled fingers back toward the root end, slice across the cuts made in Step 2 above. Keep the knife blade pressed against your finger joints and do not raise the cutting edge higher than the knuckles, lest you cut into your hand.

Making Slices, Strips and Dice

1 **Cutting slices.** To keep a rounded vegetable from rolling about, cut a thin strip from one side and set that side on the cutting board. Then slice the vegetable — a stemmed eggplant, in this case — to the thickness you want the finished dice to be.

2 **Cutting the slices into strips.** Stack the slices on top of one another, setting aside the rounded outer slices. Cut through the stack at intervals equal to those of the slices in Step 1.

3 **Dicing the strips.** Holding the strips firmly together at one end, cut across the stack of strips to produce dice. Slice the reserved rounded vegetable pieces into strips, then dice them too.

Shredding Leafy Vegetables with a Knife

Tight heads of leaves. Halve the vegetable — cabbage, here — and core it (page 66). Place a half on a cutting board with its flat side down. Then, slice the vegetable vertically with a large chef's knife. The closer together you make the slices, the finer the shreds will be.

Loose leaves. To cut individual leaves of lettuce and spinach into the fine shreds known as a chiffonade, stack the leaves one on top of another; lettuce leaves are used in this demonstration. Roll the leaves into a tight cylinder *(above, left)*. Place the cylinder on a cutting board with the seam down. Holding the cylinder tightly to keep it in shape, cut vertically through the roll at 1/16-inch [1 1/2 -mm.] intervals to produce fine shreds *(above, right)*.

Chopping Up Leafy Herbs

1 Bunching the herb. Wash the herb — parsley, here — and dry it with paper towels so that it will not stick together when you chop. Push the herb leaves into a tight clump and secure the clump by pinching the stems together just below the leaves.

2 Coarse chopping. Grip the knife handle as shown in Step 1, page 29. Press the stems of the herbs down onto the cutting board with your free hand, and slice through the clump of leaves at small intervals until you reach the stems. Discard the stems.

3 Fine chopping. Gather the chopped leaves into a mound. Hold the knife tip against the board. Then — without moving the tip — cut the leaves by raising and lowering the knife handle while moving it from side to side in an arc. Gather the bits and repeat the process until the bits reach the desired size.

Slicing for Surface Area

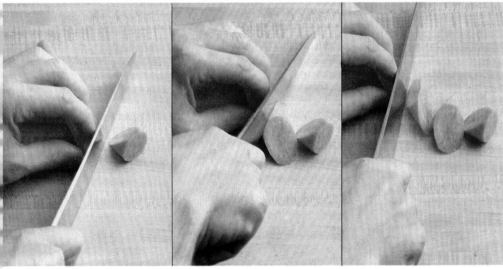

Making the roll cut. Place a peeled, cylindrical vegetable, such as the carrot shown here, on a cutting board. Make a diagonal cut across the carrot to sever its flat stem end *(above, left)*. Keeping the knife in the same position, roll the carrot over and slice through it diagonally again to form a piece with two slanted sides *(center)*. Roll the carrot again and make another diagonal cut to form the second piece. Continue rolling and cutting *(right)* until the entire carrot has been sectioned.

Cutting on the diagonal. Place a trimmed stalk, such as the celery rib above, on a cutting board. Position the knife blade about ¾ inch [2 cm.] from the free end of the vegetable. Slanting the blade away from you, slice the stalk with a sharply angled cut. Discard the first irregular piece. Continue cutting at the same slant at small, regular intervals to produce thin, flat slices.

Shaping Garnish Vegetables

Firm-textured root vegetables such as potatoes, carrots and turnips may be readily carved into shapes that make attractive garnishes. One of the simplest ways is to scoop out small spheres of flesh with a melon baller.

But a variety of other rounded shapes can be quickly carved with an ordinary kitchen knife, using the cutting technique shown at right. First, curve your index finger around the top of the knife blade *(right, center)* to ensure maximum control during cutting. Then hold the knife in a fixed position and push the vegetable against the blade: moving the vegetable rather than the knife makes shaping both easier and safer.

With this technique, you can fashion vegetables into the cylindrical shapes shown here. By paring the cylinders down, you can produce the olive-sized ovals known as *olivettes,* or the smaller ovals called *noisettes* (hazelnuts).

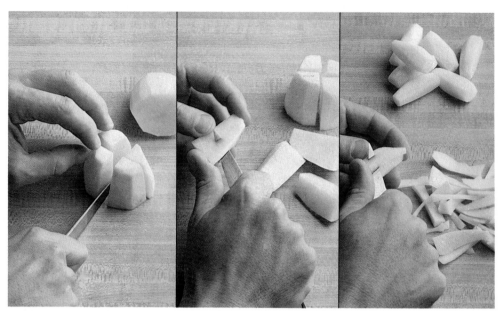

Turning potatoes. Slice off the ends of a peeled potato, halve it crosswise, then quarter the halves lengthwise *(left)*. Push each quarter against the knife to pare off long, curved slices *(center)*. Turn the potato after every cut to form a cylinder *(right)*.

Fancy Names for Simple Shapes

In the lexicon of vegetable cookery, garnish shapes *(above)* are not the only ones with picturesque names. Simple shapes *(right)* have them, too. Julienne, for example, might be called *allumettes,* French for matchsticks, if they are fine, and shoestrings if they are coarse.

Finely chopped food is termed mince or *émincé.* When coarsely chopped, it is said to be cut into bits or *haché.* Coarse dice can be described as cubes. Fine dice can be called *brunoise,* after the French town Brunoy; *salpicon,* after the sauced dishes made with them; even *mirepoix,* for a flavoring base *(opposite).*

For the cook, selecting dimensions for all these shapes is literally a matter of taste. With small pieces, flavors mellow and marry; with large pieces, vegetables keep their texture.

The cook's choice. Cut vegetables fine for pan frying, coarse for boiling and braising. The coarse julienne here are ¼ inch [6 mm.] wide, the fine ones ¹⁄₁₆ inch [1 mm.]; both are about 1 inch [2½ cm.] long. Chopped pieces vary in size. The coarse dice are ½ inch [1 cm.] on a side, the fine dice ⅛ inch [3 mm.].

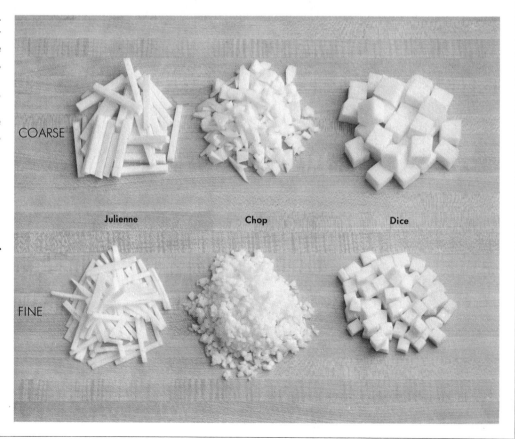

COARSE

Julienne   Chop   Dice

FINE

Classic Flavoring Mixtures

Flavor-rich vegetables ranging from onions to mushrooms are often chopped or diced and used in combinations, perhaps with fresh herbs or other ingredients, to enhance dishes made with other vegetables. Four of the most useful of these aromatic mixtures—three of them French in origin—are demonstrated below.

A *mirepoix (top row, left)* includes finely diced carrots and onions—and sometimes celery—seasoned with fresh parsley, thyme and bay leaf. Often a *mirepoix* is spread on the bottom of a braising vessel to enrich both the cooking liquid and the vegetable being braised.

Duxelles (top row, right) is a mixture of finely chopped mushrooms and onions or shallots, cooked in butter until it reaches a thick, purée-like consistency. This aromatic blend is used in stuffings, mixed vegetable bakes and gratins.

Sofrito (bottom row, left), a common flavoring in Spanish cookery, is primarily composed of tomatoes and onions, although it may include ham, sausage, peppers or garlic. It is used in vegetable stuffings and gratins.

A *persillade (bottom row, right)* combines garlic and parsley. Although the mixture can be included in stuffings and marinades, it is most commonly added to sautés or grills a minute or two before they are served. When heated, the ingredients of a *persillade* quickly suffuse a dish with their flavor.

Cooking mirepoix. Melt butter in a sauté pan and add equal amounts of finely chopped onions and diced carrots *(left)*. Flavor with chopped parsley and thyme, bay leaf and salt. Fry over very low heat for about 30 minutes, stirring occasionally *(right)* to prevent sticking. The ingredients should soften, but not brown.

Making duxelles. Wring finely chopped mushrooms dry in a towel. Fry chopped onions gently in butter until soft. Add the mushrooms *(left)*. Cook, stirring, over medium heat until any mushroom liquid evaporates. Add chopped parsley *(right)*, pepper, salt and lemon juice; cook for 2 more minutes.

Making sofrito. Gently fry finely chopped onions in olive oil until soft but not brown. Add peeled, seeded and chopped tomatoes *(left)*. Salt lightly and cook for 15 to 20 minutes, until the mixture reduces to a thick sauce *(right)*.

Mixing a persillade. Using a ceramic or marble mortar and pestle, pound raw, peeled garlic cloves to a purée *(left)*. Add 2 tablespoons [30 ml.] of chopped parsley for each garlic clove, and mix thoroughly with your fingers *(right)*.

Monthly Availability

	January	February	March	April	May	June	July	August	September	October	November	December
Artichokes												
Asparagus												
Bean Sprouts												
Beans: Broad/Lima												
Beans: Green/Wax												
Beets												
Belgian Endive												
Bok Choy												
Broccoli												
Brussels Sprouts												
Cabbage												
Carrots												
Cauliflower												
Celeriac												
Celery												
Chayote												
Corn												
Cucumber												
Eggplant												
Fennel												
Garlic/Shallots												
Greens: Beet/Collard/Mustard/Turnip												
Jerusalem Artichokes												
Kale												
Kohlrabi												
Leeks/Scallions												
Lettuce												
Mushrooms												
Okra												
Onions												
Parsnips												
Peas												
Peppers												
Potatoes												
Potatoes: New												
Potatoes: Sweet												
Rutabaga												
Salsify												
Snow Peas												
Sorrel												
Spinach												
Squash: Spaghetti												
Squashes: Summer												
Squashes: Winter												
Swiss Chard												
Tomatoes												
Turnips												

Summary of Options for Shopping and Cooking

Cooking Methods

Boil	Steam	Pan Fry	Deep Fry	Batter-coated Deep Fry	Braise/Stew	Bake	Stuff	Gratin	Pudding/Soufflé	Broil/Grill
•		•		•	•	•	•	•		
•	•	•		•		•		•	•	
•	•	•						•	•	
•	•	•			•			•	•	
•	•	•			•					
•		•			•	•		•		
•	•	•			•			•		
•	•	•			•			•		
•	•	•		•				•	•	
•	•	•		•	•			•		
•	•	•			•		•	•		
•	•	•		•	•			•	•	•
•	•	•		•	•			•	•	
•	•	•		•	•			•	•	
•	•	•			•			•		•
•	•	•			•		•	•		
•	•	•			•	•			•	•
•	•	•		•	•	•	•		•	
•	•	•		•	•	•	•	•	•	•
•	•	•			•			•		•
•	•	•			•	•			•	
•	•	•			•				•	
•	•	•		•	•			•	•	
•	•	•			•			•		
•		•			•	•		•		
•	•	•		•	•	•		•	•	
•	•	•			•		•	•	•	
	•	•		•		•	•	•	•	•
	•	•			•					
•	•	•		•	•	•	•	•		
•	•	•		•	•			•	•	
•	•	•			•			•	•	
•	•	•		•	•		•	•		•
•	•	•	•		•	•	•	•	•	•
•	•	•			•	•	•	•	•	•
•	•	•	•		•	•	•	•	•	•
•	•	•			•			•	•	
•	•	•		•				•	•	
•	•	•		•	•					
•	•			•	•			•	•	
•	•	•		•	•			•	•	
•	•				•			•		
•	•	•		•	•	•	•	•	•	
•	•	•			•	•	•	•		
•	•	•		•	•		•	•		
	•			•	•	•	•	•	•	•
•	•	•		•	•	•	•	•	•	•

The chart at left shows at a glance the monthly availability and cooking methods for each vegetable in this volume. You can use it first as a guide to shopping and menu planning, then as a help to choosing recipes from the Anthology or experimenting with the techniques demonstrated on the following pages.

The month-by-month calendar section of the chart indicates when a vegetable is in the greatest supply in American markets—and therefore likely to be best in quality and lowest in price. Many vegetables can be bought at any time of year. The finest, however, remain those that are locally grown, and harvested and sold as they ripen. Depending on where you live, these vegetables may be marketed at times other than the peak seasons shown: in Florida home-grown tomatoes appear as early as January; the Michigan crop does not appear until August.

The Cooking Methods section of the chart provides a general guide to the many possible ways of handling different vegetables. It lists all the methods by which each vegetable is most commonly cooked, but does not describe the steps that may be needed to prepare the vegetable for these methods. Always check the techniques section of this book to find out any required preparations.

Using the chart. Locate the vegetable you want in the list at far left and read across the chart. In the Monthly Availability section, a white space means that less than 1 per cent of the annual supply of that vegetable is available in the month noted at the top of the column; a light green bar means that 1 to 9 per cent of the supply is available; a medium green bar signifies 10 to 14 per cent; and a dark green bar, more than 15 per cent. In the Cooking Methods section, a black dot means that the vegetable may be cooked by the method indicated at the top of the column.

1
Boiling and Steaming
A Matter of Good Timing

Of all the cooking methods suitable for vegetables, boiling is the most used and the most abused. Too often, vegetables lose their tastes, textures and vitamins through overboiling. Properly treated, they will retain freshness and much nutritional value. Crisp green beans, firm new potatoes, tender asparagus—all are the rewards of proper boiling.

Hot water can produce a number of undesirable changes in a vegetable's chemical structure: it leaches out water-soluble nutrients and it releases compounds that dull the colors of green vegetables, rob sweet ones of their sugar and produce sulfurous tastes in cabbages. These changes may be minimized in several ways, but no single tactic can prevent them all. Immersing green and strong-flavored vegetables in a large quantity of boiling water *(pages 38-39)* in an uncovered pot best preserves natural color, flavor and texture. Cooking vegetables in a small amount of water in a covered pot preserves nutrients, as does steaming *(page 40)*. For all of these approaches, though, the cooking time should be as brief as possible; the longer a vegetable cooks, the more pronounced the changes in it will be.

Success in boiling or steaming may depend on additional treatments. Many vegetables should be completely peeled to shorten the cooking time; in the case of broccoli and asparagus, only the tough stems are peeled. Other vegetables, such as beets, should not be peeled at all. A few vegetables require precautions against discoloration: artichokes, celeriac and asparagus, for example, must be cooked in stainless-steel or enameled pans if they are to keep the right color and taste. A list of boiling hints for individual vegetables, along with recommended cooking times, appears on page 41.

Vegetables may be completely cooked by boiling or the technique may be a preliminary to other preparations. Parboiling—boiling vegetables until they are partially cooked—is used to soften dense vegetables such as carrots before they are fried. Vegetables to be puréed *(pages 44-45)* are almost always boiled first. Whatever the treatment, boiled vegetables are commonly served as side dishes. They can, however, become meals in themselves. A large cabbage hollowed out, filled with a hearty stuffing and then gently poached *(pages 46-47)* makes a satisfying supper for a table of hungry people.

Green beans spill from their boiling pan into a colander with all their color, crispness and flavor intact. Once they have been drained, the beans should be returned to the pan and dried quickly over high heat, then buttered, placed in a warm dish and brought to the table.

A Maximum of Water — or a Minimum?

The boiling of individual vegetables differs considerably in details *(page 41)*, but there are only two basic methods, each with adherents convinced that their way is best. Professional chefs prefer the French method of using large quantities of water and an uncovered pan, as shown with broccoli at right. Nutritionists, on the other hand, often insist on a minimum amount of water and a covered pan. In truth, both methods have advantages and disadvantages.

With green vegetables—leaves, most stalks and some seeds and pods—the use of a large, uncovered volume of water has the special virtue of preserving colors. During immersion, the green vegetables release natural acids that dull their color, but the deeply filled, open pan permits the acids to disperse in the air and water. A similar dispersal occurs with sulfurous compounds that would otherwise intensify the flavors of cabbages and other strong-tasting vegetables. On the minus side, the large amount of water used in this method leaches out some of the nutrients of vegetables.

Such leaching is minimized when the vegetables are cooked in only a small amount of water, with the pan covered to ensure all-around heat and even cooking. To obtain some of the dispersing effects of the other approach, the pan can be left uncovered for the first few minutes of cooking; even so, the color of green vegetables and the flavor of strong-tasting ones will never be quite as good as with the open-pan, deep-water method. The vegetables must be carefully watched when cooked covered, because the water can evaporate, leaving them to scorch.

Either method of boiling works well when color and strong taste are not problems—with mild-flavored roots such as potatoes and carrots, for example. So does a middling amount of water, usually described as "enough to cover the vegetable"; but for most vegetables, water to cover is a compromise that does not take full advantage of the benefits of either basic technique.

1 **Starting in boiling water.** Bring a large quantity of salted water to a vigorous boil. Slip the trimmed vegetable into the water. Broccoli *(above)* should have its stalks peeled — and sliced if they are very thick — as shown on page 11. Leaving the pan uncovered, bring the water back to a boil over high heat. Then reduce the heat somewhat, but keep the water boiling.

2 **Testing for doneness.** Continue boiling uncovered until the vegetable is tender but not soft. Peeled broccoli will cook in about 5 minutes, timed after the water returns to the boiling point. Test broccoli by piercing the thickest part of a stalk with the point of a knife; the point should enter the stalk easily.

3 **Draining and serving.** Drain the vegetable in a colander. Return the vegetable to the pan and shake over high heat to dry it. Serve immediately. Some cooks refresh green vegetables by plunging them into cold water to stop their cooking; but they must then be reheated, and may get overdone.

Keeping Asparagus Firm

Asparagus demand special handling during cooking, not only because of their long and slender shape, but also because their firm stalks take longer to cook than their fragile tips. To shorten the cooking time for the stalks and to prevent them from being stringy, they first must be peeled, as shown on page 21.

The standard cooking method is to immerse the peeled stalks in a large quantity of boiling water, as shown at right. But the asparagus may cook unevenly when treated this way, so some cooks use the partial-immersion method, shown below, to keep the tips from overcooking. In this method, the stalks are boiled, but the tender tips are gently steamed.

For either approach, asparagus stalks are tied in bundles before cooking; this prevents the delicate tips from knocking against one another and breaking. Once cooked, the bundles can be lifted out by the string and drained on paper towels. The string should be cut and the stalks separated on the serving plate, minimizing damage to individual stalks.

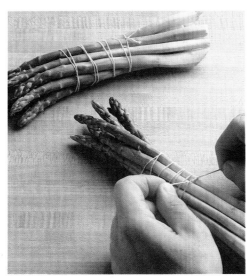

1 **Tying bundles.** Gather six to eight peeled asparagus stalks into a bundle and place them in the middle of a length of string about 30 inches long. Staying below the tips, wind the halves of the string several times around the stalks in opposite directions, and knot the ends near the bases. Reserve one loose stalk to taste for doneness.

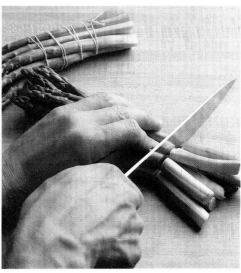

2 **Trimming the ends.** If you have not snapped off the woody ends of the stalks as described on pages 20-21, trim them to the same length with a sharp knife. Cut through the stalks with one stroke, making sure you remove the woody sections where the color changes to a darker green.

A Tandem Technique

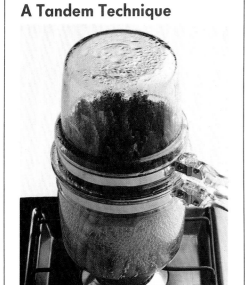

Steam boiling. Pour 3 inches [8 cm.] of boiling water into the bottom section of a double boiler. Place the bundled asparagus upright in the boiling water. Invert the boiler's top section over it to trap the steam. Steam the tips and boil the stalks until they are tender — about 8 minutes.

3 **Boiling asparagus.** Lift the bundles by slipping a fork through the string wrapping, and lay them, along with the loose stalk, in a large pot or deep skillet of boiling water. Cook uncovered for about 8 minutes after the water returns to a boil. Remove the asparagus when the single stalk is tender yet firm to the bite.

Strategies for Steaming

Any vegetable that can be boiled can also be steamed—cooked over boiling water *(right)* or in the aromatic steam released from lettuce leaves *(below)*. Steaming takes longer than boiling, but because it requires a covered pan and because the vegetables do not touch the water, it does a better job of preserving nutrients. The covered pan, of course, can discolor green vegetables and intensify the tastes of strong-flavored vegetables. These problems can be minimized by decreasing cooking time: tender vegetables or those cut into small pieces will cook before their colors or flavors change.

Quick-cooking, small vegetables such as young peas or green beans are the best candidates for cooking in lettuce leaves. When heated, the leaves release moisture that steams the vegetables they enclose; if vegetables require long cooking, however, that moisture may evaporate, allowing the leaves to scorch.

The safest technique is to suspend vegetables over boiling water in a steaming pan with a perforated insert or the collapsible metal basket shown at right.

1 **Adjusting the steamer.** Place the steamer basket in a pan and put the vegetables into the basket. Pour in 1 to 2 inches [2½ to 5 cm.] of water; the water must not touch the basket bottom. To shorten cooking times, cut dense vegetables such as carrots into thin pieces; soft vegetables such as zucchini may be left in larger pieces.

2 **Steaming the vegetables.** Cover the pan, bring the water to a boil over medium heat and steam the vegetables gently, following the cooking times specified on the opposite page. When the vegetables can be pierced with a sharp knife, they are done.

Exploiting the Moisture of Leaves

1 **Positioning the leaves.** Rinse two or three large lettuce leaves and arrange them so that they cover the bottom of the pan, extending partway up the sides. Boston lettuce is shown here, but any large-leafed lettuce may be used.

2 **Enclosing the vegetables.** Put small, quick-cooking vegetables, such as the young peas shown here, in the center of the leaves, leaving a ½-inch [1-cm.] margin so the vegetables do not spill out as the leaves shrink during cooking. Cover with more leaves.

3 **Steaming the vegetables.** Cover the pan tightly and place it over low heat. When the lettuce leaves are completely wilted, after about 10 minutes, their rendered moisture will have steamed the vegetables within.

How to Boil or Steam Any Vegetable

The following guide summarizes boiling and steaming instructions for the vegetables in this book. Because a vegetable's cooking time varies with its size, age and tenderness, both minimum and maximum times are listed. These times will produce vegetables that retain as much of their natural texture—and nutrients—as possible. For softer texture, you may want to increase the times for certain vegetables.

When the way a vegetable is prepared affects its cooking time, this is noted. The term "cut up" refers to vegetables reduced to equal-sized pieces—either 1-inch [2½-cm.] dice or slices ½ inch [1 cm.] thick. If your pieces are larger or smaller, adjust the cooking times.

Cooking times for boiling are the same for both the open-pan, deep-water method (at least 2 quarts [2 liters] of water to each pound [½ kg.] of vegetables) and the covered-pan, shallow-water technique (1 cup [¼ liter] of water to each pound of vegetables). For either method, boil the water, add the vegetables and begin timing when the water returns to a boil. To parboil, reduce the times to one third.

Most vegetables should be boiled in salted water; allow 1 teaspoon [5 ml.] salt to each quart. Vegetables boiled in shallow water should be left uncovered for the first few minutes of cooking to minimize color and flavor change.

Some vegetables—indicated below—discolor when they are prepared in cast-iron or aluminum pans. Cook these vegetables in nonreactive enameled, glass or stainless-steel pans. Other vegetables—also indicated—discolor in plain water; boil them by the open-pan, deep-water method, using acidulated water *(page 13)* or a *blanc*—water to which flour, oil and lemon juice have been added in the proportion of 1 tablespoon [15 ml.] of each to 1 quart of water.

Artichokes. Boil whole in a *blanc* for 20 to 40 minutes. Use a nonreactive pan. Do not steam.
Asparagus. Boil whole for 5 to 8 minutes, 3 to 4 minutes if cut up. Steam whole for 10 to 15 minutes, 5 to 7 minutes if cut up. Use a nonreactive pan.
Bean sprouts. Boil whole for 2 to 3 minutes. Steam whole for 3 to 5 minutes.

Beans: broad or lima. Boil whole for 10 to 15 minutes. Steam whole for 15 to 25 minutes.
Beans: green or wax. Boil whole for 5 to 10 minutes, 4 to 7 minutes if cut up. Steam whole for 15 to 20 minutes, 10 to 15 minutes if cut up.
Beets. Boil whole and unpeeled for 40 minutes to 3 hours. Do not steam.
Belgian endive. Boil whole for 15 to 20 minutes. Steam whole for 30 to 40 minutes.
Bok choy. Boil leaves for 2 to 3 minutes, ribs for 7 to 10 minutes. Steam leaves for 5 to 7 minutes, ribs for 15 to 20 minutes.
Broccoli. Boil whole stalks for 5 to 10 minutes, 3 to 7 minutes if cut up. Steam stalks for 15 to 20 minutes, 10 to 15 minutes if cut up.
Brussels sprouts. Boil whole for 5 to 7 minutes. Steam whole for 15 to 20 minutes.
Cabbage. Boil quarters for 10 to 15 minutes, 5 to 7 minutes if shredded. Steam quarters for 25 to 35 minutes, 10 to 15 minutes if shredded. For red cabbage, use a nonreactive pan and acidulated water.
Carrots. Boil whole for 15 to 20 minutes, 5 to 15 minutes if cut up. Steam whole for 25 to 40 minutes, 15 to 35 minutes if cut up.
Cauliflower. Boil whole for 15 to 20 minutes, 5 to 8 minutes if cut up. Steam whole for 45 to 50 minutes, 20 to 30 minutes if cut up.
Celeriac. Boil cut up for 15 to 20 minutes. Do not steam.
Celery. Boil whole ribs for 12 to 15 minutes, 10 to 15 minutes if cut up. Steam whole ribs for 20 to 25 minutes, 15 to 20 minutes if cut up.
Chayote. Boil quarters for 15 to 20 minutes. Steam quarters for 25 to 30 minutes.
Corn. Boil whole for 3 to 5 minutes, omitting salt but adding ½ teaspoon [2 ml.] of sugar for each quart [1 liter] of water. Steam whole for 20 to 30 minutes.
Cucumber. Boil peeled, seeded halves for 7 to 10 minutes, quarters for 5 to 6 minutes, cut-up pieces for 3 to 5 minutes. Steam halves for 15 to 20 minutes, quarters for 10 to 15 minutes, pieces for 10 to 15 minutes.
Eggplant. Boil whole and unpeeled for 15 to 20 minutes, 5 to 10 minutes if peeled and cut up. Steam peeled and cut up for 20 minutes.
Fennel. Boil whole for 30 to 35 minutes, 10 to 15 minutes if quartered. Steam quartered for 20 to 25 minutes.
Garlic or shallots. Boil peeled or unpeeled for 10 to 15 minutes. Do not steam.
Greens. Boil whole beet, collard, mustard or turnip leaves for 7 to 10 minutes. Steam whole leaves for 15 to 20 minutes.
Jerusalem artichokes. Boil whole for 10 to 15 minutes, 5 to 8 minutes if cut up. Steam whole for 20 minutes, 15 minutes if cut up.
Kale. Boil whole leaves for 10 to 15 minutes. Steam whole leaves for 15 minutes.
Kohlrabi. Boil whole for 30 to 40 minutes, 20 minutes if quartered. Do not steam.

Leeks or scallions. Boil whole for 10 to 15 minutes, 2 to 3 minutes if cut up. Steam whole for 30 minutes, 7 to 10 minutes if cut up.
Lettuce. Boil separated romaine leaves and whole butterhead for 2 to 3 minutes, whole romaine for 5 to 10 minutes. Steam separated romaine leaves and whole butterhead for 10 to 15 minutes, whole romaine for 20 to 25 minutes.
Mushrooms. Do not boil. Steam whole for 3 to 8 minutes.
Okra. Boil whole for 10 to 15 minutes. Steam whole for 20 minutes.
Onions. Boil small yellow or white onions for 15 to 30 minutes. Steam for 25 to 40 minutes. Do not steam or boil large onions.
Parsnips. Boil whole for 10 to 15 minutes, 5 to 10 minutes if cut up. Steam whole for 25 to 35 minutes, 20 to 30 minutes if cut up.
Peas. Boil large mature peas for 4 to 10 minutes, small young peas for 2 minutes. Steam large peas for 15 to 20 minutes, small peas for 5 to 7 minutes.
Peppers. Boil halves for 6 to 7 minutes, 4 to 5 minutes if cut up. Steam halves for 15 minutes, 8 to 10 minutes if cut up.
Potatoes. Boil whole and unpeeled for 20 minutes, 10 to 15 minutes if cut up. Steam cut up for 35 to 40 minutes.
Potatoes, new. Boil whole and unpeeled for 7 to 15 minutes, 10 minutes if quartered. Steam whole and unpeeled for 25 to 35 minutes.
Potatoes, sweet. Boil whole and unpeeled for 25 to 30 minutes, 20 to 30 minutes if cut up. Do not steam.
Rutabaga. Boil whole for 30 to 40 minutes, but for 15 to 20 minutes if cut up. Steam cut up for 30 minutes.
Salsify. Boil whole for 25 to 35 minutes, 20 to 30 minutes if cut up. Use acidulated water or a *blanc*. Do not steam.
Snow peas. Boil whole for 30 seconds. Steam whole for 5 to 7 minutes.
Sorrel. Do not boil or steam. Parboil whole leaves for 1 minute. Use a nonreactive pan.
Spinach. Boil whole leaves for 1 to 2 minutes. Steam whole leaves for 15 to 20 minutes.
Squash, spaghetti. Boil whole for 35 to 45 minutes. Steam halves for 30 to 45 minutes.
Squashes, summer. Boil whole and unpeeled for 5 to 20 minutes, 7 to 10 minutes if cut up. Steam whole and unpeeled for 10 to 20 minutes, 10 to 15 minutes if cut up.
Squashes, winter. Boil cut up for 10 to 15 minutes. Steam cut up for 25 to 35 minutes.
Swiss chard. Boil leaves for 1 to 2 minutes, ribs for 10 to 12 minutes. Steam leaves for 5 to 7 minutes, ribs for 5 to 20 minutes.
Tomatoes. Do not boil or steam.
Turnips. Boil whole for 10 to 15 minutes, 5 to 10 minutes if quartered. Steam whole for 25 to 30 minutes, 15 to 20 minutes if quartered.

A Spectrum of Sauces

The sauces that enrich boiled vegetables can range from a spoonful of olive oil or butter to one of the three classic mixtures—vinaigrette, hollandaise and butter sauce—demonstrated here. Whatever your choice, the vegetables should be freshly cooked and carefully dried; otherwise the sauce will turn watery.

To dry firm vegetables such as green beans and potatoes, drain them in a colander, then toss them in a pan over high heat until the water clinging to them evaporates. If the sauce is to be butter, add small pieces to the hot pan, tossing until the butter melts. Vegetables such as asparagus that are too fragile to toss should be drained on a kitchen towel; pour melted butter over them in the serving dish. For any vegetable, olive oil and a little lemon juice can be a fragrant substitute for butter.

From olive oil and lemon juice it is a short step to vinaigrette: a blend of oil, vinegar and seasonings *(opposite, bottom)*. A temporary emulsion, vinaigrette quickly separates; stir it before serving.

Hollandaise sauce *(opposite, top; recipe, page 166)* is a longer lasting emulsion made by beating butter into warmed egg yolks; lemon juice gives the sauce its tart flavor. If the yolks are to absorb the butter without curdling or separating, they must stay fluid, they must never be overheated and the butter must be added slowly. To keep the yolks fluid, mix them with water. To avoid overheating, make the sauce in a bain-marie *(opposite)* or double boiler. Hollandaise separates if left standing, but if you set the pan in warm water, it can wait up to an hour.

Butter sauce, or *sauce bâtarde (below; recipe, page 166),* is also thickened with egg yolks, but is based on a roux of butter and flour blended over low heat. Add warm water to a roux for a plain sauce; add egg yolks for a rich, creamy one.

The trick with butter sauce is to make it very quickly. Stir water into the roux as soon as it is smooth. Add the egg yolks just after the water and roux have boiled and slightly cooled. Take the sauce from the stove as soon as it thickens and finish it immediately with butter chunks.

Sauce Bâtarde: Starting from Butter and Flour

1 **Beating the egg yolks.** Drop the egg yolks into a bowl, pour in a little cold water and beat the mixture until it is smooth. Set the mixture aside.

2 **Making the roux.** Melt butter in a heavy pan and add an equal amount of flour *(above)*. Stir the mixture over low heat until it begins to bubble.

3 **Pouring in water.** Remove the pan from the heat and whisk in lightly salted warm water *(above)*. Return to the heat and whisk until the mixture boils.

4 **Adding the egg.** Remove the sauce from the heat, let it cool for a minute, then whisk in the beaten egg mixture. Continue to whisk over low heat.

5 **Adding lemon juice.** When the sauce thickens, but before it boils, take it off the heat and add lemon juice. Whisk in some butter chunks.

6 **Finishing.** Remove the pan from the heat and gradually add the rest of the butter, whisking steadily. Adjust the seasoning and serve immediately.

Hollandaise: A Mixture of Butter and Egg Yolks

1 **Making a bain-marie.** Put the egg yolks in a pan. Next, half-fill a larger pan with water and place a trivet in it. Then heat the water to a slow simmer.

2 **Whisking the egg yolks.** Add a spoonful of cold water to the egg yolks. Set the pan on the trivet and whisk the yolks until they are smooth.

3 **Adding butter.** Whisk in butter chunks in batches. Allow the yolks to absorb each batch — you should see no butter — before adding the next.

4 **Thickening the sauce.** When all the butter has been added, continue whisking until the sauce becomes thick and creamy. Keep the heat low.

5 **Adding lemon juice.** Season with white and cayenne pepper and salt. Add lemon juice to taste *(above)*; squeeze the juice through a strainer into the pan.

6 **Adjusting consistency.** Whisk the sauce over low heat until it is as thick as heavy cream. If it becomes too thick, whisk in a little warm water to thin it.

Vinaigrette: Blending Oil with Vinegar

1 **Seasoning the vinegar.** Put salt and pepper in a bowl and pour in vinegar — in this case, red wine vinegar. Stir until the salt dissolves.

2 **Pouring in oil.** Add about four or five times as much oil as vinegar; exact proportions will depend on the acidity of the vinegar, and your taste.

3 **Combining the ingredients.** Stir to barely mix the oil and vinegar; excess beating allows volatile flavoring elements in the oil to escape.

Five Ways to Produce a Purée

Once they are made tender by cooking, all vegetables can be mashed or sieved to make a smooth pulp, or purée. A vegetable purée not only constitutes a light side dish by itself, but also can provide the primary ingredient for such elaborate preparations as the cauliflower pudding demonstrated on pages 88-89.

The actual mashing or sieving can be accomplished in various ways *(right)*, depending on your vegetables and the texture you want the purée to have. The coarsest-textured purée is produced by pounding vegetables with a potato masher. For a finer, lighter purée, use a large pestle to press them through a sieve. For especially fine purées, scrape the vegetables through a drum sieve.

A food mill will ease the labor of puréeing vegetables. So, of course, will electrical devices such as blenders, portable mixers and processors, but they should be used with care since their rapid action can reduce vegetables to a homogeneous pulp without texture or character.

All vegetables to be puréed should be well drained after they are boiled or steamed; this ensures that the purée will be thick and firm. Most vegetables have enough water content after draining to provide ample moisture for the purée. Potatoes, however, contain so much starch and fiber that they will be too dry without the addition of milk, cream or simply a little of the water in which they were boiled. Add the liquid after puréeing so that you will be able to judge how much the mixture needs.

Naturally starchy vegetables, such as potatoes and peas, can be puréed alone; but vegetables with a low starch content, such as young green beans, should be combined with a small amount of cooked rice or potato to give their purées the necessary starchy body.

To give any purée a smoother consistency and a shiny surface, incorporate butter after the purée has been reheated and has been removed from the heat for serving. Instead of simply melting, butter added at this point will bind the vegetable purée into a creamy whole.

Using a potato masher. Any cooked vegetable that does not have tough fibers or skin, such as the peeled potatoes shown here, can be puréed with a potato masher. Pound the vegetable, a little at a time, until all of it is smooth. Then use the masher or a spoon to blend butter into the purée.

Sieving with a pestle. Pumpkin *(above)* and other soft-textured cooked vegetables can be puréed by using a large pestle to press them through the mesh of a fine metal sieve into a bowl or pan. Green beans and other more fibrous vegetables are too firm to purée by this method.

New Flavors from Judicious Mixes

In the composite purée demonstrated here, starchy potatoes give body to an all-white mixture of turnips, celeriac, onions and garlic. As in all mixed purées, the separate flavors of the individual ingredients merge into a new and unique whole. With the exception of the garlic, which is added to taste, the vegetables used for the purée are combined in roughly equal proportions. By following this formula, you can select other combinations of vegetables to create your own mixture.

In this demonstration, the first step is to parboil the turnips briefly and separately to tame their strong flavor and draw out some of their excess moisture. After parboiling, stew the turnips in butter until they are tender and most of their remaining moisture has evaporated. All the other vegetables are boiled together, then puréed with the turnips. Finally, the mixed vegetable purée is reheated and, immediately before serving, bound with butter.

Boiling the vegetables. Parboil peeled and quartered turnips for 5 to 10 minutes, then drain them. Peel the celeriac, potatoes and onions, and cut them into large pieces. Boil the celeriac for 10 minutes, add other vegetables and several garlic cloves *(above)*, then cook for 30 to 40 minutes.

Using a food mill. Firm-textured vegetables — such as the cauliflower here — are easily broken up by the blades of a food mill. The blades, rotated by turning the handle, gradually force food through a perforated plate in the machine's base. Food mills are also ideal for breaking up peas and beans before sieving them *(far right)*.

Puréeing in a processor. Any vegetable can be reduced to pulp in seconds by a food processor. But part of the load — here, carrots — will be flung out of reach of the blades. For an even consistency, operate the machine in short bursts, stopping often to scrape the bowl with a spatula. Processors are not recommended for potatoes or other starchy vegetables; the rapid blade movement will turn them pasty.

Using a drum sieve. Vegetables such as celery or string beans, with fibers or skins that are not removed before cooking, can be chopped in a food mill, then puréed through a drum sieve, or tamis, with very fine, nylon mesh. Here, peas are pressed through the mesh with a plastic scraper; their skins do not pass through the sieve, so the resulting purée is smooth.

2 **Straining off the stock.** While the other vegetables are cooking, stew the turnips gently in enough butter to keep them from sticking to the saucepan; do not let them color. When the other vegetables become tender, strain off the water into a bowl *(above)*. Reserve it for use in a soup or as a stock.

3 **Making the purée.** Add the butter-stewed turnips to the other vegetables and purée them all together. Since onions are not easily puréed through a conventional sieve, push all the cooked vegetables through a food mill, as demonstrated here.

4 **Binding with butter.** Reheat the purée for serving, stirring constantly with a wooden spoon to keep it from sticking and to distribute the heat evenly. When the purée is hot, remove it from the heat and stir in chunks of butter *(above)*, then serve at once.

Whole, Stuffed Cabbage: A Course in Itself

Cabbage—that staple of peasant cooking throughout the world—is often simply shredded, boiled briefly and served as a garnish vegetable. But the size and structure of a cabbage head offer the cook a special opportunity: the tightly furled center leaves, or heart, can be removed, producing a capacious hollow for stuffing. Boiling the stuffed cabbage produces a meal in one dish *(recipe, page 107)*.

Any green or white cabbage weighing 2 to 2½ pounds [1 kg.] or more is suitable for such treatment. A preliminary blanching softens its outer leaves so that they can be peeled back to expose the tightly layered heart *(Step 1, far right)*. When the heart is removed, it is chopped up and mixed with meat, other vegetables and herbs to make the stuffing.

Among the types of meat that might be used for stuffing, bacon and pork have a special affinity with cabbage—and their fat helps to keep the filling moist. If you use lean meat, such as veal, or cooked meat leftovers, you should add a little fat—butter, oil, pork fat or bone marrow.

You can include almost any vegetable in the stuffing. In the demonstration here, parboiled, chopped chard leaves, peeled, seeded and chopped tomatoes and sautéed onions are combined with bacon and the chopped cabbage leaves. But lettuce, peas or spinach leaves would also blend well with the cabbage heart. Boiled rice binds and lightens this stuffing; or you may use bread crumbs. Similar stuffings can serve for chard or for vine or individual cabbage leaves *(pages 68-69)*.

To keep the stuffed cabbage in shape as it cooks, enclose it in an undyed-cotton string net *(right)*. These nets are sometimes sold at kitchenware shops; cheesecloth may be substituted. Submerged in stock or salted water, the cabbage can then be simmered safely for the 2 to 3 hours it takes to cook.

1 **Removing the heart.** Trim the stem of the cabbage and remove any damaged leaves *(left)*. Simmer the cabbage in salted water for 10 to 15 minutes, until the outer leaves are just supple. Take the cabbage out of the pot and drain it. Set aside any leaves that become detached. When the cabbage is cool enough to handle, place it on a string net or a large piece of cheesecloth. Gently pull back the outer leaves *(center)*. Cut the firm heart of inner leaves from the stem *(right)*, leaving the outer leaves attached.

5 **Tying up the bag.** With a trussing needle, thread uncoated cotton string through the mesh around the top of the string net *(above)*. Pull the string tight and tie it. If you use cheesecloth, pull the edges together at the top and tie them. Lower the cabbage into a pot of boiling, salted water or stock, then reduce the heat to a simmer.

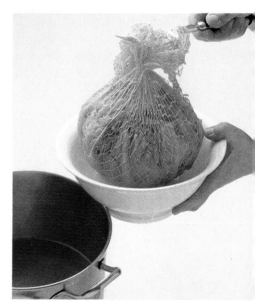

6 **Completing the cooking.** Leaving the pot lid ajar to keep the liquid simmering slowly, cook the cabbage for 3 hours. To remove the cabbage from the pot, push the prongs of a fork through the top of the bag. Use a bowl to catch the dripping liquid *(above)*, and transfer the cabbage to a colander to drain for 5 to 10 minutes.

2 **Stuffing the cabbage.** Chop the heart finely, squeeze out excess water with your hands and mix the chopped leaves with the other ingredients of the stuffing. Place the string net with the outer cabbage leaves on it in a bowl. Pack stuffing into the hollow center, molding it into a ball about the same size and shape as the cabbage heart.

3 **Capping the stuffing.** To help keep the stuffing intact, press one or two large leaves over it. Use the leaves that broke off during the preliminary simmering or detach a few outer leaves. If you have extra stuffing, press it around their edges and fold a few outer leaves over it (above).

4 **Closing up the cabbage.** Gently fold all the remaining outer leaves back into place. Overlap them to enclose the stuffing completely and to give the cabbage its original rounded shape.

7 **Unwrapping the cabbage.** Place the drained cabbage in a bowl, cut the string and pull back the edges of the net (left) or cheesecloth. Lay a plate on top of the cabbage, then turn over plate and cabbage together. Lift away the bowl (center) and remove the net or cheesecloth. Finally, replace the bowl on the cabbage and invert the plate and the bowl once more so that the cabbage is stem side down and ready to serve (right).

8 **Serving the cabbage.** Serve the stuffed cabbage directly from the bowl so that it retains its shape as it is cut into portions. Slice it into wedges as if it were a cake, then pour a little of the cooking liquid over each wedge.

2
Frying
Suiting the Method to the Material

Pan-frying tactics
The basics of deep frying
Perfect French fries
Sculpting potato shapes
Making batter coating

Vegetables can be fried in two basic ways: quick frying, which means cooking vegetables in the minimum amount of hot oil or fat, and deep frying—cooking them in a large amount of even hotter oil or fat. Either way, the vegetables will retain their crispness, since they are cooked only briefly and do not come into contact with water during the process. They also will taste delicious; the coating of oil, fat or batter that vegetables receive in frying acts as a flavoring while sealing in the vegetables' own flavors. To achieve good results, you need only adapt the frying method to the vegetables you have and carefully prepare those vegetables for cooking.

For frying, vegetables must be in small pieces that will cook through quickly: at temperatures up to 390° F. [195° C.], it is all too easy to scorch the surfaces before the interiors are even heated through. Slices, cubes, julienne or rough chunks may be either quick fried or deep fried. The only rule is that all vegetables that are fried together should be cut into pieces of approximately equal size so that they will cook in the same amount of time. Shredded vegetables may be cooked in a mass as a kind of cake by combining quick frying with steaming *(pages 52-53)*. And shredded, finely chopped or puréed vegetables may be bound together with a batter and quick fried as pancakes *(pages 52-53)* or bound with a thick sauce and deep fried as croquettes *(page 54)*.

Most vegetables can be quick fried straight from the cutting board. However, moisture-rendering vegetables such as tomatoes must be coated with crumbs or flour to seal in their liquid and protect their delicate flesh from the heat of the fat and pan. And dense vegetables that require a long time to cook—cauliflower and carrots, for example—should be parboiled before quick frying to minimize their cooking time. Dense vegetables also need parboiling before deep frying, and all vegetables except potatoes must be coated with a protective batter that will keep them from burning and drying in the sizzling oil. In the case of potatoes, a high starch content serves to seal in their moisture.

Potatoes, in fact, would seem to be the perfect frying vegetable—almost any method suits them. But most vegetables, from Jerusalem artichokes to asparagus, can be fried in one way or another, as shown in the chart on pages 34-35.

Deep-fried onion rings tumble from the towel used to drain them onto a serving platter lined with a napkin that will blot up the last traces of fat. Each ring of onion is moist and tender under its protective coating of crisp batter.

49

Easy Steps to Perfect Pan Frying

The rules and results of pan frying—or sautéing—are the same, whether the cooking is done in a skillet, a sauté pan or a wok. The vegetables are cooked quickly in a small amount of very hot oil or fat. The brief cooking and the coating of oil or fat the vegetables receive ensure that they retain their flavor, texture and color. Almost any vegetable can be pan fried, alone or with others. If carefully prepared and cooked, each will emerge crisp and delicious.

Vegetables to be fried together should be cut into small, uniform pieces that cook in only moments. Quick-cooking vegetables such as snow peas and mushrooms need no further preparation. Vegetables that take longer to cook, such as carrots, should be parboiled first—and dried to prevent spattering—to decrease cooking time. Fragile vegetables, such as tomatoes, benefit from a coating that will harden during cooking to protect their flesh from the heat and seal in their moisture *(box, opposite, bottom)*.

Coated vegetable slices are protected to some extent from the heat and should be turned only once to brown the coating on both sides. Uncoated vegetables, however, should be kept moving briskly in the oil or fat—flip them with a spatula or shake the pan—so that they do not overcook or cook unevenly.

The oil, plus a little salt, provides the essential flavoring for pan-fried vegetables. Butter adds sweetness, but it must be clarified or mixed with oil to prevent burning; olive oil contributes a fruity taste and bacon fat or lard an aromatic one. For stir frying, mild peanut oil is customary. You may vary flavors further by adding chopped shallots or onions, sliced ginger root or—as with the green beans here—whole cloves of garlic, unpeeled to restrain their sharpness. Or, as shown in the demonstration with mixed vegetables *(right, below)*, you may add seasoning at the end of cooking in the form of a pungent *persillade (page 33)*, lemon juice or a sprinkling of freshly chopped herbs. For contrasting texture, add bread crumbs during the last few seconds of cooking.

Pan frying a single vegetable. Place a shallow skillet containing a thin layer of butter and oil over moderate heat; add crushed unpeeled garlic cloves. When the garlic begins to brown, add the vegetables — here, green beans. Cook for 3 to 4 minutes, shaking the pan constantly; add bread crumbs *(right)* and cook for a moment more, until the crumbs have browned.

Pan frying a mixture of vegetables. Cut the vegetables — here, raw scallions, mushrooms, asparagus and celery, along with parboiled artichoke bottoms — into small, thin pieces. Place them in a pan in which a film of oil has been heated to the sizzling point. Cook for 3 to 4 minutes over moderate heat, shaking the pan every few seconds. Season with a *persillade* and freshly squeezed lemon juice *(right)*.

Stir Frying in a Wok

Stir frying—pan frying done Chinese style—uses very high heat and very brief cooking to produce vegetables that are almost as crisp as when they were raw. Quick-cooking vegetables such as summer squashes and asparagus need no more advance preparation than thin slicing. Slower-cooking root vegetables such as turnips can be stir fried if cut finely and parboiled briefly.

For stir frying, the oil may be flavored ahead of time with fresh ginger or, as here, with garlic cloves, but these seasonings must be removed almost immediately to prevent them from burning. At the end of cooking, the oil may be turned into a sauce by adding 1 teaspoon [5 ml.] of cornstarch mixed with 1 tablespoon [15 ml.] of water.

The best pan to use for stir frying is a carbon-steel wok *(right)*. Its small bottom area enables the cook to keep the vegetables well coated while using a minimum of oil; its curving sides make it easy to keep the vegetables moving.

Stir frying. Coat a heated wok with oil. When the oil almost smokes, add peeled garlic cloves, removing them as they begin to brown—after about 10 seconds *(left)*. Add the vegetable — here, broccoli florets and sliced, peeled broccoli stems — and flip it constantly *(right)* until the pieces become tender. Broccoli will be ready to serve in about 3 minutes.

A Shield for Fragile Vegetables

Sliced cucumbers, summer squashes or the green tomatoes shown below are all fragile vegetables that exude their moisture when heated. To keep them intact for pan frying, these vegetables can be dipped in a coating that will seal in their moisture and, at the same time, brown to a crisp crust.

Preparations for coating are simple: cut the rinsed, unpeeled, raw vegetables into ½-inch [1-cm.] slices that will cook quickly. The cut surfaces will be moist enough to make the coating adhere, so the coating may be a simple one—flour, dried bread crumbs, cornmeal or cracker crumbs. Season the coating with salt and pepper and, if you wish, pulverized herbs.

1 **Coating the slices.** Press both sides of each tomato slice into the coating — in this case, cornmeal. Let the slices dry on a rack for a few minutes.

2 **Pan frying the slices.** Heat a thin film of fat — here, rendered bacon fat — in a shallow pan over moderate heat. Add the coated slices.

3 **Turning the slices.** When the bottoms are lightly browned, turn the slices with tongs or a spatula. Cook until the second side is browned.

A Crisp Cake of Shredded Potato

If you shred vegetables instead of slicing them for pan frying, they will be malleable and so easily penetrated by heat that you can fry them in a solid mass. Most shredded vegetables must be combined with a batter to give them body and hold them together; they then are fried as pancakes *(box, below)*. Shredded potatoes, however, have an abundance of natural starch to hold them together and no other binding is required if they are pressed together to form a *paillasson,* or straw cake *(right; recipe, page 118).*

The straw cake illustrates a variation of the basic frying technique. The skillet is covered for half the cooking time so that the steam that rises from the vegetables when they are heated helps to cook them, producing a soft, moist interior. During the steaming phase, excess moisture that condenses on the underside of the pan lid must be wiped off from time to time so that it does not drip onto the cake and make it soggy. The cake is then turned over and fried uncovered. During this phase, it develops a crisp crust.

Although a *paillasson* is composed primarily of potatoes, you can vary its taste by sandwiching different ingredients between layers of potatoes. Use shredded carrots or cheese, sliced, precooked artichoke bottoms, chopped onions, or one of the flavorings demonstrated on page 33.

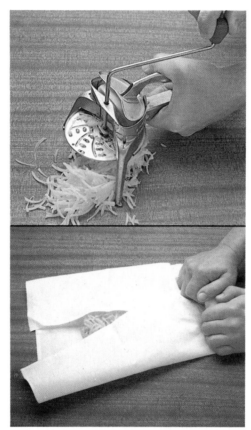

1 **Preparing the potatoes.** Shred peeled potatoes with a rotary shredder *(top).* Rinse the shreds in cold water, then drain; repeat both steps. Place the shreds on a towel and roll them up as tightly as you can *(above)* to dry them.

2 **Forming the cake.** Over a medium-to-low heat, melt enough butter to form a thick coating on the bottom of a heavy, shallow skillet. Put the potato shreds into the pan. Gently press them with a fork to form a single, firm cake.

Old-fashioned Potato Pancakes

Shredded vegetables such as spinach *(recipe, page 102)* often are added to batter and fried to produce pancakes with a mild vegetable flavor. Starchy potatoes, however, can become pancakes with the simple addition of egg and a little flour to bind them and give them body.

Successful potato pancakes *(recipe, page 120)* require thoroughly dried potato shreds, since excess moisture will make the mixture too thin. Press the shredded potatoes in a sieve to drain them, as shown here, or wring them dry in a towel. Work quickly: potatoes turn gray when exposed to the air.

For a different flavor, add shredded cheese, grated onion or fresh, chopped herbs to the potato mixture.

1 **Making the batter.** Mix eggs and flour in a bowl. Peel and shred the potatoes and put the shreds in a sieve. Press the shreds to remove their liquid *(above)*; stir them into the egg mixture.

2 **Forming pancakes.** Heat ¼ inch [6 mm.] of fat or oil in a skillet over medium heat. When the fat sizzles, drop in spoonfuls of the potato batter. Flatten the batter into thin cakes about 5 inches [13 cm.] in diameter.

3 **Cooking the first side.** Salt and pepper the cake. To prevent it from sticking to the pan, distribute thick slices of butter around its edges *(above)*. Cover and cook for about 20 minutes, removing the lid two or three times to wipe off condensation on its underside. When the edges of the cake begin to brown, shake the pan to loosen the cake or loosen it with a spatula.

3 **Turning the pancakes.** After about 2 minutes, when the pancake bottoms brown, turn the cakes over *(above)*. Brown the second side, then remove the pancakes and drain them on paper towels.

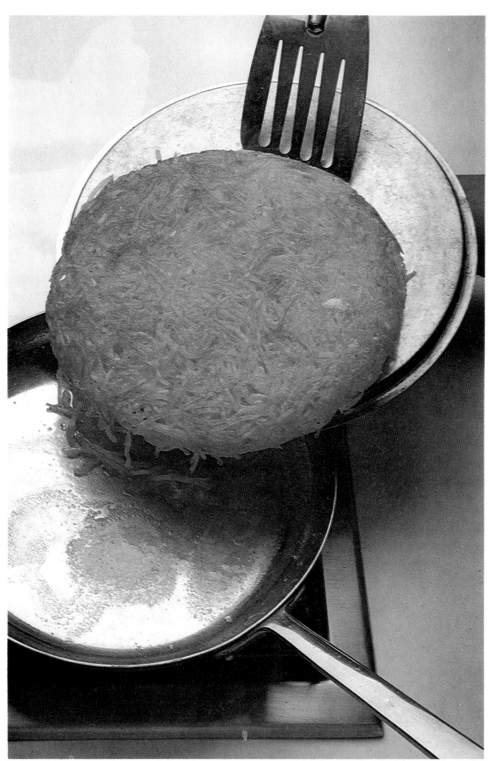

4 **Turning the cake.** Dry the underside of the pan lid and hold it tightly on the pan; turn pan and lid over together so that the cake falls gently onto the lid. If the skillet you are using does not have a flat lid, use a flat plate instead. Return the pan to the heat, melt a little more butter in it and slide the cake, uncooked side down, from the lid back into the pan *(above)*. Fry the cake, uncovered, for about 15 minutes to brown the uncooked side.

Mixing and Molding Croquettes

A cooked vegetable—finely chopped or puréed, and bound with butter, cream, egg yolks or a thick sauce—can be molded into small cylinders or balls, then coated with egg and bread crumbs, and deep fried to produce croquettes (from the French verb *croquer,* "to crunch").

Crunchy outside, soft and moist inside, croquettes are an ideal way to serve potatoes *(recipe, page 118).* Puréed potatoes require only a light binding with egg and butter to hold their shape when molded. Puréed cauliflower, too, can be made into croquettes; although, since it has less body than potatoes, cauliflower must be bound with a stiff sauce—such as a white sauce *(recipe, page 165)*—that will help the croquettes hold their shape. Other vegetables—notably green beans, carrots and broccoli—that may have too thin a consistency when puréed to hold their shape can be chopped or sliced, then combined with potatoes.

You can add chopped leftover meat, grated cheese or bread crumbs to any croquette mixture. And you can season it with mixed herbs, onion, or a flavoring such as *duxelles* or *persillade (page 33).*

1 **Preparing the vegetable.** Boil the vegetable—here, potatoes—until it is just done. Purée it *(pages 44-45)* and, to give the vegetable a light texture, push it with a pestle through a fine sieve.

2 **Firming the croquettes.** In a mixing bowl, combine the warm purée with the binding ingredients—here, egg yolks and butter—and with seasonings. Spread the mixture thinly on a platter and put it in the refrigerator for about 1 hour to make the purée firm and easier to shape.

3 **Coating the croquettes.** Take a spoonful of the chilled mixture for each croquette and roll it on a floured surface, gently shaping it by hand into a cylinder *(above).* Dip each croquette in beaten egg, then roll it in bread crumbs. Set the croquettes aside for about 1 hour to dry and firm the coating.

4 **Frying.** Fill a deep-frying pan with enough fat or oil to cover the croquettes and place over moderate heat. If you do not have a deep-frying thermometer, test the temperature by dropping a bread cube into the pan; if the cube browns within a minute, the fat is hot enough—375° F. [190° C.]. Gently drop in the croquettes—do not crowd the pan—and increase the heat to maintain the temperature. Turn the croquettes to brown them evenly. When they are well browned, remove them with a wire spoon *(above)* and drain them on paper towels.

Doing Justice to French Fries

There are several ways to prepare potatoes for French frying. Some cooks wash the potatoes beforehand, as shown here, to remove their surface starch, and then dry them to keep them from spluttering in the hot fat. Some cooks simply wipe unwashed potatoes with a towel, and other cooks neither wash nor dry them. Unwashed potatoes will be browner than washed ones when fried, but will tend to stick together in the hot fat.

When it comes to the actual frying, there are two different approaches. Potatoes can be fried once, as in this demonstration, in fat heated to 375° F. [190° C.]. Or they can be fried twice: first in 360° F. [185° C.] fat, to cook them through without browning, then a second time, just before serving, in very hot fat—390° F. [195° C.]. The second frying browns the potatoes quickly and may make them puff up. Either way, cook the French fries in small batches, so that the temperature of the fat does not fall too much as each new batch of potatoes is added to the deep-frying pan.

1 **Preparing the potatoes.** Peel the potatoes — mealy baking ones (page 12) are best suited for frying — and cut each one lengthwise into slices about ½ inch [1 cm.] thick. Cut each slice into strips ½ inch thick (left). Rinse the potatoes in plenty of cold water (center), rubbing them gently with your fingers to remove their surface starch. Finally, dry the potatoes thoroughly in a kitchen towel (right) or with paper towels.

2 **Heating the fat.** Put enough fat or oil into a deep-frying pan to immerse a small batch of potatoes; do not fill the pan to more than half its depth. Place the pan over moderate heat. You can test the fat's temperature by touching the end of a raw potato to it: if the potato sizzles (above), the fat is hot enough for frying — 375° F. [190° C.].

3 **Adding the potatoes.** Lower an empty deep-frying basket into the hot fat to coat it, so that the potatoes will not stick to its wires as they fry. Lift out the basket, add a batch of potatoes and carefully lower them into the fat.

4 **Frying.** Leave the potatoes in the fat for 8 to 10 minutes, adjusting the heat to maintain a constant, gentle sizzling in the pan. When the potatoes are golden, lift the basket and hold it over the pan to drain. Empty the basket onto several layers of paper towels, which will soak up excess fat. Fold the towels over the French fries to keep them warm.

Six Forms for Deep-fried Potatoes

Shoestrings or straw potatoes. Peel the potatoes, cut them into large pieces and shred them using one of three devices: the large-holed drum of a rotary grater *(left)*, the large-holed disk of a rotary shredder *(page 52)* or the shredding disk of a food processor *(page 45)*. Rinse the shoestrings well to wash off surface starch; then dry them thoroughly and deep fry a small batch at a time *(page 55)* in very hot fat until they are crisp and golden.

Matchstick potatoes. Peel the potatoes and cut them lengthwise into slices about ⅛ inch [3 mm.] thick. Stack a few slices at a time and cut them lengthwise again into strips about ⅛ inch wide *(left)*. Rinse the strips and dry them thoroughly. Deep fry them in small batches in very hot fat until they are golden.

Potato chips. Wafer-thin potato chips are fashioned most easily with a mandolin. Adjust the mandolin's slicing blade to the thinnest cutting width. Press one side of a peeled potato against the mandolin with the palm of your hand. Slide the potato down the frame repeatedly to cut the slices, keeping your fingers spread for safety *(left)*. Soak the slices in water for a few minutes, dry them thoroughly and then deep fry them until they are crisp.

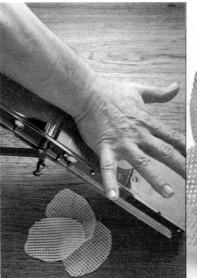

Potato waffles. Use the corrugated slicing blade of a mandolin. Slide a peeled potato lengthwise down the mandolin to remove a slice and cut a ridged pattern. Then rotate the potato 90° and slide it down the mandolin crosswise to produce a thin slice with ridges cut on both sides, but in opposite directions *(left)*. Repeat, rotating the potato after each waffle-cut slice. Rinse, then dry the waffles well before deep frying them.

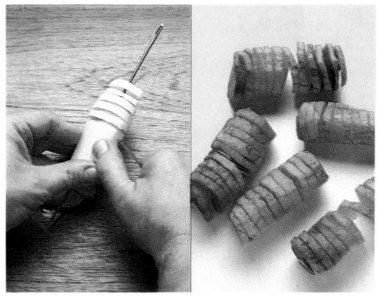

Potato shavings. Remove the skins of the potatoes and, with a vegetable peeler, pare each potato lengthwise into long, thin shavings *(left)*. Since the shavings will be too fragile for thorough washing and drying, let them drop into a bowl of cold water as you pare them; that way some of the surface starch will be washed off with a minimum of handling. Gently pat the shavings dry with paper towels before you deep fry them.

Potato spirals. Peel medium-sized potatoes and form each into a cylinder. If you do not have a device for making potato spirals, shape the potatoes as follows: push a trussing needle, as here, or a skewer through the long axis of each cylinder. With a paring knife, cut one end of the potato cylinder down to the needle. Keeping the blade of the knife against the needle, rotate the potato, cutting around it in a spiral as it turns *(left)*, until the knife reaches the other end. Remove the needle. Rinse and dry the spirals, and deep fry them until they are crisp.

Choosing the Right Oil or Fat

Two factors must be weighed in choosing a proper fat or oil for deep frying vegetables: heat tolerance and flavor. First, and most important, any fat or oil used must be of a kind that will not smoke or burn when it is heated to temperatures of 375° F. [190° C.] or more. Among the fats and oils that tolerate high heat, some impart a distinctive taste to the foods cooked in them, while others have almost no flavor. Additionally, of course, the costs and storage life of fats and oils vary.

Pure olive oil has the richest flavor, but it is costly and its smoking point is too low for most deep frying. Other vegetable oils—from corn, soy beans, sunflower seeds and peanuts—stand up well to high temperatures. Many chefs prefer peanut oil: its faint flavor does not mask that of the vegetables, its smoking point is 425° F. [220° C.], it is fairly inexpensive and it stores well.

Many commercial cooking oils are clear, flavorless blends of several vegetable oils and most produce satisfactory, if undistinctive, results in deep frying. Avoid oils that are sold as "salad oils." Their smoking points are too low for deep frying and heat makes them turn rancid quickly.

Most animal fats—especially butter, chicken fat and goose fat—have burning points too low for deep frying. The exceptions are suet and lard, the fats from beef kidney and pork, respectively. Both are inexpensive and store well but they have distinctive flavors that may not suit every palate.

To keep fats and oils fresh, store them in airtight containers in a cool, dark place. Do not use any fat or oil whose smell or taste has changed—that is usually a sign of rancidity.

In using oil or fat for deep frying, pour in, or melt, enough to immerse the food completely but, to prevent dangerous spattering, fill the pan no more than half full. Use a heavy pan, preferably deeper than it is wide: the more surface area exposed to air, the more quickly the oil or fat reaches its smoking point.

A removable basket is convenient for lifting foods such as French fries *(page 55)* in and out of the pan. But the fragile potato shapes described here or vegetables that are deep fried in batter *(pages 58-59)* might be damaged if crowded in a basket. Remove and drain such foods with a wire skimmer.

After deep frying, oil or fat can be reused, although its smoking point will be lower each time. Let the oil cool, then strain it into a container through a funnel that has been lined with a double thickness of cheesecloth. Straining removes food particles that would burn when the fat is reheated; the particles would also speed spoilage.

Sealing in Moistness

Vegetables other than potatoes will dry out rapidly in the very hot oil or fat that deep frying requires: their natural moisture—unlike that of potatoes—is not bound in by starch. You can protect a vegetable's moistness during deep frying, however, by sealing it in with a starchy batter *(box, below)*. The result is a fritter—a vegetable encased in a crisp, delicious coating.

Almost any vegetable, ranging from fragile spinach and chard to sturdy green beans and cauliflower, can be deep fried this way. The great French chef Escoffier even applied the method to tomatoes *(recipe, page 142)*. You may prefer to fry only one kind of vegetable at a time; fried onions, because of their strong flavor, are usually done alone. Or you can combine many vegetables: here, cauliflower, broccoli, artichoke bottoms, zucchini, mushrooms, scallions and sorrel.

Whether you deep fry one vegetable or many, each type must be properly prepared ahead of time to ensure that it is easy to handle and easy to coat with bat-

ter. Leave small vegetables whole—the mushrooms, scallions and sorrel leaves pictured here are simply cleaned and trimmed. Divide large vegetables into pieces: broccoli and cauliflower should be broken into small clusters or florets; artichoke bottoms should be quartered and zucchini cut lengthwise into thin slices.

Because firm, dense-textured vegetables of any size will not cook through in the time that it takes the batter to crisp, they should be tenderized by precooking. The cauliflower, broccoli and artichoke bottoms shown here have been parboiled. Green and wax beans, carrots and parsnips would require the same treatment.

After parboiling, but before deep frying, you can give any bland or sweet vegetable a sharper flavor by marinating it. In this demonstration, the marinade is composed of lemon juice, olive oil and mixed fresh herbs. You could substitute wine for lemon juice, choose a milder-tasting vegetable oil, or spice the mixture with soy sauce, mustard, ginger or—discreetly—cayenne pepper.

1 Marinating. Place all the vegetables except the sorrel in a bowl. Dribble olive oil over them; add lemon juice, salt, pepper and fines herbes *(page 26)*. Mix everything with your fingers to coat each piece. Leave at room temperature for up to 1 hour, turning the pieces two or three times.

A Fritter Batter

To ensure that it will coat the vegetable pieces evenly, fritter batter should be made well in advance of frying. It must stand undisturbed—or rest, as this procedure is called—for about an hour at room temperature so the flour absorbs the liquid and thickens the batter.

The batter shown here *(recipe, page 167)* contains flour, salt, egg yolks and oil—plus beer and beaten egg whites, which give the batter lightness. If you prefer, however, you can use plain water or milk instead of beer.

The proportions of the ingredients

can be varied to taste. The addition of more liquid will produce a thinner batter that is crisp and light when fried but tends to spread out in the fat; a thicker batter, on the other hand, will cling to the vegetables, but will have a spongier, more breadlike texture.

1 Combining the ingredients. Sift flour and salt into a bowl. Make a well in the flour and pour in oil, egg yolks and liquid—here, beer. Whisk the ingredients, starting in the well and working toward the bowl edges *(above)*.

2 Mixing the batter. Continue to whisk the batter until it is smooth *(above)*. Cover the bowl and let the batter rest at room temperature for about 1 hour.

3 Adding egg whites. Immediately before using the batter, beat the egg whites until they begin to form peaks. Use your fingers to fold the beaten whites gently into the batter.

2 **Coating the vegetables.** Make the batter in advance *(box, opposite)*, and prepare the deep-frying pan: put just enough fat or oil into it to allow the vegetables to float freely; do not fill the pan more than half full. Place the pan over a high heat. Drop the marinated vegetables, a few pieces at a time, into the batter *(left)* and spoon over more batter to cover them completely. Fragile sorrel leaves should be dipped separately, one by one, just before you deep fry them *(right)*.

3 **Deep frying.** If you do not have a deep-frying thermometer, drop a little batter into the fat: when the batter sizzles on contact, the fat is sufficiently hot for frying —375° F. [190° C.]. Carefully lower each coated vegetable piece into the pan, using your fingertips *(above)* or a wire skimmer.

4 **Turning the fritters.** Do not fry more vegetable fritters at one time than can float on the surface of the fat without touching one another. When the batter around the edges of a fritter is browned, turn the vegetable over carefully with a fork *(above)* or a skimmer so that it can brown evenly on the other side.

5 **Removing the fritters.** When the vegetables are brown, lift them with a wire skimmer that allows the fat to drain off. Drain the fritters on paper towels and place them on a napkin on a heated platter to keep them warm as you fry the remaining vegetables. Garnish the vegetable fritters with lemon wedges and with parsley sprigs that have been rinsed, thoroughly dried (but not coated with batter) and briefly fried in the hot fat.

3
Braises and Stews
The Merging of Flavors

Snow peas that have been parboiled for a few seconds are added to a stew of young vegetables. Already cooking in butter are small onions and wedges of artichoke bottoms combined with shredded lettuce — whose juices provide cooking liquid for all of them.

In stewing and braising, vegetables cook slowly in a relatively small amount of liquid. Unlike boiling *(pages 36-47)*, where the aim is to cook vegetables as rapidly as possible to conserve their individual tastes and textures, braising requires slow cooking because the object is to mingle the flavors of the ingredients. The inevitable transfer of some of the vegetables' flavor to the braising liquid is not a loss since that liquid, reduced during cooking to a light sauce, is as much an integral part of the finished dish as the smooth, soft texture of the braised vegetables.

Although the dividing line between braises and stews is blurred, most cooks make a convenient distinction: a braise usually consists of only a single vegetable, cooked with a little added liquid; a stew is a mixture of different vegetables, often cooked in their own juices.

The choice of liquid obviously plays an important part in the flavor of the finished braise. Veal stock provides a mild-tasting complement to any sort of vegetable. Wine or other acid liquids such as lemon juice will help keep soft vegetables intact while they cook and, like tomato sauce, contribute zest to the finished dish. Even plain water serves as a satisfactory moistener for strong-tasting or lavishly seasoned vegetables. Both stews and braises generally include seasoning elements—garlic, herbs, salt-pork pieces or aromatic vegetable mixtures such as mirepoix or *sofrito (page 33)*. Sugar is often added to counterbalance naturally acid vegetables, such as tomatoes, or to produce a rich glaze. And for maximum enrichment, vegetables may be filled with savory stuffings before they are braised.

Vegetables braised singly can be served either as an accompaniment to meat or fish, or as a separate course; the blend of flavors drawn from a mixed vegetable stew is best appreciated on its own. Certain vegetables have a natural affinity for one another that is celebrated in stews such as *ratatouille*—a mélange of eggplants, tomatoes, zucchini, onions and peppers *(recipe, page 165)*. Stews of young vegetables *(left, and pages 72-73)* include improvisational but equally successful combinations: whole small onions, lettuce, peas or broad beans, and artichoke bottoms, for example, supplemented with other vegetables according to the season. Provided each vegetable is added to a stew at the right moment so that all of them will be ready together, the choice is almost limitless.

Altering the Formula for Different Effects

Braising always involves long, slow simmering, but preparations and flavoring ingredients can be altered to suit different vegetables or to vary the effect of the finished dish. Celery, celeriac, turnips or Brussels sprouts, for example, are so assertive they usually are parboiled before braising to tame their strong flavors. Fennel is often treated the same way, but like mild-tasting zucchini or eggplant, it may instead be browned in olive oil (*Step 2, right*) or butter. If it is, the finished dish will taste strongly of fennel: browning seals the surface of a vegetable so that its flavor is not lost in the liquid.

The braising liquid itself is a critical flavoring element. Water is used here with fennel *(recipe, page 152)* for a braise that will taste primarily of the vegetable. But fennel, celery *(below, right; recipe, page 150)* and other vegetables often are braised in stock or tomato sauce.

Other flavorings may be added. Unpeeled garlic complements mild vegetables; a mirepoix *(page 33)* sets off those with pronounced flavor such as celery.

Fennel Braised in Water

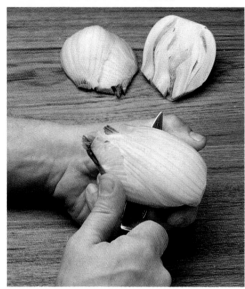

1 **Preparing fennel.** Trim and string fennel bulbs *(page 21)*, reserving their feathery leaves to sprinkle over the dish at the last minute. Halve the bulbs, as shown here, or quarter large ones if you wish to reduce the cooking time.

2 **Preliminary cooking.** Place the fennel pieces, flat side down, in a heavy pan coated with hot oil. Add some garlic cloves, unpeeled to prevent them from burning and becoming bitter. Lightly salt the vegetable and cook over medium heat for about 10 minutes, turning the fennel *(above)* occasionally until the pieces are browned.

Enriching with Veal Stock

The ideal stock for braising vegetables is one that enriches them without imposing too much of its own character. It should also have so much body that by the end of cooking it will have reduced to a syrupy sauce that needs no thickening.

A stock that is made from meaty veal bones fulfills these requirements; thickened naturally by the abundant gelatin that is dissolved from the bones and sinews, it is full-bodied yet unassertive in flavor. To prepare the stock, simmer a meaty veal knuckle with a bouquet garni and aromatic vegetables for several hours *(recipe, page 166)*.

Peppers, onions and celery are among the vegetables enhanced by a veal stock. Fennel can also be cooked in it, although the distinctive taste of this vegetable will be more evident if the braising liquid is plain water *(opposite, top)*.

Celery Braised in Stock

1 **Parboiling celery.** Make celery hearts by trimming bunches to a length of about 5 inches [12 cm.] and removing the outer ribs. Cut off only the discolored surfaces from the bases; if you cut too deeply, the inner ribs will separate. Halve each heart lengthwise. Parboil the celery hearts for 8 to 10 minutes *(above)* and then drain them well.

2 **Adding the flavorings.** Peel a few onions and carrots and chop them coarsely. Remove the cores *(page 13)* before chopping the carrots, unless they are very young. Strew the onions and carrots over the bottom of a heavy pan and lay the celery hearts on top.

3 **Braising in water.** Pour water over the fennel *(left)* and gently scrape up all the deposits on the bottom of the pan. Bring the water to a boil, reduce it to a simmer, then cover and cook for 20 minutes to 1 hour, or until the fennel is soft and the sauce reduced to a thin coating. Season with pepper and chopped fennel leaves *(above)*.

3 **Cooking and serving.** Pour in veal stock just to cover the vegetables *(left)*; bring it to a boil, then simmer gently, covered, for about an hour, or until the hearts are very tender. If, when the celery is ready, the sauce has not reduced to a coating consistency, put all the vegetables on a warmed dish and boil down the sauce rapidly. Pour it over the vegetables and sprinkle chopped parsley on top *(above)*.

Providing the Finishing Touch

Firm, sweet vegetables acquire an extra richness when braised in sugar, butter and liquid—a process known as glazing. During the cooking period, the liquid evaporates, leaving the vegetables coated with a shiny film of syrup. Here, carrots *(right)* and small white onions *(box, below)* are used to show the basic techniques. Parsnips, chayotes and beets are also good candidates for glazing.

During cooking the glaze may be further reduced so the sugar caramelizes, coloring the vegetables a rich brown. The treatment is particularly appropriate for small white onions, as shown at right, below. In this variation on glazing, the onions are cooked in butter until they color; then sugar is added, along with liquid that prevents the sugar from scorching.

For both clear and caramelized glazes, use a sauté pan or skillet large enough to hold the vegetables in one layer. If the pan is overcrowded, the vegetables will steam in the juices, preventing the evaporation that forms the glaze.

Sugar-coating Carrots

Readying the vegetable. Prepare carrots for cooking as described on page 13. Put the carrots in a single layer in a sauté pan or skillet. Add about 2 tablespoons [30 ml.] of butter and 1 tablespoon [15 ml.] of sugar for every 1 pound [½ kg.] of carrots. Season with salt and pour in cold water until the vegetables are halfway covered *(above)*. Bring the water to a boil, then reduce the heat to very low, cover the pan and simmer.

White-glazed Onions

Adding stock for flavor. To glaze small white onions so that they emerge pale in color, with their natural flavor barely altered, follow the steps described for glazing carrots *(top, right)*. Prepare the onions for cooking *(page 23)*. Add sugar and butter at the beginning of cooking, along with a little liquid to prevent the sugar from caramelizing and browning the onions. Use veal stock, as shown here, instead of water to enhance the onions' mild flavor.

A Caramelized Brown Glaze for Onions

Cooking in butter. Melt a generous amount of butter in a heavy sauté pan or skillet. Put in a layer of peeled, whole onions and season with salt. Cook the onions gently until they soften and their surfaces color evenly. Allow about 20 minutes for the onions to cook to this stage. Shake the pan occasionally *(above)* to prevent their sticking; do not stir the onions, lest they fall apart.

2 **Perfecting the glaze.** By the time the carrots are tender — up to 45 minutes or so for older ones — almost all the water should have evaporated. Remove the lid and boil hard to evaporate all the remaining liquid *(above)*, shaking the pan to prevent the vegetable from sticking. Take the pan off the heat and add a knob of butter, shaking the pan so that each carrot piece is evenly coated as the butter melts. Sprinkle the glazed carrots with finely chopped parsley or fresh lemon juice just before serving *(right)*.

2 **Caramelizing the sugar.** Scatter a spoonful of sugar over the onions. Continue cooking for a few minutes over very low heat. When the butter-and-sugar mixture begins to turn golden brown, add a few tablespoons [30 to 45 ml.] of stock or water to dissolve any caramel sticking to the pan and prevent scorching. Shake the pan constantly until the onions are thickly coated with a syrupy glaze *(above)*, then serve them *(right)*.

The Advantages of Braising in Wine

Vegetables braised with wine taste different from those braised in water or stock—and not just because of the flavor of the wine. A second, less obvious, influence is the wine's acidity; it keeps vegetables firm during cooking so that they may be simmered for longer periods than usual, and long simmering means a more thorough blending of flavors.

The type of wine to use depends on the vegetables that you are braising. Strong-flavored vegetables—leeks, for example, or the red cabbage used along with chestnuts in this demonstration *(recipe, page 110)*—may be cooked in either red or white wine. But mild-flavored vegetables such as zucchini or artichokes will be overpowered by red wine; braise them in a less assertive white. Any wine should be tempered by an equal amount of stock (beef, veal or chicken) or water. As always the wine should be of good quality: its taste will be apparent in the dish.

1 **Coring the cabbage.** Halve the cabbage. Hold one half upright and cut down both sides of the white triangular core, angling the knife so that the cuts intersect to form a wedge around the core *(above)*. Lift out the wedge. Repeat for the other cabbage half. Then shred the cored cabbage.

2 **Preparing the salt pork.** Remove the rind from salt pork, cut the pork into julienne and blanch them for 5 minutes in boiling water. Drain the strips, then sauté them in an enameled casserole over medium heat until they render their fat and turn gold. Remove the pork strips *(above)* and reserve them.

3 **Adding the cabbage.** Soften chopped onion slowly in the pork fat over medium heat. Then add the shredded cabbage, stirring to coat it with fat.

4 **Pouring in wine.** Cover the pot and cook the cabbage over low heat for 10 minutes. Add the wine—red in this case—and an equal amount of beef stock or water. Stir in spices and the reserved strips of salt pork.

5 **Braising the cabbage.** Cover the pot and braise the cabbage for 2 hours over low heat or in a preheated 325° F. [160° C.] oven. Check the cabbage occasionally and add more stock or water if the liquid threatens to cook away. Stir in peeled chestnuts and cook for 1 more hour, until the chestnuts are tender and most of the liquid has been absorbed *(above)*.

A Rich and Creamy Binder

Any braising liquid may be turned into a thick sauce by adding to it either flour or a mixture of egg yolks and cream. If you use flour, add it at the start of cooking: long simmering will prevent the finished braise from having a floury taste.

Egg yolks and cream, on the other hand, can stand neither long simmering nor high temperatures. You may thicken a braise with egg yolks alone, but adding cream will give the sauce a richer flavor. In either case, add these ingredients just before serving, and above all do not allow the sauce to approach the boiling point once you have added them. Otherwise, the egg yolks will curdle instead of forming a smooth emulsion.

In this demonstration, egg yolks and cream thicken a braise made of broad beans, winter savory—an herb especially suited to beans—and salt pork. The salt pork would be a fine addition to cabbage, onion or leek braises and the thickener could be used to enrich braises of cauliflower, carrots and turnips.

1 Precooking the salt pork. Trim the rind from a piece of salt pork, cut up the pork, parboil it for 5 minutes and drain it. Cook the pork gently in butter or lard in a fireproof casserole; do not let it become crisp. Add a bunch of winter savory, or a little dried savory, and shelled, peeled beans *(page 15)*.

2 Braising the beans. Pour in water to a depth of no more than ¼ inch [6 mm.]. Add salt. Cover the casserole, bring the water to a boil, then lower the heat and simmer the beans very gently. Braise them for 8 to 10 minutes, shaking the casserole from time to time to prevent sticking.

Blending a Liaison

Handling yolks and cream. First blend the egg yolks and heavy cream together in a bowl *(above)* and season the liaison. If, as shown at right, you use only a small amount of braising liquid, blend the yolk-and-cream mixture into the braise directly—but slowly. If you want to thicken a larger amount of liquid, first warm the egg yolks and cream by stirring into them a few spoonfuls of the hot braising liquid.

3 Mixing in eggs and cream. Remove the pan from the heat and let it cool. Prepare the yolk-and-cream mixture *(box, left)*. Pour it over the beans *(above)*, stirring gently to blend the sauce evenly.

4 Thickening the sauce. Return the casserole to low heat; a fireproof pad underneath will help give you better control of the heat. Cook for a minute or two, until the sauce thickens slightly; do not let the sauce approach a boil.

Leaf-wrapped Packages of Stuffing

A sturdy vegetable leaf, wrapped neatly around a savory filling and braised, makes an attractive and edible package. And each element of the assembly—the leaf, the filling and the braising liquid—is available for imaginative variation. Among the leaves commonly used as wrappings are the cabbage, Swiss chard and vine leaves shown here. But spinach leaves also are suited to the purpose, and even fresh or dried inner husks of corn—although themselves inedible—are used in Latin America as envelopes for fillings such as the mixture of chopped tomatoes, corn kernels and white cheese in the box below *(recipe, page 131)*.

Other fillings for vegetable leaves can include many different combinations of cooked ground meats, chopped vegetables and nuts, dried fruits, cheeses, and herbs and spices. Most fillings are bound together by bread or parboiled rice; these ingredients also swell during cooking to plump up the assembled packages.

The braising liquids for leaf packages range from the tomato sauce *(box, opposite)* used here to cook the stuffed cabbage leaves, to veal or other meat stock, wine or plain water. Cooking times vary from 45 minutes to 2 hours, depending on the type of leaf and the stuffing you use.

1 **Preparing the leaves.** Parboil large cabbage leaves for about 1 minute to make them supple. Drain them well. Use a knife to shave away part of the thick, central ribs *(above)* so that the leaves will be easy to roll.

2 **Stuffing the leaves.** Put a handful of stuffing—here, cooked rice, chopped cabbage leaves, tomatoes, parboiled chard, sautéed onions and salt pork—on the stem end of the leaf *(left)*. Fold the leaf end and sides over the stuffing *(center)*. Roll up the leaf from the stem end *(right)* to make a neat parcel.

How to Roll Three Kinds of Leaves

Vine leaves. Rinse preserved grapevine leaves in hot water; parboil fresh ones. Put stuffing—here, rice, onions, peppers and parsley—on a leaf's stem end. Fold over the end and sides. Roll the leaf up from the stem end.

Chard leaves. Parboil the leaves to make them flexible. Cut the stems from the leaves *(page 21)*. Place stuffing—here, saffron rice, pine nuts, chopped bacon and celery—at the stem ends and roll up the leaves from those ends.

Cornhusks. Cross one parboiled inner husk on top of another and put stuffing in the center. Alternately fold the lower and upper husks over the stuffing to form a package. Tie it with thin strips of the tough outer husks.

3 **Braising the leaves.** Holding the packages carefully to prevent them from unwrapping, put them in a casserole with the free ends of the leaves underneath. Pack them closely so that they cannot unroll *(above)*. Pour in braising liquid — here, tomato sauce and stock — until it barely covers the packages. Cover the casserole and cook in a preheated 350° F. [180° C.] oven for about 1 hour. Serve the leaf packages from the casserole, using the braising liquid as a sauce.

An All-Purpose Tomato Sauce

A sauce made from fresh, ripe summer tomatoes makes an excellent braising liquid for many stuffed leaves. Out-of-season tomatoes lack flavor; use canned plum tomatoes instead.

To make a sauce from fresh tomatoes, chop them coarsely and put them in a stainless-steel, enameled or tin-lined pan. Add salt and herbs — basil, parsley and thyme — and, if you like, chopped onion or garlic *(recipe, page 165)*. Taste the tomatoes before cooking: the ripest ones are naturally sweet, but others have an acid taste that can be countered with a pinch of sugar.

Simmer the chopped tomatoes gently, stirring occasionally to prevent them from sticking. When the tomatoes have softened — this will take 30 to 40 minutes — push them through a sieve or purée them through a food mill to remove the skins and seeds. The sieved sauce should have the consistency of heavy cream; if necessary, reduce it to the desired consistency *(right)*.

To make a sauce from canned tomatoes, pass them through a sieve, with their juices, then season to taste with salt, herbs, and perhaps sugar. Simmer the tomatoes to reduce them to the desired consistency. To shorten the reduction process, drain off the juices before sieving the tomatoes, and save the juices for later use.

Testing for consistency. Reduce the sauce over medium heat just until it has the consistency of heavy cream *(above)*. Watch carefully to prevent the sauce from thickening too much.

A Vegetable Filling for Hollowed Onions

Many vegetables, including large onions, peppers *(opposite)*, eggplant and zucchini, are the appropriate size and shape for stuffing and can be made into firm shells that keep their shapes during braising. Among these candidates for stuffing, onions are perhaps the least familiar; they are usually thought of as a complement to other foods or as a flavoring. But if onions are hollowed out, filled with stuffing and braised in stock, they make a fine dish in their own right. As they cook, the onions develop a mild, sweet flavor that contributes to the tastes of both the stock and the stuffing.

Choose onions 3 inches [8 cm.] in diameter for the best results. Trim the roots to create a flat base for each onion to rest on during cooking. Skin the onions *(page 23)* and peel off any slippery membrane so that you can grip them firmly when you are scooping out the inner flesh with a spoon *(right)*.

Reserve the scooped-out onion flesh. Chopped and fried gently in butter, it can be combined with a wide variety of stuffing ingredients, including the mixture of mushrooms and bread crumbs shown in this demonstration.

1 **Stuffing the onions.** Cut off the top of each peeled onion and dig into the center with a metal spoon. Scoop out the flesh *(above)*, leaving two or three layers to form a solid shell. Spoon the stuffing into the onions *(right)*, heaping it about ½ inch [1 cm.] above the tops.

2 **Assembling the braise.** Put the onions in a shallow, ovenproof dish that holds them snugly. Pour in stock — or stock combined with wine — until the liquid reaches nearly halfway up the onions. Sprinkle bread crumbs over the stuffing *(above)*; the crumbs will form a crust during the final stages of cooking.

3 **Braising the onions.** Cover the dish loosely with aluminum foil; do not press the foil down or you will crush the stuffing. Place the dish in a preheated 400° F. [200° C.] oven. After 20 minutes, reduce the temperature to 350° F. [180° C.]; cook for 25 minutes, and remove the foil from the dish *(above)*.

4 **Finishing the onions.** Continue to cook the onions, uncovered, for up to 30 minutes, until they are brown and the liquid is syrupy. Baste them frequently with the cooking liquid to keep them moist. If the onions brown too quickly, reduce the heat. Serve the onions with the liquid poured over them *(above)*.

Packing Flavor into Peppers

Vegetables vary greatly in the amount of preparation they require before stuffing and braising. For example, while zucchini and eggplant both must be halved and hollowed out, the flesh of zucchini can be scooped out raw with a spoon, but the eggplant has to be precooked to soften its firm flesh for easy removal. After halving the eggplant, score crosses in the cut sides so that the flesh will cook evenly; then sauté the halves in olive oil. As with zucchini, save the scooped-out eggplant flesh to add to the stuffing.

Peppers, which should be firm and square-shaped to stand upright, need only the simple preparations shown on this page. Like eggplant and zucchini, peppers lend themselves to a variety of stuffings. If you base your filling on leftover or ground meat, the vegetables become a substantial main course. Or use vegetable fillings, such as mushrooms, onions or tomatoes, for a lighter dish. Rice or bread crumbs bind the ingredients and add bulk, and nuts or currants can contribute contrasting flavors and textures.

1 **Preparing the peppers.** Slice off the pepper tops, leaving the stems intact, and reserve them *(top)*. Pull out the seeds and ribs *(above)*. Parboil the pepper shells and tops for 4 to 5 minutes, or until they are supple.

2 **Stuffing the peppers.** Prepare the stuffing: here, sliced onion has been sautéed in oil and simmered with rice, chopped tomato, pine nuts and dried currants *(recipe, page 162)*. Pack the peppers in an ovenproof dish, then fill each to its rim with stuffing *(above)*.

3 **Braising the peppers.** Replace the pepper tops. Pour water or stock into the dish *(left)*. Cover the dish with foil and cook for 15 to 20 minutes in a 400° F. [200° C.] oven. Reduce the heat to 325° F. [160° C.] and bake 40 minutes more. When done, the peppers will be wrinkled but still intact *(below)*.

Stewing Vegetables in Their Own Juices

In most mixed vegetable stews, the vegetables themselves render the liquid that serves as the braising medium. The vegetables of some stews, such as *ratatouille (bottom)*, release so much moisture that the liquid must be reduced *(box, below)* before the stew is served. Stews composed mainly of firm, dry vegetables always include one that renders moisture, and generally need a little water as well to help steam them. The stew at right, for example, uses shredded lettuce to help moisten onions, artichokes and other firm vegetables *(recipe, page 164)*.

Almost any vegetable can form part of a mixed stew, although different vegetables should be added at different times, according to the amount of cooking they need, and preliminary preparations will differ. Tender young vegetables are usually added raw, but old vegetables should be parboiled. Parboiling also attenuates the strong flavors of vegetables such as leeks and fixes the crispness and color of snow peas, which would become limp and gray if they were braised raw.

Mixed Vegetable Stew: A Mélange of Young Produce

1 **Cooking in butter.** Melt a large chunk of butter in a shallow pot over very low heat; if you use an earthenware one, as here, protect it from direct heat with a fireproof pad. Add the vegetables that need the most cooking — here, small whole onions, quartered artichoke bottoms and unpeeled garlic cloves.

2 **Stewing with lettuce.** Mix the vegetables with the butter, bury a bouquet garni among them and cook them slowly, covered, while you shred the lettuce coarsely. Add the lettuce to the pot. Salt lightly, cover and stew gently for about 30 minutes. Shake the pot occasionally; add a little water if you see no syrupy juice in the pot.

Reducing a Cooking Liquid

Producing a syrup. The vegetable fruits in a *ratatouille (right)* release a great deal of liquid as they cook. To reduce this liquid to a sauce, do not raise the heat while the vegetables are in the cooking vessel: the agitation caused by fast boiling would damage the vegetables. Instead, strain off the liquid, pour it into a shallow saucepan *(left)* and boil until it has reduced to a syrupy consistency *(right)* before returning it to the vegetables.

Ratatouille: A Mediterranean Blend of Tastes

1 **Cooking the onions.** Peel onions and chop them coarsely. Cook them gently in plenty of olive oil until they soften; do not let them brown. Peel, seed and quarter ripe tomatoes and add them to the onions. Cook for a few minutes more until the tomatoes disintegrate, forming a liquid in which the other vegetables will stew.

2 **Adding eggplant and peppers.** Put a bouquet garni of parsley, thyme, leek, celery and a bay leaf into the pot, together with a few peeled, sliced garlic cloves. Cut up the eggplants and peppers and tip them into the mixture *(above)*. Salt lightly, cover the pot and cook over low heat for about 45 minutes.

3 **Adding snow peas.** Plunge snow peas into a pan of boiling salted water, cooking them only until the water returns to a boil. Drain them well. Slice zucchini thinly and sauté the slices in butter for 5 to 6 minutes, until they begin to color. Stir the drained, parboiled snow peas into the stew.

4 **Adding the zucchini.** As soon as you have mixed in the snow peas, tip the zucchini into the pot and add any other quick-cooking vegetables you have chosen. If you use young peas or broad beans, add a little water to help produce the steam that will cook them.

5 **Mixing in more butter.** Stew very gently for a few minutes to mingle the different flavors and to complete the cooking of the last vegetables added. Remove the bouquet garni; season the vegetables to taste. Turn off the heat and add pieces of butter. Shake and tilt the pot until the butter has melted and mixed with the vegetable juices.

3 **Adding zucchini.** Cut the zucchini into large chunks, but do not peel them. Add the zucchini chunks to the other vegetables. Cook, covered, for another 45 minutes or so. Do not add any liquid; the vegetables themselves will provide ample moistening.

4 **Straining off the liquid.** Turn the vegetable mixture into a colander set in a bowl and allow the juices to drain through. Reduce the liquid to a syrup (box, left); meanwhile, discard the bouquet, return the vegetables to the pot and keep them warm. Season to taste.

5 **Preparing to serve.** Pour the reduced liquid back over the *ratatouille* (above). You can serve the dish hot, barely warm or cold. If the *ratatouille* is to be eaten cold, let it cool and then pour some good, fruity olive oil over it. Stir with a wooden spoon to blend in the oil without mashing the vegetables.

4
Baking, Broiling and Grilling
Opportunities Unlimited

The simple approach: baked whole
Mixed bakes: medleys of flavor
Gratins: straightforward or elaborate
Tips on puddings and soufflés
Advantages of marinating

Baked whole and unadorned, vegetables develop mellow yet concentrated flavors. Buttered and broiled, vegetables take on an appetizing brown color outside while keeping their just-picked freshness inside. Oiled and grilled over a fire, they become juicy and tender while absorbing the aromas of the smoke. And the imaginative cook can elaborate on these simple bakes and grills to produce the most elegant of vegetable dishes.

Hollowing out vegetables and stuffing them is the most obvious elaboration. Stuffings may be delicate or substantial, mild or strongly seasoned; they can be made from leftovers as well as from fresh ingredients. The only limitation to invention is that the stuffing must complement the vegetable: soft-fleshed, moisture-rendering tomatoes need a stuffing that will absorb excess liquid; drier vegetables such as artichokes require a moist stuffing that will help baste them during cooking.

The mingling of flavors can be approached another way by marinating vegetables before broiling them or by wrapping them in foil, along with seasonings, before putting them on a grill. Still another tactic is to bake cut-up vegetables together to produce a composite dish. In the covered, mixed bake on pages 80-81, eggplant, artichokes and tomatoes actually steam in their own aromatic juices. The demonstration explains how to combine vegetables not only on the basis of compatible flavors, but also for the moisture that some must contribute to prevent others from drying out during baking.

Textures as well as flavors can be blended and varied by preparing vegetables of almost all kinds, from spinach to turnips, in a gratin, pudding or soufflé. The ingredients for all three of these dishes are essentially the same; how they are handled makes the difference. Depending on the texture a cook wants, the vegetables may be sliced, cubed, julienned, shredded, chopped or puréed. For a moist gratin, the vegetables then are simply coated with cream or a sauce and baked; they retain their own distinctive textures while the coating forms a crisp crust on top of them *(pages 84-87)*. If the sauce is enriched with eggs and the mixture is cooked in a mold, the vegetables emerge from the oven in a hearty pudding *(pages 88-89)*. And if the eggs are separated so that the whites can be beaten stiff before they are folded into the mixture, the result will be an airy vegetable soufflé *(pages 90-91)*.

Belgian endive is lifted from beneath a golden-brown crust, formed by masking the braised vegetables *(recipe, page 96)* with cream and baking them. Gratinéing may serve to cook raw vegetables, or it may be used for a finishing step, as here.

Baking Vegetables in Their Skins

Cooking vegetables whole in their skins is the simplest baking technique, ideal for root vegetables as well as for eggplant and winter squashes. All these vegetables have tough skins that protect their flesh from the drying oven heat as they cook. If whole bulbs of garlic are baked, they can be made into the mild puréed flavoring described in the box opposite.

Among these vegetables, potatoes are the ones most often baked, undoubtedly because they require the least preparation. Simply scrub them with a vegetable brush and pierce their skins in several places. The holes serve as escape vents for steam that builds up inside the baking potatoes and might burst them.

Sweet potatoes should also be scrubbed before cooking, but they need not be pierced, since they do not produce excessive steam. They create another sort of internal moisture during cooking, however: their starch is converted to sugar syrup, making the vegetables moist and sweet. Since the conversion will not occur if the potatoes reach too high a temperature, they should be baked in an oven heated no higher than 375° F. [190° C.]. White potatoes, however, may be baked at any temperature from 325° to 450° F. [160° to 230° C.].

When you bake an onion in its skin, first slice off its root end to keep the onion steady. Because sugary juices may leak from this cut, place the onion in a shallow baking pan (opposite, below right), and add a little water to the pan so that the onion juices will not burn.

Beets take three to four times as long to bake as potatoes of comparable size, so you may decide to bake them only when you are using the oven for other foods.

Nevertheless, baked beets are so tasty that it is worth heating the oven specially for them. Their skins, while helping to retain the beets' juices, are not thick enough for protection against drying. To keep beets moist, wrap each one in aluminum foil (opposite, below left).

After cooking, the inedible skins of onions and beets are peeled, but potato skins usually are not. All these vegetables may be served simply with butter, salt and pepper. Potatoes and sweet potatoes may be enriched by scooping out the flesh, mixing it with butter, cream and seasonings, then spooning it back into the potato skins for a brief reheating (below, right; recipe, page 120). Or flavor white potatoes or eggplants by inserting bacon or garlic through their skins before baking (recipe, page 138).

Baking potatoes. Scrub the potatoes, pierce the skins with a fork and bake on an oven rack; in a 375° F. [190° C.] oven, they will take about an hour. To test for doneness, squeeze each potato, using a pad to protect your hand from a burn; if the potato yields to the pressure, it is cooked through. Gently roll the hot potato on a counter to crumble the flesh inside the skin (above, left). With a fork, punch holes in the top of the potato in the shape of a cross. Then hold the potato at both ends and squeeze it until it pops open along the cross to reveal the crumbly flesh (above, right).

Stuffing baked potatoes. After baking potatoes — here, sweet potatoes — cut an oblong section from the top of each one and scrape the flesh off the section. Scoop the flesh out of the skin, leaving a layer ¼ inch [6 mm.] thick next to the skin to hold the potato in shape (above, left). Purée the flesh with a fork, a potato ricer or an electric mixer. Beat butter, cream and seasonings into the flesh; the more cream you add, the smoother and lighter the mixture will become. Refill the skins with the mixture (above, right). Return the potatoes to a 400° F. [200° C.] oven for about 10 minutes until the tops brown and the potatoes are heated through.

Oven-baked Garlic for a Purée

Bulbs of garlic, baked in their skins, develop a mild, sweet flavor without a trace of harshness. They also are easy to peel and soft enough to purée. When blended with olive oil, the purée can be stored in a jar and used as a flavoring with many meat or vegetable dishes, or added to a vinaigrette *(page 43)*. A little more oil, poured on top of the mixture *(far right)*, will protect it from the air and enable you to keep it, refrigerated, for up to three months.

To make 1 cup [¼ liter] of purée, you will need 20 to 25 bulbs of garlic. Do not separate them into individual cloves or peel them; the skins keep in the flavor. After baking, separate the bulbs into cloves, peel the cloves and pass them through a sieve. Combine this purée with the oil to make a smooth paste.

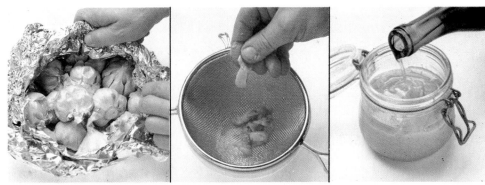

Baking garlic bulbs. Wrap the garlic in aluminum foil *(above, left)* and bake it in a preheated 375° F. [190° C.] oven for 1 hour. Then separate the cloves. Squeeze each clove — it will pop out of its skin — and discard the skin *(above, center)*. Purée the garlic through a sieve and add olive oil — about 1 tablespoonful [15 ml.] to every 10 garlic bulbs — and salt to taste. Mix the purée well. For storage, smooth the top of the mixture, cover it with a thin film of olive oil *(above, right)* and refrigerate.

Baking beets. Wash each beet; to avoid losing juices and color, do not trim or peel it. Wrap each beet in foil and bake in an oven, preheated to 325° F. [160° C.], for 3 to 4 hours. Do not increase the heat to speed cooking; high heat will dry out beets even in foil wrapping. Peel back the foil *(above, left)* and, with a knife point, test a beet for doneness; the knife tip should penetrate easily. Unwrap and peel each beet *(above, right)* before serving.

Baking onions. Arrange the onions, unpeeled but with slices cut from the root ends to keep them upright, in a baking dish just large enough to hold them in one layer. Pour sufficient water into the dish to cover the bottom. Bake the onions in a preheated 400° F. [200° C.] oven until they are soft — 1 to 1½ hours. Test for doneness by squeezing the onions *(above, left)*; they should compress slightly. With a knife, peel off the outer skins *(above, right)* before serving the onions with salt, pepper and butter.

Hearty Fillings for Tomato Cases

Any vegetable that can be stuffed and braised (*pages 70-71*) can also be stuffed and baked; the group includes eggplant, large onions, zucchini, peppers and artichokes (*opposite*). Other candidates are vegetables that cannot survive the slow, moist cooking braising demands. Mushroom caps, for example, would become rubbery if braised, but are crisply tender when baked. Tomatoes would disintegrate in a braising liquid, but hold their shapes during baking (*below, right*) provided they are slightly underripe.

Choose good-sized tomatoes for stuffing. Make sure your stuffing includes absorbent ingredients that will soak up rendered tomato juices. In this demonstration, the stuffing is a combination of corn, onions and parsley topped with bread crumbs; a simple mixture of bread crumbs and *persillade (page 33)* would be another good choice. With any stuffing, dribble a little oil or melted butter over the top to help it become an appetizing brown as it bakes.

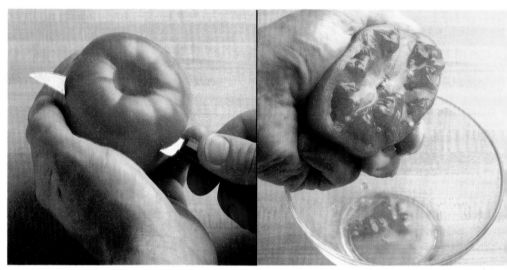

1 **Coring and seeding the tomatoes.** With a stainless-steel knife, core each tomato by cutting a conical plug from the stem end. Cut a thin slice from the tomato's top *(left)*. Gently squeeze the tomato's base to push out the seeds and juice *(right)*. Use a finger or a teaspoon handle to remove clinging seeds. Put the tomatoes in an oiled, shallow, fireproof dish.

2 **Stuffing the tomatoes.** Fill the tomatoes loosely with stuffing, cover with bread crumbs and dot with butter. Warm the dish over low heat for a few minutes, then transfer it to an oven preheated to 375° F. [190° C.]. Bake for 30 minutes, basting with butter. Serve when the tomatoes are tender and the stuffing has browned *(below)*.

The Art of Stuffing an Artichoke

Stuffed artichoke recipes often call for the cuplike shape of a turned artichoke bottom *(page 25)*, but whole artichokes also can be stuffed and baked. Once the outer leaves have been trimmed or removed *(right)*, a gentle thump is all that is needed to loosen the artichoke's tightly packed leaves so that layers of stuffing can be forced between them.

Artichokes exude little liquid during cooking and, since they require up to 1½ hours of baking, can dry out in the oven. To prevent this, stuff them with a moist mixture that will provide some liquid. A moist stuffing, incidentally, is easier to press between the leaves than a dry one would be. Here, bread crumbs soaked in water are mixed with chopped anchovy and a *persillade (page 33)*.

Stuffed artichokes need frequent basting. A glass of white wine added to the baking dish will provide flavor and serve as a basting liquid: the thick bottoms braise in the liquid while the tops bake to a rich, crusty finish.

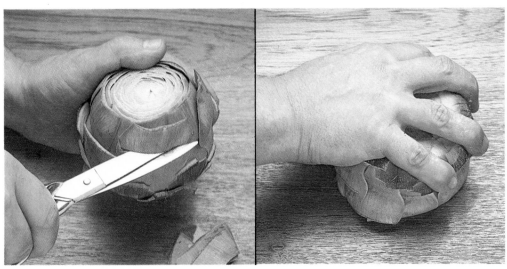

1 **Preparing the artichokes for stuffing.** Slice off the spiky upper third of each artichoke. Snap off the stem and tough outer leaves. Use scissors to trim off the tips of the rest of the leaves *(left)*. Cut a thin slice from the bottom to make a level base for the artichoke. To loosen the leaves, hold the bottom and press the artichoke firmly on the work surface *(right)*.

2 **Stuffing the artichokes.** With the aid of a spoon *(above)*, press the stuffing between the loosened leaves; you may have to open the leaves further with your fingers. When the artichokes will hold no more, place them in an oiled baking dish and sprinkle them with olive oil. Add white wine and place the dish in an oven that has been preheated to 375° F. [190° C.].

3 **Cooking and serving the artichokes.** Baste the artichokes with oil and wine from the baking dish about every 15 minutes. Mature artichokes will be ready to serve in about 1½ hours. Eat a baked artichoke leaf by leaf, scraping off the stuffing and flesh with your teeth. Finally, scoop out the stringy choke, cut up the tender artichoke bottom and eat it with a fork.

A Fan That Melds a Mixed Bake

When you bake vegetables that have been peeled or cut up so that their flesh is no longer protected by their skins, you must ensure that they will stay moist in the dry heat of an oven. Almost any vegetable can be cooked in liquid as described on pages 84-87. But some vegetables—notably vegetable fruits (such as eggplants, tomatoes and sweet peppers) and summer squashes (such as zucchini)—can also be baked without added moisture because they render water during cooking. When they are baked in a covered vessel, they will actually cook in the aromatic steam from their own juices.

Certain procedures should be followed if the vegetables are to steam successfully. The vegetables should be tightly packed into their baking dish to conserve as much moisture as possible—and to expose as little of their flesh as possible. A little olive oil dribbled over them at the start of cooking will keep them from scorching before they begin to render their juices. And the cover to the baking dish—whether it is a lid or a sheet of aluminum foil—should be as tight as possible to keep steam from escaping.

If you cut up several different vegetables and cook them together, their moisture and flavors will mingle as they cook. A particularly attractive way of combining ingredients is to make the vegetable fans shown here *(recipe, page 137)*. Eggplant halves are sliced so that they resemble fans when opened *(Step 1, right)*; good-sized zucchini can be treated the same way. The fans are combined with tomatoes and packed into a well-oiled baking dish between layers of onions.

To protect the vegetables further—and to add even more flavor—spaces between the fans can be filled with other vegetables: the artichoke bottoms and black olives shown here, parboiled celery chunks or whole mushrooms. The eggplant—or zucchini—and tomatoes will moisten these vegetables during the baking period; about an hour for eggplant, half that for zucchini.

Vegetables prepared this way are good hot, but they taste even better if they are presented tepid or cold—one fan for each serving—garnished with wedges of fresh lemon as a first course.

1 Shaping the fans. Choose elongated eggplants; wash them and lop off both ends. Halve the eggplants lengthwise. Place each half skin side up and slice it lengthwise, making the cuts about ⅓ inch [1 cm.] apart and leaving the slices attached at the stem end.

2 Preparing the tomatoes. Halve unpeeled tomatoes lengthwise, through their stem ends; remove the tough cores. Cut the tomato halves into thin lengthwise slices *(above)* that will fit neatly between the segments of the fans.

3 Stuffing the fans. Insert the tomato slices, skin side up, between the sections of the eggplant fans *(above)*. In addition to making an attractive presentation, this arrangement ensures a minimum loss of moisture during the cooking period.

4 Arranging the fans. Coat a shallow, ovenproof dish with olive oil and cover its bottom with aromatic vegetables—here, thinly sliced onions and garlic. Lift the fans *(above)*, supporting them from the bottom, and place them in the dish skin side up, packing them in without crushing them.

5 **Adding other vegetables.** Tuck in other vegetables: here, parboiled, quartered artichoke bottoms *(page 25)* and olives. Cover the vegetables with onions and garlic, then press down gently to pack all of the ingredients. Add bay leaves, mixed herbs and coriander seeds. Dribble olive oil over the vegetables *(left)*.

6 **Testing for doneness.** Cover the dish with aluminum foil and put it in an oven, preheated to 450° F. [230° C.], for 10 minutes. Then lower the heat to 350° F. [180° C.] and cook for 1 hour and 20 minutes more. Test for doneness by piercing the fans with a knife *(below)*; the stem ends should feel soft.

Gratins: Crisp on Top, Moist Underneath

Gratin means crust; all dishes prepared au gratin have a crisp, brown topping produced by baking or broiling them. To form a dry, crunchy crust, sprinkle food with grated cheese, bread crumbs or both. To form a delicate, chewy crust, coat the food with cream (pages 84-85) or sauce (pages 86-87).

Many foods, including vegetables, are gratinéed only as a finishing touch; the Belgian endive pictured on page 74, for example, was braised, then coated with cream and briefly baked to give color and crispness to the top. But the making of a crust can also be an integral part of a dish's preparation.

The trick in creating an integral gratin with raw vegetables is to cook the vegetables without burning them, yet still achieve an appetizingly crisp crust. To this end, quick-cooking vegetables are usually arranged in a shallow baking dish—the gratin dish used here is the classic choice—so that a maximum surface area is exposed to the browning heat.

To heat the dish quickly and speed the baking, the cooking process begins in a hot oven; then the temperature is reduced to bake the vegetables to tenderness. The crust does not form until the last few minutes of the cooking time, and it may be necessary to raise the heat at that point to develop the crust fully.

Vegetables that readily render their own water may be gratinéed without adding any other liquid to the container. For the gratin demonstrated below (recipe, page 103), raw spinach is chopped, packed tightly into an oiled gratin dish, sprinkled with bread crumbs and baked. Underneath the bread-crumb crust, the leaves cook down into a delicious near-purée. Other moisture-rendering vegetables that may be cooked this way include leaf vegetables like Swiss chard, as well as tomatoes, zucchini and eggplant.

Gratins may also be made from vegetables such as sliced artichoke bottoms (opposite, below), which render comparatively little moisture. These vegetables need added liquid to prevent them from shriveling and drying out in the oven.

Sandwiched between layers of moistened bread, as here (recipe, page 158), the artichokes cook gently; only the topmost bread dries out to produce the gratin. Chopped onion, garlic, herbs and anchovies may be added to the bread; mushrooms or young peas may be mixed with the artichokes; or vegetables such as celeriac may serve as the basic ingredient.

Slow-cooking vegetables like pumpkin or winter squashes require different handling. In a shallow dish these vegetables would parch and char before they were cooked through. As shown in the demonstration opposite, at top (recipe, page 145), cubes of Hubbard squash, tossed in flour, oil and spices, should be packed into a deep dish and baked in a 325° F. [160° C.] oven for 2 to 2½ hours. The slow cooking and the thickness of the vegetable layer allow the evaporation of just enough moisture to reduce the squash's bulk and intensify its flavor. The cubes at the top of the dish brown to a crust without the aid of bread crumbs.

A Crumb Topping for Delicate Leaves

1 **Chopping spinach.** Strip the stems from the spinach and wash the leaves (page 9). Drain the leaves thoroughly and pat them completely dry with paper towels. Hold them tightly together and use a large, well-sharpened knife to chop the leaves coarsely.

2 **Assembling the gratin.** Rub a generous film of olive oil around the inside of a gratin dish to prevent sticking. Fill the dish with the chopped spinach, pressing it down tightly. Season well and sprinkle the top with dried bread crumbs (above).

3 **Baking the gratin.** To ensure that the gratin browns evenly, dribble olive oil over the surface. Put the dish in a preheated 450° F. [230° C.] oven. After 10 minutes, reduce the heat to 375° F. [190° C.]. After 40 to 50 minutes, the spinach will be cooked through beneath a golden crust of bread crumbs.

Keeping Slow-cooking Squash from Drying Out

1 **Preparing the squash.** Peel and seed Hubbard squash, and cut it into ½-inch [1-cm.] cubes. Put the cubes in a large bowl. Add a handful of *persillade* *(page 33)* and toss the cubes in it. Sprinkle the vegetables with flour and toss them again, tumbling them between your fingers until they are coated.

2 **Filling the baking dish.** Rub the inside of a deep baking dish with a generous amount of olive oil. Season the squash cubes with salt and pepper, tossing them once more to distribute the seasonings. Put the squash mixture into the baking dish. Trickle more olive oil over the top of the mixture.

3 **Baking the gratin.** Cook the squash mixture in a preheated 325° F. [160° C.] oven for 2 to 2½ hours. A brown crust will form on the uppermost layer of squash. The layers underneath should be soft and juicy, but the pieces of squash should still retain their shapes.

Layers of Herbed Bread to Conserve Moisture

1 **Preparing the bread layer.** Trim the crust from a large chunk of stale bread. Soak the bread in warm water or milk for a few minutes; when it swells, squeeze out the excess liquid *(above)* and mix the bread pulp with finely chopped onion, garlic and parsley. Oil a gratin dish and line it with a little more than half of the bread mixture.

2 **Preparing the artichokes.** Trim artichoke bottoms *(page 25)* and cut them into thin slices. (If you prepare the artichokes in advance, immerse the bottoms in olive oil to keep them from discoloring.) Lay the sliced artichoke bottoms on top of the bread layer in the gratin dish, and cover them with the remaining bread mixture.

3 **Baking the gratin.** Cover the artichokes and bread with grated Parmesan cheese, and dribble oil over the top. Put the gratin in a preheated 425° F. [220° C.] oven for 10 minutes, then lower the heat to 375° F. [190° C.] and bake for 1 hour. Serve with a fork and spoon to keep the layers together.

Gratins Moistened with Cream

A Rich Finish for Grated Roots

Rich sauce and a crusty, golden surface distinguish moist gratins. They may be made several ways. The easiest of these is to put prepared vegetables in a baking dish as shown here, then cover them with cream or with milk topped with cream. The cream will keep the vegetables moist during baking and provide a sauce for them when they are done. Furthermore, the cream undergoes a chemical reaction during cooking: its natural sugar forms a browned crust on top of the sauce.

This basic combination—vegetables, cream and oven heat—can be endlessly varied. The gratin of thinly sliced potatoes shown opposite (*recipes, page 121*) is a case in point. In its simplest version, called scalloped potatoes in America and *gratin dauphinois* in France, its primary ingredient is waxy potatoes (*pages 12-13*), which retain their firm texture during baking. The potatoes are cut into slices ⅛ inch [3 mm.] thick, layered in a buttered gratin dish, then covered with milk and cream.

In the version shown, a cut garlic clove rubbed on the inside of the gratin dish adds flavor. But the flavoring could just as easily be thyme or basil. You can add sliced onions or carrots to the potatoes, or even replace them with whole, peeled and parboiled white onions. Here, bits of butter are scattered across the gratin to add richness, but scalloped potatoes often are topped with grated cheese, which, like the cream, browns to a golden crust.

Besides cheese, cream gratins may be topped with bread crumbs, as in the turnip gratin demonstrated at right (*recipe, page 127*). The crumbs provide a crisp contrast to the sauce beneath and will brown evenly during baking if they are first sautéed in butter.

The turnip gratin is made with grated vegetables instead of sliced ones, and grating is yet another way to vary the texture of a gratin. After grating, the turnips must be salted and drained of excess moisture, then briefly sautéed in butter to dry them out even more before they are covered with cream and crumbs. Zucchini or yellow squash can be prepared for a gratin the same way. So can parsnips, carrots and beets, although you need not remove their moisture.

1 **Preparing the turnips.** Peel the turnips, grate them coarsely and salt them. After 30 minutes, squeeze them in your hands to draw out their moisture. Cook the turnips in butter over low heat, stirring to prevent sticking *(above)*.

2 **Assembling the gratin.** After 10 minutes the sautéed turnips will be tender and permeated with the butter. Transfer the turnips to a buttered gratin dish and pour in enough heavy cream to cover them *(above)*.

3 **Finishing the gratin.** Sauté fresh bread crumbs in butter over low heat until they are golden. Use plenty of butter; the bread crumbs will absorb a surprising amount. Scatter the buttered crumbs over the cream *(above)*, then bake the gratin in a preheated 375° F. [190° C.] oven for 30 minutes. When the surface is a deep golden brown, remove the dish and serve the gratin bubbling hot.

A Classic Bake of Thinly Sliced Potatoes

1 **Layering the potato slices.** Rub the inside of a gratin dish with a cut garlic clove. Let the garlic juice dry, then smear the dish thickly with butter. Arrange potato slices in the dish in rows, slightly overlapping both the slices and the rows. Salt each layer of potato slices. Do not fill the dish more than two-thirds full.

2 **Adding milk and cream.** Pour milk into the dish until the potatoes are about half-covered, then top the gratin mixture with a layer of cream deep enough to cover the slices. To enrich the gratin, scatter thin shavings of butter over the cream.

3 **Baking the gratin.** Put the dish in a preheated 400° F. [200° C.] oven. After 15 minutes, reduce the heat to 350° F. [180° C.] and bake for a further 45 minutes, until the potatoes have absorbed the milk and the cream has formed a golden crust over the surface. The potatoes will be very tender. Serve them carefully, lifting them out with a fork and a spoon (left).

Flour-based and Custard Sauces

Topping vegetables with a sauce before baking them will yield a hearty and moist gratin. Sauces made with flour—either a white sauce or the related velouté—produce a light but substantial crust. Or an especially airy crust can be created with cheese custard sauce, which puffs up like a soufflé. Either treatment will suit almost any vegetable, from the chard ribs and eggplant shown here to cucumbers or leftovers. The only rule is that the vegetable must be partly precooked so that it will be done by the time the sauce develops a crisp surface.

White sauce, the basis of the béchamel of French cuisine, is made by cooking flour and butter together over low heat and whisking in milk to form a lightly thickened blend *(box, top right; recipe, page 165)*. In a velouté, stock is substituted for the milk. Be sure to simmer either sauce for at least 40 minutes to eliminate the taste of raw flour.

When white sauce or velouté is poured over precooked vegetables and baked in the oven, it will produce a thin crust without further embellishment. For a richer, thicker crust, you can add a topping of bread crumbs and grated cheese *(opposite, top)*. Or you can sharpen the flavor of a white sauce by adding grated cheese. The result is a mornay sauce, named after the 16th Century French cook who supposedly invented it. For cheese sauce, use aged, hard cheese such as Parmesan; it will not form gummy strings when cooked. Cheese sauce produces an excellent cauliflower gratin, and it suits celery or leeks as well.

A cheese gratin that puffs as it bakes is made with custard—a mixture of soft white cheese such as ricotta, plus Parmesan, eggs and heavy cream *(box, bottom right; recipe, page 138)*. The eggs in the gratin—and steam from the vegetables cooking beneath the custard—force the topping up into a golden dome.

In the demonstration opposite, below, the custard is poured over eggplant slices layered with *sofrito (page 33)* and basil; zucchini may be substituted for the eggplant. Watery vegetables like these are sautéed in oil before the gratin is assembled; other vegetables—carrots and small white onions, for example—should first be parboiled until almost tender.

Preparing a White Sauce

Adding milk to a roux. Melt the butter in a pan over a low heat *(left)*, then add the flour *(center)*. With a wooden spoon, stir the mixture into a smooth paste, or roux. When the roux begins to bubble, but before it can brown — after 2 to 5 minutes — pour in the milk, whisking at the same time *(right)*. Bring to a boil, and continue to whisk so lumps do not form. Then lower the heat and keep the mixture at a bare simmer. Cook the sauce over very low heat for 40 minutes, until it is thickened and smooth, occasionally stirring and scraping the sides and base of the pan.

Mixing a Cheese Custard

Blending cheese and eggs. Place ricotta cheese and grated Parmesan in a bowl with eggs, salt and pepper. Whisk the ingredients together *(left)* and beat them into a thick paste. Pour in heavy cream *(center)* and stir the mixture *(right)* until it is free of lumps. The mixture should have a thick pouring consistency; if it is too thick to pour, stir in a little more cream.

A Light, Thin Covering

1 **Preparing the chard ribs.** Cut Swiss chard ribs *(page 21)* into 2-inch [5-cm.] lengths and parboil them in lightly salted water for 10 to 12 minutes, until they are cooked but still firm. Drain the ribs, then tip them into a buttered gratin dish *(above)*, arranging them to form a level, shallow layer in the dish.

2 **Adding the sauce.** Pour white sauce over the chard ribs until they are just covered. Mix fine bread crumbs with grated Parmesan cheese and sprinkle the mixture on the sauce.

3 **Baking the gratin.** Scatter slivers of butter over the cheese and bread-crumb mixture. Put the dish in a preheated 475° F. [250° C.] oven for about 20 minutes, until a golden brown crust has formed on the top. Serve from the gratin dish *(above)*.

A Golden, Puffed Crown

1 **Combining the vegetables.** Cut unpeeled eggplants lengthwise into slices ½ inch [1 cm.] thick and fry them in oil over medium heat until they are golden brown. Put half the slices in a gratin dish and cover with a layer of *sofrito*. Add fresh, torn-up basil leaves. Lay the rest of the eggplant on top.

2 **Adding cheese custard.** Pour thick cheese custard over the eggplant slices and, if you like, sprinkle a thin coating of bread crumbs or freshly grated Parmesan cheese over the surface.

3 **Baking the gratin.** Put the dish in a preheated 450° F. [230° C.] oven. Bake for 10 minutes, then lower the temperature to 375° F. [190° C.]. Allow about 25 minutes more for the topping to swell and brown, then serve the gratin from the dish *(above)*.

A Decorative Pudding Baked in a Mold

The ingredients that go into sauced gratins—vegetables, white sauce, eggs and cheese—can be used in combination to produce a different sort of dish: a molded vegetable pudding. Creamy and light, a pudding is striking enough to become a separate course.

Vegetables for a pudding must be puréed *(pages 44-45)* to create the proper texture. The pudding demonstrated here *(recipe, page 111)* is based on cauliflower, but it could be made with almost any puréed vegetable, either alone or in combination with others. Both zucchini and spinach make especially good puddings, as does the mixed purée demonstrated on pages 44-45. Whatever the vegetable, the purée will be thicker and more richly flavored if the vegetable is parboiled, well drained, then sautéed in butter to soften it and evaporate excess water.

The purée is then further thickened with a thick white sauce and eggs. The sauce adds volume as well as body. The eggs set as the pudding cooks, making it firm. You can beat the eggs smooth before you use them, or add them whole and beat them with the mixture. Finally, the pudding is seasoned with spices and grated Parmesan cheese, which adds a slightly sharp flavor.

Because the pudding will expand as it cooks, use a mold big enough to hold the mixture with room to spare—the mold should be about three-quarters full when you put it in the oven. To decorate the surface of the unmolded pudding, first smear the inside of the mold thickly with butter, and lay thin parboiled strips of differently colored vegetables—and perhaps some finely chopped raw vegetables—in the butter. Chill the mold so that the butter will harden and keep the decorations in place when you ladle in the pudding mixture.

Like most baked puddings, this one is set in a bain-marie *(page 91)*, and protected from the drying heat of the oven by a sheet of buttered wax paper *(Step 4)*. The bain-marie helps the pudding cook evenly, and prevents the eggs from setting so quickly that the pudding becomes dry and rubbery.

1 **Preparing the cauliflower.** Break a trimmed, washed head of cauliflower into florets and parboil them for 4 to 5 minutes. Drain the florets well, and sauté them in butter *(above)* until they are tender, breaking up the pieces with a spoon as they soften. Then purée the cauliflower and measure the amount of purée.

2 **Blending the ingredients.** Whisk the puréed cauliflower into half its volume of thick white sauce *(below, left)*. Add eggs, salt, pepper, grated nutmeg and grated Parmesan cheese. Continue whisking *(below, right)* until all the ingredients blend thoroughly.

3 **Decorating the mold.** Butter the inside of the mold, then arrange a pattern of parboiled and thoroughly drained vegetables — here, strips of carrots and green beans — around the bottom and sides, augmenting the pattern with finely chopped, raw vegetables. Chill for 20 to 30 minutes to set the butter.

4 **Filling the mold.** Ladle the cooled pudding into the mold *(above, left)*. Tap the mold on a work surface to settle its contents. Lay a piece of buttered wax paper, slightly larger than the mold, on the pudding. Press the paper against the mold's edges *(above, right)*. Set the mold in a large pan and place the pan in an oven, preheated to 375° F. [190° C.]. Pour enough hot water into the pan to come two thirds of the way up the sides of the mold.

5 **Baking the pudding.** The pudding is cooked when it is firm to the touch; allow about 40 minutes. Let the pudding settle for 7 to 8 minutes, then peel off the wax paper *(above)* and place a serving dish upside down on the mold. Invert the dish and mold together and lift the mold off *(right)*.

Turning a Pudding into a Soufflé

The ingredients for the vegetable pudding demonstrated on pages 88-89 can be used to make a soufflé pudding possessing some of the lightness of a soufflé, some of the creaminess of a pudding and the golden crust of a gratin. Beaten egg whites, folded into vegetables and white sauce, give the dish its lightness. The whites expand during cooking, causing the vegetable mixture to puff as it bakes in its mold. The pudding is then unmolded onto a baking dish and coated with a cream-based sauce. A second baking puffs the pudding even more, and the sauce browns to a crisp topping.

To keep the soufflé pudding firm and light, the vegetables used in it must be drained of liquid. Turnips or the zucchini used here (recipe, page 148) are salted, squeezed dry and sautéed. Mushrooms are prepared as described on page 33. Spinach is parboiled and squeezed dry.

Your hands are the best tools to use for squeezing vegetables dry—and also for folding the vegetables and egg whites together, since fingertips break down fewer air bubbles than a spatula would.

Bake the soufflé pudding in any dish that will be easy to unmold; a ring mold is used here, but a charlotte mold or soufflé dish would do as well. If you wish to use individual ramekins, decrease the baking time by about a quarter.

1 **Preparing the zucchini.** Wash and trim the zucchini and shred them coarsely. Arrange the shreds in layers in a bowl, sprinkling salt on each layer (above, left). Leave them for about 30 minutes while the salt draws out their liquid. Then squeeze as much liquid as you can out of the zucchini (above, right). Press the shreds in a sieve to draw out more liquid, then squeeze again with your hands. If the zucchini tastes too salty at this point, rinse it in cold water and repeat the squeezing process.

2 **Sautéing the zucchini.** Melt a little butter in a pan and add the shredded, squeezed zucchini. Tossing it frequently (above), cook over medium heat for 7 to 8 minutes, or until it is lightly browned. Shake the pan to spread the zucchini evenly after tossing.

3 **Making the basic sauce.** Prepare a thick white sauce. Remove the pan from the heat and allow the sauce to cool for a minute or two; then—still off the heat—stir in the egg yolks (above).

4 **Adding the zucchini.** When the mixture is smooth, season it with pepper only; the zucchini will contribute sufficient salt. Stir in the shredded zucchini (above); continue stirring until the vegetable has been evenly dispersed throughout the mixture.

5 **Folding in the egg whites.** Whisk the egg whites until they form soft peaks. Pour the zucchini mixture down the sides of the bowl and use your hands to fold it gently into the whites (above). Do not blend the mixture too thoroughly, or you will deflate the whites.

6 **Filling the mold.** As soon as the egg whites have been incorporated, pour the soufflé mixture into a well-buttered mold, filling it no more than two-thirds full so that the pudding has room to expand *(above)*. Tap the mold lightly to settle the mixture, then smooth the surface of the pudding.

7 **Cooking in a bain-marie.** Place the mold in a bain-marie *(pages 88-89)* in an oven preheated to 350° F. [180° C.]. Cook for 20 to 25 minutes, until the surface is firm and springy to the touch. Remove the soufflé from the oven and from the bain-marie, and let it stand for 10 minutes; it will shrink slightly and become easier to unmold. Raise the oven temperature to 450° F. [230° C.].

8 **Saucing the soufflé.** Using the method described on page 89, unmold the soufflé onto a shallow baking dish *(above, left)*. Coat the soufflé with heavy cream or, as here, with a sauce made by whisking the cream with a thick tomato purée that has been seasoned with a pinch of sugar, salt, black pepper and cayenne pepper, then sieved. Sprinkle freshly grated Parmesan cheese over the top of the soufflé *(above, right)*.

9 **Finishing the soufflé.** Return the soufflé to the oven and cook it for about 20 minutes. It will swell, gaining more volume than it lost while it stood before unmolding. When the soufflé has risen and the topping has browned, remove it from the oven and serve it at once.

Broiling: Dealing with a Broiler's Intense Heat

Broiling is a simple process, but when vegetables cook under a broiler's intense heat—550° F. [290° C.]—special precautions are needed to retain their juiciness.

Most vegetables are prepared for broiling by being thinly sliced to expose a maximum of surface area; this method ensures that vegetables will cook quickly, with minimal drying. Another way to cook them rapidly is to cut them into small pieces and skewer them (*opposite, bottom*). Mushrooms inspire yet another variation; the caps can be stemmed and then broiled stem side up to trap their copious liquid (*below*).

Before broiling, soft vegetables—such as eggplant, summer squashes and tomatoes—should be oiled or marinated to help keep them moist. Dense or fibrous vegetables—such as celery, fennel, potatoes or carrots (*opposite, top*)—must be coated with butter and repeatedly basted to keep the surfaces from drying out before the interiors cook.

For any vegetable, remove the broiler pan and rack, then preheat the broiler for 15 minutes to ensure a high, even temperature. If vegetables brown too quickly, lower the rack or oven shelf; do not adjust the broiler temperature.

Moist Mushroom Caps

Preserving juices. Twist the stems out of the mushrooms. Arrange the caps stem side up on a broiler rack and put a sliver of butter*(above)* or a drop of olive oil in the center of each cap. Broil 6 inches [15 cm.] from the heat for 4 to 5 minutes, until the mushrooms are full of liquid, but still firm to the touch.

1 **Oiling vegetable slices.** Cut the unpeeled vegetable—in this case, eggplant—into slices ½ inch [1 cm.] thick. Place the slices on a rack and brush the top of each slice with oil (*above*). Season the slices with salt, pepper and freshly chopped herbs.

2 **Broiling the slices.** Place the rack about 5 inches [13 cm.] below the preheated broiler unit. Broil for 5 minutes, or until the slices begin to brown. Turn each slice (*above*), then oil and season its uncooked side. Broil for 3 minutes more before adding a topping (*Step 3, below*). Or, for plain slices, broil about 5 minutes more.

3 **Adding a topping.** To enhance the flavor of a grilled vegetable, add a topping of grated cheese or of thick—not runny—sauce. The eggplant slices shown here have been topped with tomato sauce*(recipe, page 165)*. Grated mozzarella and Parmesan cheese sprinkled over the tomato sauce add a contrasting layer of flavor and texture.

4 **Testing for doneness.** Slide the slices back under the broiler and cook for about 2 minutes, or until the sauce is hot and the cheese is bubbly. Test for doneness by squeezing each slice gently between your thumb and forefinger (*above*). The vegetable should be slightly resistant—soft on the outside, but still firm in the center.

A Butter Coating for Slow-cooking Vegetables

1 **Melting the butter.** In a shallow, fireproof dish placed 6 inches [15 cm.] below the heat, melt a generous amount of butter. Cut vegetables into thin slices and add them to the melted butter *(above)*. Here, carrots and fennel are both sliced ⅛ inch [3 mm.] thick to ensure equal broiling times.

2 **Broiling the vegetables.** Toss the vegetables in the melted butter to coat them thoroughly. Slide the dish back under the broiler and cook the vegetables for 12 to 15 minutes, stirring carefully every 3 minutes to keep them coated with butter *(above)*. Add fresh butter if the vegetables begin to look dry.

3 **Adding a garnish.** When the vegetables are tender — a fork should pierce them easily — remove the dish from the broiler. Before serving, garnish the vegetables with freshly chopped herbs — in this case, dill.

Creating Vegetable Kebabs

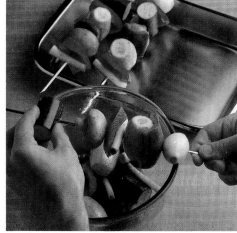  

1 **Marinating the vegetables.** Cut quick-cooking vegetables into small pieces of equal size that will cook evenly. Yellow squash, zucchini, peppers, mushrooms, scallions and small white onions are used here. Soak the pieces in a marinade *(page 58)* for half an hour; then push them onto skewers, packing them closely together.

2 **Broiling the vegetables.** To catch drippings, balance the skewers over a shallow pan. Baste the vegetables with marinade and slide the pan under the broiler, 6 inches [15 cm.] below the heat. Broil until the vegetables brown — about 5 minutes. Turn and baste. Broil until done, adding cherry tomatoes to cook during the final 2 to 3 minutes.

3 **Serving the vegetables.** When the vegetables are browned and fork-tender, remove from the broiler the pan that supports the skewers. To serve, grip the end of each skewer with a hot pad. Place the skewer tip on a plate. Use a large fork to push off the vegetables, two or three at a time *(above)*.

Protective Measures for Grilling

Because the heat of the charcoal fire is harder to control than that of an oven broiler, vegetables grilled outdoors require particular care in both preparation and cooking. One approach is to cut vegetables into slices ½ inch [1 cm.] thick that will cook rapidly and be easy to turn with tongs. Liberally coat the slices with oil before cooking to help keep the juices from escaping, and baste the slices frequently when they are on the grill to prevent them from burning.

Another approach is to seal vegetables in packages that protect them from the drying heat; cooked this way, they will partly steam in their own juices. Corn—one vegetable that demands this treatment—even provides its own package: the husks, presoaked in water to prevent burning and provide additional moisture for steaming, may be tied around the cobs, as shown at right.

For other vegetables to be grilled under wraps, heavy-duty foil, sealed with double folds at the top and ends, is the best protection (below, right). The vegetables may be cooked whole or cut into pieces, and you may grill several different types of vegetables in the same package. For added flavor, put fresh herbs, cooked bacon or pats of butter into the foil bundles before you seal them.

Vegetables should be grilled 6 inches [15 cm.] above coals that have been allowed to burn for 30 to 45 minutes until they are covered with white ash. Cooking times for grilling will vary with the way you trim the vegetables. Wrapped in foil, fleshy whole or cut-up vegetables such as eggplant, onions and tomatoes will cook through in 20 to 30 minutes; beets, carrots and potatoes will take 45 minutes to an hour. Sliced, unwrapped vegetables such as summer squashes and eggplant will take 15 to 20 minutes to cook.

Vegetable slices are done when they can be easily pierced with a fork. Vegetables that have been wrapped in foil packages are done when they yield easily to gentle pressure. Corn is done when the husks are browned all over.

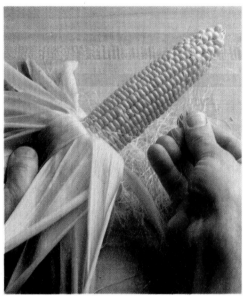

1 **Removing the silk.** One leaf at a time, carefully peel the husks down to the stalk end of the ear of corn. Pull off the threadlike silk inside.

2 **Reassembling the husks.** Return each husk leaf to its original position. Secure the husk around the cob by tying string around the loose tips.

3 **Grilling the corn.** Soak the tied ears of corn in cold water for 10 minutes. Drain and cook on the grill for 25 to 30 minutes, turning every 5 minutes to ensure even cooking. The corn here is grilled with oil-coated yellow-squash halves and whole new potatoes wrapped in foil; a belt of skin was removed from each potato to serve as a steam vent and prevent the potato from bursting.

Anthology
of Recipes

Drawing upon the cooking traditions and literature of more than 24 countries, the Editors and consultants for this volume have selected 232 published vegetable recipes for the Anthology that follows. The selections range from the simple to the unusual—from an informal vegetable stew to an elaborate soufflé pudding.

The Anthology also spans nearly 200 years and includes recipes by 140 writers, many of them distinguished exponents of the culinary art. But there are also recipes by little-known authors of out-of-print books held in private collections; a number of these recipes have never before been published in English. Whatever the sources, the emphasis is on authentic dishes prepared with fresh, natural ingredients that blend harmoniously.

Since many early recipe writers did not specify amounts of ingredients, the missing information has been judiciously added. Where appropriate, clarifying introductory notes have also been supplied; they are printed in italics. Modern terms have been substituted for archaic language; but to preserve the character of the original recipes, and to create a true anthology, the authors' texts have been changed as little as possible. Some instructions have been expanded, but in cases where recipes may seem abrupt, the reader has only to refer to the appropriate demonstration in the front of the book to find the technique explained in words and pictures.

For ease of use, the Anthology is organized according to the same vegetable categories described in the guide at the front of the book—with an additional category for mixed vegetable dishes. Recipes for standard preparations—stock, pastry, batter and basic sauces—appear at the end. The serving suggestions and accompaniments included in some of the recipes, are, of course, optional.

Apart from the primary vegetables, all recipe ingredients are listed in order of use, with both the customary U.S. and the new metric measurements provided in separate columns. The metric quantities supplied here reflect the American practice of measuring solid ingredients, such as flour or sugar, by volume—rather than by weight, as Europeans do. To make the quantities simpler to measure, many of the figures have been rounded off to correspond to the gradations that are now standard on metric spoons and cups. (One cup, for example, equals 237 milliliters; in most of these recipes, however, a cup appears as a more readily measurable 250 milliliters or ¼ liter.) Similarly, weight, temperature and linear metric equivalents are rounded slightly. For these reasons, the American and metric figures are not equivalent—but if you carefully use one set or the other, you will produce equally good results.

Leaf Vegetables

Braised Belgian Endive

To serve 4

8	heads Belgian endive, trimmed and cored	8
10 tbsp.	butter	150 ml.
	salt and pepper	
2 to 3 tbsp.	fresh lemon juice	30 to 45 ml.
5	slices bacon, cut into small strips (optional)	5

Lightly cover the interior surfaces of a fireproof casserole with 1 tablespoon [15 ml.] of the butter. Lay the Belgian endive in the casserole and add the remaining butter, cut into small pieces. Sprinkle with salt and pepper.

Put the casserole over moderate heat and, once the butter has started to sizzle, reduce the heat. Cover and cook gently until the endive is tender, 20 to 30 minutes. Alternatively, cook in a moderate oven, preheated to 350° F. [180° C.], for 1 hour. Before serving, sprinkle with lemon juice.

Small pieces of bacon can be browned beforehand in the casserole and left to finish cooking with the endive.

MARIE STONE
THE COVENT GARDEN COOKBOOK

Belgian Endive Baked with Ham and Cheese

Chicorée mit Schinken und Käse

The technique of removing the bitter core of Belgian endive is demonstrated on page 9.

To serve 4

8	large Belgian endives, cores removed	8
1 cup	milk	¼ liter
1 tsp.	salt	5 ml.
8	thin slices precooked ham, each about 4 by 6 inches [10 by 15 cm.]	8
8	thin slices Gruyère or Emmentaler cheese, each about 4 by 6 inches [10 by 15 cm.]	8
1 tbsp.	butter	15 ml.

Arrange the Belgian endive in one layer in a 12-inch [30-cm.] stainless-steel or enameled skillet, and pour the milk and 1 cup [¼ liter] of cold water over it. Add the salt, and

heat until small bubbles appear around the rim of the pan. Reduce the heat to low, cover the pan tightly, and simmer for 20 minutes, or until the Belgian endive is tender but not falling apart.

Preheat the oven to 400° F. [200° C.]. Remove the Belgian endive from the pan with tongs, and drain it on a double thickness of paper towels. Wrap each head of Belgian endive in a slice of ham, then in a slice of cheese. Generously butter a shallow 8-by-10-inch [20-by-25-cm.] baking dish, and arrange the Belgian endive rolls in it side by side. Bake undisturbed in the middle of the oven for 10 minutes, or until the cheese softens and melts. Serve immediately, directly from the baking dish.

FOODS OF THE WORLD/THE COOKING OF GERMANY

Belgian Endive Pie

Tortino di cicoria

To serve 3 or 4

3	heads Belgian endive, cored, parboiled for 15 minutes, drained and coarsely chopped	3
	short-crust pastry *(recipe, page 167)*	
2	eggs	2
½ cup	freshly grated Cheddar cheese	125 ml.
⅔ cup	milk	150 ml.
⅔ cup	light cream	150 ml.
	salt and pepper	
⅛ tsp.	grated nutmeg	½ ml.

Line a 6-inch [15-cm.] piepan with the short-crust pastry. Lay the Belgian endive in the piepan. In a bowl, mix together the rest of the ingredients. Pour the mixture over the Belgian endive and bake in a moderate oven, preheated to 350° F. [180° C.], for about 30 minutes, or until the cheese custard has set.

JANET ROSS AND MICHAEL WATERFIELD
LEAVES FROM OUR TUSCAN KITCHEN

Belgian Endive, Flemish-Style

Endives à la Flamande

To serve 2 or 3

2 to 2½ lb.	Belgian endive, cored and sliced into rounds ½ inch [1 cm.] thick	1 kg.
4 to 5 tbsp.	butter	60 to 75 ml.
	salt	

Butter generously a shallow ovenproof casserole just large enough to contain the Belgian endive, and arrange the slices in the casserole. Cover with a piece of buttered parchment paper and seal the casserole tightly with a close-fitting lid. Bake in an oven, preheated to 300° F. [150° C.], for at least 2 hours, or until the juices have evaporated. Turn the Belgian endive out upside down onto a warmed serving platter as you would a pudding: the endive should be golden brown in color. Season with salt and serve.

MADAME SAINT-ANGE
LA BONNE CUISINE DE MADAME SAINT-ANGE

Stuffed Chard Rolls
Paupiettes of Chard

To serve 4

15	large, perfect chard leaves and stems	15
2	large leeks, including 1 inch [2½ cm.] of the green tops	2
1	small head Boston lettuce	1
2 or 3	sorrel leaves	2 or 3
6 tbsp.	unsalted butter	90 ml.
1	egg	1
½ cup	heavy cream	125 ml.
½ cup	freshly grated Parmesan cheese	125 ml.
	salt and pepper	
	grated nutmeg	

The chard leaves must be flexible enough to roll up; so, with a paring knife, remove the excess rib from about the center of each leaf down to the stem. Cut off the stems and reserve. Bring a saucepan of water to a boil and, holding the leaves with tongs, parboil each leaf until it is bright green and limp. Spread out the leaves, rib side up, on paper toweling. Select the eight best leaves for the *paupiettes*.

Slice the chard stems and the leeks into thin julienne (matchsticks). Cut the lettuce, sorrel and unselected chard leaves into chiffonade (fine shreds).

Melt 4 tablespoons [60 ml.] butter in a skillet, add ⅓ cup [75 ml.] of water and gently stew the julienne and the chiffonade until the liquid has evaporated.

Mix the egg, cream, Parmesan cheese and seasoning. Add the cooked greens.

Spread an eighth of this mixture down the center of each *paupiette* leaf. Fold the long edges over the filling and roll up each leaf. Place the *paupiettes* in a well-buttered gratin dish. Add ½ cup [125 ml.] of water, and place a shaving of cold butter on each *paupiette*. Bake in a moderate oven, preheated to 350° F. [180° C.], for 25 to 30 minutes. Baste two or three times during cooking. Serve each *paupiette* with a spoonful of the buttery juices.

JUDITH OLNEY
SUMMER FOOD

Chard Swiss-Style

Spinach or any other green may be prepared in this manner. If a sharper flavor is desired, half of the grated cheese may be Parmesan instead of Gruyère.

	To serve 4	
1½ lb.	chard leaves, parboiled for 5 minutes, thoroughly drained and coarsely chopped (about 4 cups [1 liter] after chopping)	¾ kg.
2	slices firm, white bread with the crusts removed, broken into small pieces	2
¼ cup	milk	50 ml.
1 oz.	dried mushrooms (about ⅓ cup [75 ml.]), soaked for 5 minutes in warm water, squeezed dry and finely chopped	50 g.
2	leeks, white parts only, finely chopped	2
3 tbsp.	finely chopped fresh parsley or chives	45 ml.
½ cup	finely chopped celery leaves	125 ml.
1	small garlic clove, crushed	1
⅓ cup	grated Gruyère cheese	75 ml.
	salt and pepper	
	freshly grated nutmeg	
4	eggs	4
1 tbsp.	butter	15 ml.
3 tbsp.	olive oil	45 ml.
½ cup	fine fresh bread crumbs	125 ml.

Place the bread in a mixing bowl and pour the milk over it; allow to stand until the milk is absorbed. Add the chard, mushrooms, leeks, parsley or chives, celery leaves, garlic and grated cheese. Season to taste with salt, pepper and nutmeg. Add the unbeaten eggs, one at a time, mixing well after each addition.

Butter a baking dish generously, pour in 2 tablespoons [30 ml.] of the olive oil, spreading the oil well over the bottom of the dish. Mix the bread crumbs with the remaining olive oil. Spread the chard mixture evenly in the dish and top with the oiled bread crumbs. Bake in a moderate oven, preheated to 350° F. [180° C.], for about 30 minutes, or until the mixture is firm and browned. Serve from the baking dish.

LOUIS P. DE GOUY
THE GOLD COOK BOOK

Swiss Chard Pie

To serve 6 to 8

30	Swiss chard leaves, torn into pieces	30
1	small onion, chopped	1
4 tbsp.	butter	60 ml.
2	eggs, lightly beaten	2
½ cup	freshly grated Cheddar cheese	125 ml.
⅓ cup	stemmed, seeded and chopped green chilies	75 ml.

Preheat the oven to 350° F. [180° C.]. Sauté the onion in the butter until transparent. Add the chard and cook for 1 minute or until wilted. Be sure the chard is covered with butter.

Pour the chard into a buttered piepan. Mix the eggs with the green chilies and pour over the chard. Stir with a fork. Spread the Cheddar cheese on top and bake for 20 to 30 minutes or until firm.

MRS. L. V. HOUSEWRIGHT
THE GREAT GREEN CHILI COOKING CLASSIC

Gratin of Chard or Beet Greens

Polpettone di Bietole

To serve 4

2 to 2½ lb.	chard leaves or beet greens, trimmed, parboiled, rinsed under cold running water, squeezed dry and finely chopped	1 kg.
7 tbsp.	butter	105 ml.
3 tbsp.	oil	45 ml.
1 lb.	mushrooms, sliced, or ⅔ cup [150 ml.] dried mushrooms, soaked in warm water for about 30 minutes, drained, rinsed and roughly chopped	½ kg.
1	garlic clove, chopped	1
½ cup	ricotta or other fresh white cheese	125 ml.
¼ cup	freshly grated Parmesan cheese	50 ml.
	salt	
3	egg yolks	3
½ cup	dry bread crumbs	125 ml.

Melt the butter in a saucepan with 1 tablespoon [15 ml.] of the oil. Add the mushrooms and garlic, and lightly sauté them without browning the mushrooms. Add the chard or beet leaves, mix well to blend the flavors, and remove the pan from the heat. Add the white cheese and the Parmesan;

season with salt and blend in the egg yolks to make a smooth, homogeneous mixture.

Oil a shallow baking dish thoroughly and sprinkle it with some of the bread crumbs. Pour the mixture into the dish and smooth the top with the back of a spoon. Cover with the remaining bread crumbs and sprinkle with the rest of the oil. Put the gratin into an oven, preheated to 375° F. [190° C.], and cook for about 30 to 40 minutes until the top is golden brown. This dish can be served either hot or cold.

LUIGI CARNACINA AND LUIGI VERONELLI
LA BUONA VERA CUCINA ITALIANA

Collard Casserole

To serve 6

4 lb.	collard greens	2 kg.
2 tbsp.	butter	30 ml.
2 tbsp.	finely chopped onion	30 ml.
2 tbsp.	flour	30 ml.
1 cup	milk	¼ liter
½ tsp.	salt	2 ml.
	pepper	
3	hard-boiled eggs	3
1 cup	freshly grated medium sharp Cheddar cheese	¼ liter

Wash the collard greens and strip the leaves from the stems. Boil the greens in a large amount of lightly salted water. When the leaves are tender (after about 20 minutes), drain the greens and discard the water. Chop the greens coarsely and set them aside.

In a small saucepan, heat the butter. Sauté the onions just until soft. Stir in the flour and, when blended, add the milk. Whisk until the mixture is smooth and thick. Season with salt and pepper.

Put half of the greens in a buttered 1½-quart [1½-liter] casserole. Spoon half the sauce over the greens and cover with half of the sliced eggs and half of the cheese. Repeat the layers and bake for 20 minutes in an oven that has been preheated to 350° F. [180° C.].

CHARLOTTE TURGEON
OF CABBAGES AND KINGS COOKBOOK

Spring Greens

This tasty recipe costs almost nothing and can be used for beet or turnip greens, spinach, chard or any of your favorites. But by all means try it with a mixture of early spring greens, such as dandelion and wild winter cress, and the leaves of perennial herbs, such as sour sorrel, Good-King-Henry and Russian broadleaf comfrey. If you can locate them, these fresh spring greens are ready long before spinach or beet greens can be picked.

To serve 3 or 4

6 cups	greens, washed and roughly torn into pieces	1 ½ liters
1	medium-sized onion	1
2 tbsp.	oil	30 ml.
2 tbsp.	vinegar	30 ml.
1 tbsp.	molasses or brown sugar	15 ml.

Steam the greens, or cook them briefly in just the water that clings to the leaves from washing them. Drain thoroughly and reserve the liquid to use in soups. Chop the greens coarsely with a knife.

Slice the onion and sauté it in the oil until it is golden. In a small bowl mix the vinegar and molasses, then add this to the onion and heat thoroughly. Add the greens, mix well and heat again before serving.

ANNE MOYER
THE GREEN THUMB COOKBOOK

Beet-Green Pudding

To serve 6 to 8

1 quart	beet greens, boiled or steamed, drained and chopped	1 liter
2 tbsp.	butter	30 ml.
¼ cup	flour	50 ml.
¾ cup	milk	175 ml.
2 tsp.	salt	10 ml.
¼ tsp.	ground cinnamon	1 ml.
3	eggs, lightly beaten	3

Preheat the oven to 350° F. [180° C.]. Press any liquid out of the beet greens. Over low heat, melt the butter in a saucepan; add the flour, stirring constantly. Gradually stir in the milk, seasonings and beet greens. Remove from the stove and stir in the beaten eggs. Blend thoroughly. Turn into a buttered 1½-quart [1½-liter] casserole. Place the casserole in a pan of hot water in the middle of the oven and bake the mixture for 30 minutes.

Serve the pudding right from the casserole; or unmold and serve it on a warmed plate with hot, heavy cream.

GERI HARRINGTON
SUMMER GARDEN, WINTER KITCHEN

Pie of Herbs

At the time John Evelyn was writing, in the late 17th Century, all green, leafy vegetables were known as herbs. This recipe is a variation of the Tudor spinach pies, of the kind still made in Provence at Christmas. The pie is traditionally served as a dessert, but can also accompany meats.

To serve 6 to 8

1 lb.	spinach	½ kg.
½ lb.	chard	¼ kg.
¼ cup	chopped fresh chervil	50 ml.
1 cup	light cream	¼ liter
½ cup	fresh bread crumbs	125 ml.
3 tbsp.	finely crumbled macaroons or ground almonds	45 ml.
4 tbsp.	butter	60 ml.
2	eggs	2
2	egg yolks	2
¼ cup	dried currants, soaked in hot milk and drained	50 ml.
3 tbsp.	sugar	45 ml.
	grated nutmeg	
	rough puff pastry *(recipe, page 167)*	

Parboil the spinach, chard and chervil in salted water for 2 minutes, then drain and chop them. Boil the cream with the bread crumbs to thicken it, then add the chopped herbs. Next add the crumbled macaroons or ground almonds, the butter, and the eggs beaten with the extra egg yolks. Finally add the currants, sugar and a good grating of nutmeg. (More sugar and crumbled macaroons or ground almonds may be added to taste.) Stir it all together over low heat. Line a 9-inch [23-cm.] piepan with the pastry and pour in the herb mixture. Bake in an oven, preheated to 425° F. [220° C.], for 10 minutes, then lower the temperature to 350° F. [180° C.] and cook for 30 to 40 minutes. Serve hot or warm with cream.

JOHN EVELYN
ACETARIA

Baked Kale with Potatoes

Grünkohl mit Kartoffeln

To serve 4 to 6

3 lb.	kale, stems removed	1½ kg.
9 tbsp.	butter, softened	135 ml.
½ lb.	lean bacon, coarsely diced	¼ kg.
½ cup	beef or chicken stock	125 ml.
2 tsp.	salt	10 ml.
¼ tsp.	grated nutmeg	1 ml.
9	medium-sized potatoes (about 3 lb. [1½ kg.]), cut into small pieces	9
½ cup	milk	125 ml.
	freshly ground black pepper	
2	egg yolks	2

Grease the bottom and sides of an 8-by-10-inch [20-by-25-cm.] baking dish with 1 tablespoon [15 ml.] of the softened butter. Set the dish aside.

Drop the kale into enough lightly salted boiling water to cover it completely, and boil briskly for 10 minutes. Drain thoroughly in a colander and, with the back of a spoon, press the kale firmly to remove any excess liquid. Then chop the kale coarsely.

In a heavy 4-quart [4-liter] saucepan, cook the bacon over moderate heat until it is crisp and brown. Add the kale, turning it with a large spoon until the leaves are coated with the fat. Then stir in the stock, 1 teaspoon [5 ml.] of the salt, and the nutmeg, and bring to a boil over high heat. Reduce the heat to low and simmer, uncovered, stirring occasionally, for 20 minutes.

Meanwhile, preheat the oven to 400° F. [200° C.]. Drop the potatoes into enough lightly salted boiling water to cover them completely, and boil them briskly, uncovered, until they are tender but not falling apart. Drain thoroughly, return them to the pan and shake them over low heat for 2 to 3 minutes until they are dry. Then force the potatoes through a food mill set over a bowl. Gradually beat 5 tablespoons [75 ml.] of the butter into the potatoes. Beat in the milk, a few spoonfuls at a time, using as much of the milk as you need to make a purée thick enough to hold its shape in a spoon. Beat in the remaining teaspoon of salt, a few grindings of black pepper, and the egg yolks, one at a time. Taste for seasoning.

Spread the cooked kale evenly over the bottom of the prepared baking dish, smooth the potatoes over it, and dot the top with the remaining butter, cut into small pieces. Bake in the middle of the oven for 20 minutes, or until the surface of the potatoes is golden brown. Serve at once, directly from the baking dish.

FOODS OF THE WORLD/THE COOKING OF GERMANY

Lettuce Mousse

Mousse de Laitue

The lettuce hearts, not used in this recipe, may be reserved for a green salad.

To serve 4

8	heads Bibb or Boston lettuce with the hearts removed and the leaves separated, then thoroughly washed	8
	salt	
3 to 4 tbsp.	milk	45 to 60 ml.
½ cup	heavy cream	125 ml.
4 tbsp.	butter	60 ml.
	freshly ground pepper	
	croutons made from 2 slices of firm, white bread with the crusts removed, diced and fried in butter	

Bring a large saucepan of well-salted water to a boil. When the water is boiling hard, plunge in the lettuce leaves and boil vigorously, uncovered, for 5 to 7 minutes.

Drain, then rinse the leaves in cold water. Squeeze out the excess water by hand. Chop the leaves finely and put them into a blender with the milk. Purée for 30 seconds, then pour the mixture into a saucepan, and add the cream and butter. Season with salt and pepper. Reduce the purée over high heat, for 5 to 10 minutes, stirring vigorously. Serve with the croutons on top.

ANDRÉ GUILLOT
LA GRANDE CUISINE BOURGEOISE

Braised Lettuce

To serve 6

3	heads Boston lettuce	3
2 tsp.	salt	10 ml.
3 tbsp.	flour	45 ml.
1½ cups	beef stock	375 ml.
⅓ cup	Madeira or port	75 ml.

Bring a large quantity of water to a boil and add the salt. Plunge the heads of lettuce into the boiling water and cover the pot. As soon as the water comes back to a boil, remove the lettuce and plunge the heads into cold water. Drain well.

Put the flour in a small pan and slowly stir in the stock, keeping the mixture very smooth. Bring this mixture to a simmer over medium heat. Once the sauce is thick, remove it from the heat and add the wine.

Gently squeeze each head of lettuce to remove all excess water. Cut off the stem ends, then cut each head in half, from top to bottom. Lay the halves in a shallow baking dish, cut side down. Pour the sauce over the lettuce and cover them with a lid or aluminum foil.

Place the baking dish in an oven, preheated to 375° F. [190° C.], for 30 minutes, or until the lettuce is tender when tested with a sharp knife.

CAROL CUTLER
THE SIX-MINUTE SOUFFLÉ AND OTHER CULINARY DELIGHTS

───────❖───────

Sorrel Casserole
Far à l'Oseille dans la Cocotte

To serve 4

1½ lb.	sorrel, chopped	¾ kg.
2	slices bacon, chopped	2
3	heads lettuce, halved, cored and chopped	3
2	medium-sized onions, thinly sliced	2
8	garlic cloves, chopped	8
	salt and pepper	
4	eggs, lightly beaten	4
2 tbsp.	light cream	30 ml.
½ cup	dry bread crumbs	125 ml.

Lightly fry the bacon in a heavy saucepan over low heat, then add the sorrel, lettuce, onion and garlic. Mix all together; cover the pan and cook very gently for 2 hours. Season the sorrel mixture with salt and pepper and, a few minutes before serving, whisk the eggs, cream and the bread crumbs together and stir them into the sorrel.

JEAN MERCIER AND IRENE LABARRE
LA CUISINE DU POITOU ET DE LA VENDÉE

───────❖───────

Spinach Dumplings
Malfatti di Spinaci

To serve 4 to 6

2 to 2½ lb.	spinach, boiled, drained, squeezed completely dry and finely chopped	1 kg.
5 tbsp.	butter	75 ml.
1 cup	ricotta cheese	¼ liter
1	egg, beaten	1
¾ cup	flour	175 ml.
¼ cup	freshly grated Parmesan cheese	50 ml.

Sauté the spinach in 3 tablespoons [45 ml.] of the butter for about 5 minutes. Remove the pan from the heat and add the

ricotta, egg and 3 tablespoons of the flour. Mix thoroughly. Shape the mixture into small, round dumplings. Roll the dumplings in the remaining flour and cook them, a small batch at a time, by sliding them from a saucer into a large pan of simmering salted water. After about 5 to 8 minutes, when the dumplings float to the surface, lift them out with a perforated spoon, and keep them hot on a heatproof platter in an oven, preheated to its lowest setting.

To serve, melt the remaining butter and pour it over the dumplings. Sprinkle them with the grated Parmesan. Alternatively, the dumplings can be served with a tomato sauce.

GIOVANNI CAVALERA AND ODILLA MARCHESINI
LA CUCINA DELLE STAGIONI

Spinach with Rice
Spanakorizo

To serve 4

3 lb.	spinach, tough stems removed	1½ kg.
1 cup	olive oil	¼ liter
3	onions, or 1 bunch scallions (including 2 inches [5 cm.] of the green tops), coarsely chopped	3
1 tbsp.	chopped fresh dill	15 ml.
	salt and pepper	
2 cups	water	½ liter
¾ cup	raw unprocessed rice	175 ml.

Heat the olive oil in a large saucepan. Sauté the onions gently until half-cooked, but not colored. Shake the surplus water off the spinach leaves and put them in the saucepan with the onions. Cover and simmer gently for 5 minutes, then add the dill, seasoning and water, and bring to a boil.

Throw in the rice, stir well once with a wooden spoon, cover, and cook over moderate heat until the rice swells and the water is reduced. After about 10 to 15 minutes, when most of the water has been absorbed, remove the pan from the heat. Take off the lid, place a clean cloth over the pan and then replace the lid so that the steam does not escape altogether. Leave for 10 to 15 minutes until the rice is cooked and the water has completely disappeared.

JOYCE M. STUBBS
THE HOME BOOK OF GREEK COOKERY

Creamed Spinach

To serve 4 to 6

2 lb.	spinach, coarse stems removed, washed and drained	1 kg.
1 tsp.	salt	5 ml.
	grated nutmeg	
3 to 4 tbsp.	heavy cream	45 to 60 ml.
	salt and pepper	

Heat a large, heavy pan, throw in the spinach, and sprinkle with salt and nutmeg. Turn up the heat, and toss and stir for 2 or 3 minutes, by which time the spinach should be cooked. No additional water is necessary; sufficient water will adhere to the leaves.

Drain the spinach and press out any excess moisture. Place the spinach in the blender with the cream and blend until smooth. Reheat the creamed spinach in a saucepan and correct the seasoning. You may find that a little more nutmeg is an improvement.

MAURICE MOORE-BETTY
COOKING FOR OCCASIONS

Spinach with Currants and Pine Nuts

Les Épinards aux Raisins et aux Pignons

To serve 6

8 lb.	spinach, stems removed	4 kg.
	salt	
¼ cup	olive oil	50 ml.
1 cup	pine nuts	¼ liter
⅔ cup	dried currants, soaked in warm water for 30 minutes, drained and dried on paper towels	150 ml.
	pepper	

Plunge the spinach into a large pan of boiling salted water. Cook for up to 10 minutes. The spinach is ready when a leaf crushes easily on being pressed firmly between the fingers.

Drain the spinach, squeeze out the extra moisture and drain again for 2 to 3 minutes.

Heat the oil in a fireproof casserole. Toss in the pine nuts. When they begin to color, add the currants and stir briskly with a wooden spoon. Add the spinach and heat it through. Season with salt and pepper. Serve in the casserole.

JACQUES MÉDECIN
LA CUISINE DU COMTÉ DE NICE

Spinach Pancakes

Pinaattiohukaiset

To serve 6 to 8

1 lb.	spinach, blanched in boiling water, drained, squeezed completely dry and finely chopped	½ kg.
1½ cups	milk	375 ml.
1 tsp.	salt	5 ml.
⅛ tsp.	grated nutmeg	½ ml.
1 cup	flour	¼ liter
2 tbsp.	unsalted butter, melted and cooled	30 ml.
2	eggs	2
½ tsp.	sugar	2 ml.
1 to 2 tbsp.	butter, softened	15 to 30 ml.

In a large mixing bowl, combine the milk, salt, nutmeg and flour and then stir in the melted butter. (Or, if you prefer to use an electric blender, all of these ingredients can be mixed at once at medium speed.) In a separate bowl, combine the eggs and sugar, and stir this mixture into the batter. Gradually add the chopped spinach.

With a pastry brush or paper towel, coat the bottom of a heavy 10- to 12-inch [25- to 30-cm.] skillet with about a teaspoon [5 ml.] of soft butter and set the skillet over moderately high heat until the pan is very hot. For each pancake, drop 2 tablespoons [30 ml.] of the batter onto the skillet and, with a spoon or spatula, spread it out evenly to form a 3-inch [8-cm.] disk. Cook the pancakes—three or four at a time—for 2 to 3 minutes on each side, or until they have browned lightly. Keep them hot on a warmed platter, covered loosely with aluminum foil. Add more butter to the skillet as it becomes necessary while cooking the remaining pancakes. Serve the spinach pancakes as a vegetable course—accompanied, if you like, by lingonberries.

FOODS OF THE WORLD/THE COOKING OF SCANDINAVIA

Eggs and Spinach

To serve 4

2 to 2½ lb.	spinach	1 kg.
6 tbsp.	butter	90 ml.
	salt	
2 or 3	eggs, beaten	2 or 3
2 to 3 tbsp.	freshly grated Parmesan cheese	30 to 45 ml.
1 tsp.	chopped marjoram	5 ml.
4	slices French or Italian bread, fried in olive oil	4

Parboil the spinach for 1 to 2 minutes in a large pan of boiling water. Drain and squeeze dry. Melt the butter in a saucepan, add the spinach, and season with salt. Cook very gently for 15 minutes. Mix the eggs with the Parmesan cheese and the marjoram, and pour the mixture over the spinach. Stir well with a wooden spoon over low heat for 2 or 3 minutes, until barely thickened, without letting the contents of the saucepan boil and without scrambling the eggs. Remove from the heat and serve with the fried bread.

THE COOK TO A FLORENTINE FAMILY
NOT ONLY SPAGHETTI!

Frying Herbs, as Dressed in Staffordshire

In the early 19th Century, when Mrs. Rundell was writing, all green, leafy vegetables were still known as herbs.

To serve 4		
1 lb.	spinach, with the stems removed	½ kg.
⅓ cup	chopped fresh parsley	75 ml.
6	scallions, including 2 inches [5 cm.] of the green tops, chopped	6
	salt	
2 tbsp.	butter	30 ml.

Put the spinach in a large stewpan. Sprinkle the parsley and scallions among the spinach. Set them all on to stew, with some salt and the butter: shake the pan when it begins to grow warm, and let it be closely covered over low heat for about 15 minutes till done enough. It is served with slices of grilled calf's liver, small slices of bacon, and fried eggs; the latter on the herbs, the others in a separate dish.

MRS. MARIA RUNDELL
DOMESTIC COOKERY

Spinach Gratin

Gratin d'Épinards

This gratin (or *tian)* of spinach is an infinitely simple preparation that owes its originality to an important detail: the finely chopped spinach is placed raw on a bed of oil. And without doubt the spinach is best young.

To serve 4		
2 to 2½ lb.	spinach, stems removed, finely chopped	1 kg.
¼ cup	olive oil	50 ml.
	salt and pepper	
¼ cup	dry bread crumbs	50 ml.

Oil a large gratin dish with 1 tablespoon [15 ml.] of the oil. Pack in the spinach, and season with salt and pepper. Sprin-

kle with a coating of bread crumbs, and dribble the remaining oil all over the surface. Cook in an oven, preheated to 375° F. [190° C.], for about 50 minutes.

RENÉ JOUVEAU
LA CUISINE PROVENÇALE

Spinach Loaf Berthilda

Le Pain d'Épinards Berthilda

To serve 6 to 8		
2 to 2½ lb.	spinach, tough stems removed, washed	1 kg.
	salt	
10	eggs	10
⅓ cup	heavy cream	75 ml.
	pepper	
14 tbsp.	butter, melted and cooled	210 ml.
1 cup	béchamel sauce *(recipe, page 165)*	¼ liter
¼ cup	freshly grated Parmesan cheese	50 ml.
	hollandaise sauce *(recipe, page 166)*	

Cook the spinach in boiling, salted water. Drain it well, and purée it through a sieve or food mill.

Beat the eggs with the cream, and season with salt and pepper. When well beaten, pass the mixture through a fine sieve into a large bowl. Mix in the melted butter and the puréed spinach. Turn the spinach mixture into a buttered charlotte mold, and place the mold in a pan that has been partially filled with hot water. Bake in an oven, preheated to 325° F. [160° C.], for 45 minutes, or until the center of the loaf has swelled and is firm to the touch.

Turn out the loaf onto an ovenproof platter. Mix the béchamel sauce with half of the grated Parmesan, and use the mixture to coat the top and sides of the loaf. Sprinkle the remaining Parmesan over the loaf. Turn up the oven temperature to 450° F. [230° C.], and return the loaf to the oven for 10 to 15 minutes or until the coating is lightly browned.

Serve the loaf with the hollandaise sauce, passed separately in a sauceboat.

EDOUARD NIGNON
LES PLAISIRS DE LA TABLE

Spinach and Cheese Gratin

Épinards au Four

To serve 4

2 to 2½ lb.	spinach with the stems removed, chopped	1 kg.
½ cup	flour	125 ml.
	salt and pepper	
	grated nutmeg	
8 tbsp.	butter, cut into small pieces	120 ml.
1 cup	farmer or ricotta cheese	¼ liter
¾ cup	heavy cream	175 ml.
3	eggs	3

Pile the flour into a heap on a table or in a large mixing bowl, and make a well in the center. Into this, put a little salt, pepper and nutmeg, the butter, cheese, cream and eggs. Mix everything together to make a paste and then add the spinach. Put the mixture into a buttered gratin dish and cook in an oven, preheated to 375° F. [190° C.], for about 30 minutes or until a crust forms on the surface. Serve immediately.

GARLIN
LE CUISINIER MODERN

Spinach in the Old-fashioned Manner

Épinards à la Vieille Mode

It is necessary to exaggerate the amount of butter a little because the dandelion greens, spinach and, above all, the chicory absorb an enormous amount of butter and cream.

To serve 4 to 6

3 lb.	spinach, stems removed	1½ kg.
3	bunches watercress, stems removed	3
2 to 2½ lb.	dandelion greens, stems removed	1 kg.
2 to 2½ lb.	chicory, white hearts only	1 kg.
14 tbsp.	butter	210 ml.
½ to ¾ cup	leftover meat braising juices or meat stock (optional)	125 to 175 ml.
	salt and pepper	
1 cup	béchamel sauce *(recipe, page 165)*	¼ liter

Parboil each of the vegetables separately: the spinach and watercress for about 1 minute, or until softened; and the dandelion greens and chicory for 5 to 6 minutes, or until softened. Drain all the greens thoroughly, mix them together and chop them very finely. Place them in a gratin dish that has been thickly buttered on the sides and bottom. The addition of meat braising juices or stock to the greens will improve the flavor.

Taste the greens for seasoning, then pour the béchamel sauce over them. Put the dish into a hot oven, preheated to 450° F. [230° C.], for 10 minutes, then serve.

CURNONSKY
CUISINE ET VINS DE FRANCE

The Cabbage Family

Broccoli in Wine

To serve 6

3 lb.	broccoli, larger stalks trimmed and split lengthwise	1½ kg.
½ tsp.	salt	2 ml.
Wine sauce		
1 tbsp.	butter	15 ml.
2 tsp.	olive oil	10 ml.
2	garlic cloves, finely chopped	2
2 tbsp.	freshly grated orange peel	30 ml.
½ cup	fresh orange juice	125 ml.
½ cup	dry white wine	125 ml.

Prepare the wine sauce in a large, heavy stainless-steel or enameled casserole or Dutch oven, by first melting the butter with the oil over moderate heat. Add the garlic and sauté for 3 to 4 minutes, stirring frequently. Then add the orange peel, orange juice and wine. Reduce the orange mixture over high heat until it is thick and syrupy (about 6 to 8 minutes), stirring often.

Meanwhile, cook the broccoli, uncovered, in about 2 quarts [2 liters] of boiling salted water for approximately 10 minutes. Drain the broccoli, put it in the casserole and toss gently until the broccoli is coated with sauce. Serve at once.

JUNIOR LEAGUE OF PASADENA
THE CALIFORNIA HERITAGE COOKBOOK

Broccoli Amandine

To serve 4 to 6

2 to 2½ lb.	broccoli	1 kg.
	salt	
	freshly ground black pepper	
	fresh lemon juice	
⅓ cup	blanched, slivered almonds	75 ml.
4 tbsp.	unsalted butter	60 ml.
1	garlic clove, finely chopped	1

Remove and discard the large leaves and tough portions of stem from the broccoli. Wash the broccoli and soak it in lukewarm salted water for about 30 minutes, then drain and tie securely into bunches with cotton string. Cook, tightly covered, in a small amount of water, or uncovered in a large amount of boiling salted water, for 15 to 25 minutes, or until tender. Drain; remove the strings. Arrange the broccoli on a warmed platter, season with salt and freshly ground black pepper, and squeeze a little lemon juice on top.

Sauté the almonds in the butter until lightly browned, adding the garlic. Sprinkle the garlic butter and almonds over the broccoli. Serve at once.

LOUIS P. DE GOUY
THE GOLD COOK BOOK

Stir-fried Broccoli

Ch'ao Chieh Lan

To serve 4 or 5

2 lb.	broccoli, peeled	1 kg.
2 tbsp.	peanut or corn oil	30 ml.
1 tsp.	salt	5 ml.
1 tsp.	sugar	5 ml.
2 tbsp.	water	30 ml.
1 tsp.	cornstarch, combined with 2 tbsp. [30 ml.] cold water (optional)	5 ml.

Separate the broccoli florets with small stems from the large florets and stalks, and cut the large parts into thin pieces, about 1½ inches [4 cm.] long to make about 6 cups [1½ liters] in all. Rinse in cold water and drain.

Heat a wok until hot, add the peanut oil, and stir fry the broccoli for about 2 minutes. Add the salt and sugar. Mix well. Add the water and cover the wok. Cook over high heat for 2 minutes, stirring once. Serve hot. (If you are using the cornstarch-and-water mixture as a glaze, add it to the pan for the last minute of cooking.)

FLORENCE LIN
FLORENCE LIN'S CHINESE REGIONAL COOKBOOK

Broccoli Italian-Style

This classic treatment of broccoli can be applied with equally good results to a small cauliflower.

To serve 3 or 4

1 lb.	broccoli, trimmed	½ kg.
	salt	
3 tbsp.	olive oil	45 ml.
2	garlic cloves, finely chopped	2
	pepper	
	chopped fresh parsley	

Break the broccoli into small florets and cut the stems into small pieces. Boil gently in salted water for 5 or 6 minutes. The pieces must be slightly undercooked. Drain well.

Heat the olive oil in a skillet. Add the garlic and let it brown, then add the broccoli and cook for 5 minutes. Add pepper and salt to taste, and sprinkle with chopped parsley.

BERYL GOULD-MARKS
THE HOME BOOK OF ITALIAN COOKERY

Broccoli with Anchovies

Broccoli Affogati

To serve 4 to 6

3 lb.	broccoli, trimmed, broken into florets and washed	1½ kg.
⅓ cup	olive oil	75 ml.
6	leeks, white parts only, sliced lengthwise	6
1	medium-sized onion, sliced	1
12	anchovy fillets, soaked in cold water for 10 minutes and patted dry	12
2 tbsp.	chopped fresh parsley	30 ml.
	salt and freshly ground pepper	
½ cup	dry white wine	125 ml.

Cover the bottom of a sauté pan, first with the olive oil and then with half of the broccoli florets, still wet from washing. Cover the broccoli with half of the leeks, onion slices, anchovies and parsley. Season with a little salt and a generous grinding of pepper. Repeat the layers with the remaining ingredients. Cover the pan and cook over very low heat for 25 to 30 minutes. Add the wine; uncover the pan, and cook the broccoli over high heat for 10 minutes to allow nearly all of the liquid to evaporate before serving.

This dish can be served without any additions, or tossed with small noodles.

LUIGI CARNACINA AND LUIGI VERONELLI
LA BUONA VERA CUCINA ITALIANA

Brussels Sprouts with Yogurt

To toast the almonds, spread them on a baking sheet and put them in an oven, preheated to 450° F. [230° C.], or under a preheated broiler, for 3 to 5 minutes. Turn them several times with a spatula to prevent scorching.

To serve 4 to 6

2 to 2½ lb.	small Brussels sprouts, trimmed and the bases nicked with a sharp knife	1 kg.
1 tbsp.	butter	15 ml.
1	medium-sized tomato, chopped	1
2 tsp.	chopped fresh chives	10 ml.
½ tsp.	grated nutmeg	2 ml.
	salt and pepper	
1 cup	unflavored yogurt, lightly whisked	¼ liter
¼ cup	freshly grated Parmesan cheese	50 ml.
¼ cup	toasted, blanched almond slivers	50 ml.

Drop the Brussels sprouts into boiling salted water, and cook for about 10 minutes, or until they are tender. Remove the sprouts from the heat and drain thoroughly.

Place the sprouts in a buttered ovenproof casserole; cover them with the tomato and chives. Sprinkle the vegetables with the nutmeg, and season them with salt and pepper. Pour the yogurt over them. Sprinkle the top with the grated cheese and toasted almonds, and bake for 15 minutes in an oven, preheated to 350° F. [180° C.], until the top is nicely browned. Serve hot.

IRFAN ORGA
COOKING WITH YOGURT

Braised Brussels Sprouts

To serve 6

1 quart	small Brussels sprouts, trimmed (about 2 to 2½ lb. [1 kg.])	1 liter
8 tbsp.	butter, cut into small pieces	120 ml.
1 tsp.	salt	5 ml.
½ tsp.	freshly ground black pepper	2 ml.
¼ cup	fresh lemon juice	50 ml.

Put the sprouts in a heavy casserole with a tight-fitting lid. Lay the butter on the sprouts and sprinkle them with the salt, pepper and lemon juice. Cover and place in an oven,

preheated to 350° F. [180° C.], to braise for 25 to 35 minutes, or until barely tender. Every 10 minutes, remove the cover and stir the sprouts to be sure they do not stick.

The sprouts will cook in the butter and the small amount of moisture clinging to them; neither water nor stock is needed, but do keep an eye on them in case they scorch.

Baby onions and turnips can be cooked the same way; sprinkle them with 1 teaspoon [5 ml.] of sugar when adding the salt, pepper and lemon juice.

JULIE DANNENBAUM
JULIE DANNENBAUM'S CREATIVE COOKING SCHOOL

Stuffed Cabbage Leaves, Turkish-Style

Choux à la Turque

The techniques of preparing and stuffing vegetable leaves are demonstrated on pages 68-69.

To serve 4 to 6

1	large cabbage, leaves separated and ribs trimmed	1
¼ lb.	salt pork with the rind removed, blanched in boiling water for 5 minutes, drained and thinly sliced	125 g.
¼ lb.	veal, thinly sliced	125 g.
2 oz.	thinly sliced prosciutto	75 g.
1 cup	veal stock	¼ liter
Chicken and sorrel stuffing		
1	large chicken breast (about 1 lb. [½ kg.]), skinned, boned and chopped	1
¼ lb.	sorrel, stems removed, finely chopped	125 g.
3	eggs, yolks separated from whites	3
	salt and pepper	

Blanch the cabbage leaves in boiling salted water for a minute or two, then drain them. To make the stuffing, mix the chicken with the sorrel, bind with the egg yolks and season to taste with salt and pepper. Whip the egg whites until stiff and fold them into the sorrel-and-chicken mixture. Stuff the cabbage leaves with the mixture.

Line an ovenproof earthenware casserole with slices of salt pork, veal and ham. Put in the stuffed cabbage leaves, packing them tightly, and pour in enough stock to cover them. Cook, covered, for about 2 hours in a slow oven, preheated to 300° F. [150° C.]. When cooked, arrange the cabbage leaves in a warmed serving dish, strain and degrease the cooking juices and pour them over the cabbage.

LE CUISINIER GASCON

Provençale Stuffed Cabbage

Chou Farci à la Provençale

The technique of stuffing a whole cabbage and wrapping it in a string net or cheesecloth is demonstrated on pages 46-47.

	To serve 4 to 6	
1	large cabbage, trimmed	1
	salt	
½ lb.	chard leaves, blanched in boiling water for 2 minutes, drained and chopped	¼ kg.
½ lb.	salt pork with the rind removed, blanched in boiling water for 5 minutes, drained, diced and sautéed	¼ kg.
1	medium-sized onion, chopped and lightly sautéed in butter	1
2	large tomatoes, peeled, seeded and chopped	2
⅓ cup	raw unprocessed rice, boiled for 15 minutes and drained	75 ml.
1 lb.	peas, shelled (about 1 cup [¼ liter])	½ kg.
1½ lb.	sausage meat, seasoned with a crushed garlic clove	¾ kg.
2 quarts	beef stock	2 liters

Blanch the cabbage for 5 to 8 minutes in salted water, rinse it in cold water, drain it, and remove the large, tough outer leaves. Open the cabbage, spreading out the leaves, on a string net or a piece of damp cheesecloth stretched out on the table. Remove the heart of inner leaves without detaching the outer leaves from the core. Chop the cabbage heart.

Mix together the chopped cabbage and chard leaves, salt-pork dice, onion, tomatoes, rice, peas and sausage meat, and place the mixture in the center of the cabbage.

Shape the stuffing into a ball and fold the cabbage leaves around the stuffing. Tie up the net or cheesecloth.

Put the cabbage into a pan of boiling stock, cover and simmer gently for about 3½ hours. Drain the cabbage and remove the net or cheesecloth. Place the cabbage on a round dish, pour over a few tablespoons of the stock and serve.

PROSPER MONTAGNÉ
THE NEW LAROUSSE GASTRONOMIQUE

Stuffed Cabbage

Le Vrai Fassum Grassois

The technique of wrapping a whole stuffed cabbage in string net or cheesecloth is demonstrated on pages 46-47.

	To serve 4	
1	medium-sized cabbage (about 2 lb. [1 kg.]), trimmed	1
½ lb.	chard or lettuce, stemmed and finely chopped	¼ kg.
½ lb.	salt pork with the rind removed, blanched in boiling water for 5 minutes, drained and finely chopped	¼ kg.
¼ cup	boiled rice	50 ml.
¼ cup	freshly shelled peas	50 ml.
3 tbsp.	olive oil	45 ml.
	salt and pepper	
1½ to 2 quarts	beef or veal stock, or salted water	1½ to 2 liters
1	garlic clove (optional)	1
1	bouquet garni, including chervil (optional)	1

Blanch the cabbage in salted water for 10 to 15 minutes until the outer leaves are just supple. Turn back the leaves of the cabbage and remove the heart. Finely chop the heart and squeeze out any excess water. Mix the chopped cabbage heart with the chard or lettuce and the salt pork. Add the rice, peas, olive oil and seasoning. Put this mixture into the center of the cabbage and fold down the leaves to enclose it. Tie up the cabbage in a string net or cheesecloth and simmer in the stock or salted water for 2 to 3 hours. The garlic and bouquet garni may be added to the cooking liquid according to taste. Remove the cabbage from the pan, untie the net or cheesecloth and serve the cabbage in a bowl.

AUSTIN DE CROZE
LES PLATS RÉGIONAUX DE FRANCE

Southern Fried Cabbage

	To serve 4	
1	small green cabbage, cored and shredded	1
3 to 4 tbsp.	rendered bacon fat	45 to 60 ml.
2 tsp.	red pepper flakes	10 ml.
	salt	

Heat the bacon fat in a skillet, toss in the cabbage and stir until it is glistening. Lower the heat, add the pepper flakes, season with salt to taste, and continue cooking and turning the cabbage until it is barely tender—about 10 minutes.

MIRIAM UNGERER
GOOD CHEAP FOOD

Poached Stuffing in Cabbage Leaves

Le Farci au Pot ou Fars

Instructions for stuffing cabbage leaves are on pages 46-47.

To serve 6

6 to 8	large cabbage leaves, blanched in boiling water for 1 or 2 minutes, rinsed and drained	6 to 8
	Sorrel stuffing	
1 lb.	sorrel, finely chopped	½ kg.
2	heads Boston lettuce, halved, cored and finely chopped	2
½ lb.	spinach, finely chopped	¼ kg.
2	small onions, finely chopped	2
2 tbsp.	finely chopped fresh parsley	30 ml.
2	shallots, finely chopped	2
1 lb.	salt pork with the rind removed, blanched in boiling water for 5 minutes, drained and finely chopped	½ kg.
6	eggs	6
3	thick slices French or Italian bread with the crusts removed, torn into pieces	3
1 tbsp.	flour	15 ml.
⅓ cup	light cream	75 ml.

In a large bowl, blend together all the ingredients except the cabbage leaves. Spread out a string net or cheesecloth in a shallow dish, and line it with some of the cabbage leaves. Place the stuffing in the center, press the remaining cabbage leaves onto the top, and draw the string very tightly, or pull the edges of the cheesecloth together and tie securely. Transfer the cabbage-wrapped stuffing to a large pan of boiling salted water and simmer, covered, for about 2 hours. Transfer the cabbage-wrapped stuffing to a bowl and remove the string net. Serve cut into slices.

AUSTIN DE CROZE
LES PLATS RÉGIONAUX DE FRANCE

Fried Cabbage

To serve 4

1	small cabbage, cored and finely shredded	1
	salt and pepper	
1 tbsp.	lard	15 ml.
½ cup	heavy cream	125 ml.
3 tbsp.	vinegar	45 ml.

In a large bowl, season the cabbage with salt and pepper, stir well and allow to stand for 5 minutes. Drop the lard into a heated, heavy iron skillet, add the cabbage, and cook over high heat, stirring briskly until quite tender (10 to 20 minutes, depending on the quantity of cabbage in relation to the size of the pan). Add the cream and continue to stir until the cream and cabbage are well mixed. Remove the cabbage from the heat and add the vinegar. Stir and serve.

THE BUCKEYE COOKBOOK

Cabbage Quiche

This is an unusual and delicious quiche. The same cabbage mixture, baked without pastry in a bain-marie, makes a delicious accompaniment for meat.

To serve 4

1	small head cabbage (about 1 lb. [½ kg.]), cored and finely shredded	1
	short-crust pastry (recipe, page 167)	
8 tbsp.	butter	120 ml.
3	eggs	3
1 cup	light cream and milk, mixed	¼ liter
4 tbsp.	freshly grated Gruyère cheese	60 ml.
3 tbsp.	freshly grated Parmesan cheese	45 ml.
	salt and freshly ground black pepper	
	grated nutmeg	

Preheat the oven to 425° F. [220° C.]. Roll out the pastry and use it to line a 9-inch [23-cm.] quiche pan, equipped with a removable base. Line the pastry with wax paper or foil, fill with dried beans and bake for 15 minutes. Remove the paper and the beans, and let the shell dry out in the oven for 5 more minutes. Set aside the pastry shell to cool and reduce the oven temperature to 350° F. [180° C.].

Meanwhile, put the cabbage in a colander and pour a kettleful of boiling water over it gradually. Shake off the excess moisture from the cabbage. In a large, heavy saucepan melt the butter. Add the cabbage, cover tightly and cook over moderate heat until the cabbage is soft and golden, shaking the pan to prevent burning. The cooking time will depend on the type of cabbage used, but firm cabbage takes about 30 minutes. Remove the pan from the heat.

In a small bowl, beat the eggs with the cream and milk. Let the cabbage cool slightly, then stir in the egg mixture and 2 tablespoons [30 ml.] each of the Gruyère and Parmesan cheeses. Add salt, pepper and nutmeg to taste.

Carefully spoon the mixture into the baked pastry shell. Sprinkle the remaining cheese on top. Bake for 30 minutes, or until the filling is set and the top is a rich golden color.

GEORGE SEDDON AND HELENA RADECKA
YOUR KITCHEN GARDEN

Braised Red Cabbage

Kokt Rödkål

To serve 6 to 8

1	large red cabbage (about 3 lb. [1½ kg.]), shredded or cubed	1
4 tbsp.	butter	60 ml.
2 tbsp.	dark molasses	30 ml.
2 or 3	apples, peeled, cored and sliced	2 or 3
1	onion, grated	1
3 tbsp.	fresh lemon juice	45 ml.
½ cup	dry red wine or vinegar	125 ml.
	salt and pepper	

Melt the butter in a large, heavy fireproof casserole or Dutch oven. Add the cabbage and molasses, and cook over low heat for about 10 minutes, stirring constantly. Stir in the apples, onion, lemon juice, wine or vinegar, and salt. Simmer gently, covered, for 2 hours, stirring occasionally. Season to taste. Serve with roast goose or baked ham.

SAM WIDENFELT (EDITOR)
SWEDISH FOOD

Braised Cabbage with Salt Pork

Chou à la Façon des Petits Restaurants

To serve 6

2½ to 3 lb.	whole cabbage, quartered and core removed	1 to 1½ kg.
2 tbsp.	butter	30 ml.
½ lb.	salt pork, blanched in boiling water for 5 minutes, drained and diced	¼ kg.
3 to 4 tbsp.	finely chopped onion	45 to 60 ml.
	salt and pepper	

Cook the cabbage, uncovered, in plenty of boiling water for 10 to 15 minutes. Drain, press out as much moisture as possible, then chop. Melt the butter in a large saucepan and add the salt pork and the onion. Cook gently until the onion begins to brown, then add the cabbage. Season and cook, covered, over low heat for 15 to 20 minutes, stirring occasionally. Drain off any excess fat before serving.

AUGUSTE ESCOFFIER
MA CUISINE

Cabbage Rolls with Mushrooms

Bandhgobi Parcha

The spiced salt called for in this recipe can be made by seasoning table salt or crushed rock salt with a little ground coriander, cumin, mace, cayenne pepper and black pepper. Lovage and pomegranate seeds are obtainable from Indian or Middle Eastern grocers.

To serve 6

6	large green cabbage leaves, blanched in boiling water for 1 or 2 minutes and drained	6
2 tbsp.	butter	30 ml.
¼ tsp.	ground turmeric	1 ml.
½ tsp.	spiced salt	2 ml.
2 to 3 tbsp.	water	30 to 45 ml.

Mushroom stuffing

¼ lb.	fresh mushrooms, finely chopped	125 g.
2	medium-sized potatoes, peeled	2
¼ cup	heavy cream	50 ml.
4 tbsp.	butter	60 ml.
2 tbsp.	finely cut fresh chives	30 ml.
1 tbsp.	chopped fresh parsley or coriander leaves	15 ml.
⅓ cup	slivered, blanched almonds	75 ml.
⅛ tsp.	lovage seeds	½ ml.
1 tbsp.	ground pomegranate seeds or chopped capers	15 ml.

To make the stuffing, boil the potatoes, drain, and then purée them with the cream and butter. Add the mushrooms, chives, parsley or coriander, almonds, lovage seeds, and pomegranate seeds or capers. Mix well.

Place one sixth of this stuffing in the middle of each cabbage leaf. Wrap up the leaves and secure with wooden picks or tie with thread.

Heat the butter in a large skillet and put in the cabbage rolls. Sauté over high heat until the leaves brown lightly on all sides. Dust the rolls with the turmeric and spiced salt. Moisten with a few tablespoons of water. Cover the skillet tightly and raise the heat very high for 1 minute. Then reduce the heat and steam the cabbage rolls until all the moisture has dried up. Uncover the pan and continue cooking until the cabbage leaves start to stick a little to the bottom of the skillet. Serve.

DHARAMJIT SINGH
INDIAN COOKERY

Stuffed Cabbage, Greek-Style

Chou Farci à la Grecque

This dish may be served hot or cold.

There is no fixed rule for stuffings *à la grecque*. Cooked peas, even currants, may be added. Vine leaves are often used instead of cabbage leaves.

To serve 4

1	medium-sized cabbage (about 2 lb. [1 kg.]), leaves separated, blanched in boiling water for 10 to 15 minutes, rinsed and drained	1
2	small eggplants (about 10 oz. [300 g.] each), peeled and diced	2
2	peppers, halved, seeded, deribbed and coarsely diced	2
1 cup	olive oil	¼ liter
1 cup	raw unprocessed rice, boiled for 15 minutes	¼ liter
	salt and pepper	

Aromatic cooking liquid

½ cup	dry white wine	125 ml.
½ cup	water	125 ml.
4 to 6 tbsp.	fresh lemon juice	60 to 90 ml.
⅓ cup	olive oil	75 ml.
1 tsp.	mixed coriander seeds and peppercorns, tied in a piece of cheesecloth	5 ml.
15	small boiling onions	15
1	bouquet garni	1

Put all the ingredients for the aromatic cooking liquid into an enameled or tin-lined copper saucepan. Simmer for 10 minutes and set aside to cool.

To prepare the stuffing, first sauté the eggplant and peppers lightly in about ½ cup [125 ml.] of the olive oil, and mix with the rice. Season well with salt and pepper.

Spread out the cabbage leaves, two or three at a time—about 16 will be needed in all—and put a spoonful of the stuffing mixture in the center of each leaf. Roll up each leaf, tucking in the ends.

Choose a large sauté pan and lightly coat the bottom with the remaining olive oil. Arrange the stuffed leaves side by side in the pan, with no spaces between them, or fill any gap with a potato to prevent the stuffed leaves from unrolling during cooking. Pour the aromatic cooking liquid over the stuffed leaves, cover the pan with wax paper and a lid, bring the liquid to a boil and cook over low heat for 30 minutes.

CURNONSKY
CUISINE ET VINS DE FRANCE

Braised Red Cabbage in Red Wine with Chestnuts

Chou Rouge à la Limousine

To serve 6

1	large red cabbage (about 3 lb. [1½ kg.]), core removed, cut into julienne (about 3 quarts [3 liters])	1
¼ lb.	salt pork with the rind removed, blanched in boiling water for 5 minutes, drained and diced	125 g.
½ cup	finely chopped onions	125 ml.
1½ cups	dry red wine	375 ml.
1½ cups	beef stock	375 ml.
2 tbsp.	wine vinegar	30 ml.
¼ tsp.	grated nutmeg	1 ml.
¼ tsp.	ground cloves	1 ml.
½ tsp.	salt	2 ml.
	freshly ground black pepper	
2 to 2½ lb.	chestnuts, slit, parboiled for 10 minutes, outer and inner skins removed	1 kg.

Preheat the oven to 325° F. [160° C.].

In a heavy 3½-quart [3½-liter] fireproof casserole that has a tightly fitting cover, cook the salt pork over moderate heat, stirring frequently, until the dice are crisp and golden and have rendered all their fat. With a slotted spoon, remove the salt-pork dice and reserve them. Cook the onions in the fat remaining in the casserole over moderate heat, stirring frequently, for 5 minutes, or until soft but not brown. Stir in the cabbage, cover, and cook over low heat for 10 minutes.

Add to the cabbage the wine, beef stock, vinegar, nutmeg, cloves, salt-pork dice, salt and a generous grinding of pepper. Cover the casserole again and cook on the middle shelf of the oven for 2 hours. (Make sure that the liquids are not cooking away too fast; if they seem to be, add more stock.)

Gently stir in the chestnuts and cook, covered, for 1 hour more, or until the cabbage is tender and most of the liquid absorbed. Correct the seasoning and serve the cabbage from the casserole or a warmed vegetable dish.

FOODS OF THE WORLD/THE COOKING OF PROVINCIAL FRANCE

Spanish Cauliflower

Coliflor a la Española

To serve 4

1	cauliflower, trimmed and divided into florets	1
	salt	
2	hard-boiled eggs, chopped	2
1 cup	olive oil	250 ml.
2 or 3	garlic cloves, chopped	2 or 3
1 tbsp.	chopped fresh parsley	15 ml.

Boil the cauliflower florets in salted water for 10 to 15 minutes, or until tender. Drain, put them in a warmed serving dish and sprinkle them with the chopped eggs. Heat the oil in a small heavy skillet, and fry the garlic and parsley until crisp. Sprinkle over the cauliflower and serve.

VICTORIA SERRA, TRANSLATED BY ELIZABETH GILI
TIA VICTORIA'S SPANISH KITCHEN

Cauliflower Mold

To serve 4

1	medium-sized cauliflower, trimmed and broken into florets	1
4 tbsp.	butter	60 ml.
2 tbsp.	flour	30 ml.
1⅔ cups	milk	400 ml.
	salt and pepper	
	grated nutmeg (optional)	
3	eggs, beaten	3
¼ cup	freshly grated Parmesan cheese	50 ml.

Parboil the cauliflower in boiling, salted water for 4 to 5 minutes, then drain thoroughly. Lightly sauté the florets in 2 tablespoons [30 ml.] of the butter, add ⅔ cup [150 ml.] of the milk and cook for a further 5 to 6 minutes. Mash or sieve the cauliflower.

Make a roux from the remaining butter and the flour, add 1 cup [¼ liter] of the milk and whisk the mixture until it comes to a boil and thickens. Season this sauce with salt, pepper and nutmeg to taste.

Combine the sauce and the cauliflower, and stir in the eggs and cheese. Pour into a 1-quart [1-liter] mold greased with butter, and cover with a sheet of wax paper. Place the mold in a large baking pan and pour in enough hot water to reach halfway up the sides of the mold. Bake the cauliflower in an oven, preheated to 375° F. [190° C.], for about 40 minutes. Unmold onto a warmed serving platter and serve hot.

THE COOK TO A FLORENTINE FAMILY
NOT ONLY SPAGHETTI!

Benarasi Cauliflower

Benarasi Gobi

This recipe is from the Banaras district in northeast India.

To serve 4 to 6

1	large cauliflower, leaves and stalk removed, divided into bite-sized florets	1
5 tbsp.	clarified butter	75 ml.
1½ cups	coarsely chopped onions	375 ml.
2 tsp.	ground coriander	10 ml.
¼ tsp.	ground turmeric	1 ml.
½ to 1 tsp.	cayenne pepper	2 to 5 ml.
1 tsp.	salt	5 ml.
½ cup	drained canned tomatoes with ½ cup [125 ml.] of their liquid	125 ml.
½ tsp.	cumin seeds	2 ml.
¼ tsp.	caraway seeds	1 ml.
¼ tsp.	black peppercorns	1 ml.
2	whole cloves	2
2	cardamom pods, seeds only	2
1	bay leaf	1

Preheat the oven to 350° F. [180° C.]. Divide the cauliflower florets into two portions. In a medium-sized, fireproof casserole, heat the butter and fry one portion of the cauliflower at a time until each floret is lightly browned. Take the casserole off the heat; transfer the florets to a plate and set aside.

Purée the onion, coriander, turmeric, cayenne, salt and tomatoes in a blender. Off the heat, stir the purée into the butter left in the casserole. Return the casserole to medium-low heat and cook, partially covered, for about 10 minutes, or until the purée is reduced to a thick, moist sauce. Stir constantly for the last few minutes to prevent sticking. Remove the casserole from the heat.

Pulverize the cumin, caraway, peppercorns, cloves, cardamom and bay leaf in the blender, and stir them into the sauce. Fold in the reserved cauliflower until each piece is coated with sauce. Cover and bake in the preheated oven: for 15 minutes, if you prefer the cauliflower to be quite crunchy, or for up to 30 minutes, when the cauliflower will be completely tender. Serve very hot.

SHIVAJI RAO AND SHALINI DEVI HOLKAR
THE COOKING OF THE MAHARAJAS

Baked Cauliflower and Tomato Purée

Purée Gratinée De Chou-Fleur et de Tomate

	To serve 6	
1	large cauliflower (about 2 lb. [½ kg.]), divided into florets	1
1½ quarts	water	1½ liters
2 tbsp.	coarse salt	30 ml.
1 cup	puréed tomato, well seasoned	¼ liter
6 tbsp.	butter	90 ml.
1½ cups	grated Gruyère cheese	375 ml.
1 tsp.	salt	5 ml.
	pepper	

Put the water and the coarse salt in a large saucepan and bring to a boil. Add the cauliflower and let it simmer for 20 minutes, or until just tender. Drain the cauliflower and purée it. Cook the puréed tomato with 4 tablespoons [60 ml.] of the butter in a small saucepan for 5 minutes. In another saucepan, heat together the rest of the butter, the cauliflower purée and half the cheese. Add the puréed tomato to the mixture and blend well. Season to taste.

Spoon the mixed purée into a baking dish, sprinkle with the rest of the cheese, and bake in a hot oven, preheated to 400° F. [200° C.], for 10 to 15 minutes or until browned.

ALI-BAB
ENCYCLOPEDIA OF PRACTICAL GASTRONOMY

Braised Chinese Cabbage

	To serve 6	
1	Chinese cabbage, sliced into ¼-inch [6-mm.] rounds	1
3 tbsp.	butter	45 ml.
1	onion, thinly sliced	1
1 tsp.	salt	5 ml.
	freshly ground pepper	
1 cup	chicken stock	¼ liter

Melt the butter in a skillet. Add the onion and sauté until limp. Add the cabbage, season it, and add the stock. Cover tightly and simmer until the cabbage is cooked. After 7 minutes, taste for doneness. Chinese cabbage should be fairly crisp to the bite when served. Drain and serve at once.

BERYL M. MARTON
OUT OF THE GARDEN INTO THE KITCHEN

Kohlrabi Country-Style

	To serve 4	
3 lb.	kohlrabi, cut into eighths or thickly sliced	1½ kg.
	salt	
2 tbsp.	butter	30 ml.
2 tsp.	flour	10 ml.
½ cup	sour cream	125 ml.
1 tbsp.	finely cut fresh chives	15 ml.

Boil the kohlrabi in salted water for about 20 minutes, or until tender. Drain. In another saucepan, melt the butter. Add the flour and cook for 5 minutes. Then add the cream and cook, stirring, for 2 to 3 minutes. Add the kohlrabi to the cream sauce, heat through for a minute or two over low heat, or set the mixture over a pan of hot water if you are not ready to serve it at once. Pour the kohlrabi into a warmed dish, sprinkle with chives and serve.

LOUIS P. DE GOUY
THE GOLD COOK BOOK

Stuffed Kohlrabi

Gefüllte Kohlrabi

	To serve 4	
4	medium-sized kohlrabi	4
	salt	
2	hard-crust rolls, soaked in milk, squeezed and mashed	2
5 tbsp.	butter	75 ml.
1	egg yolk, lightly beaten	1
1 tbsp.	finely cut fresh chives	15 ml.
1 cup	sour cream	¼ liter
	salt and pepper	
2 tbsp.	bread crumbs, fried in a little butter	30 ml.
Kohlrabi sauce		
2 tbsp.	butter	30 ml.
2 tbsp.	flour	30 ml.
1½ cups	kohlrabi cooking liquid	375 ml.

Put the kohlrabi in lightly salted boiling water. Cook, uncovered, over medium heat for 30 minutes, or until tender.

Meanwhile, fry the mashed bread in 2 tablespoons [30 ml.] of the butter until lightly colored, then add the egg yolk, chives, 2 tablespoons of the sour cream, and salt and pepper to taste. Drain the kohlrabi, reserving 1½ cups [375 ml.] of the cooking liquid.

Make a thin sauce with the butter, flour and the cooking liquid. Hollow out each kohlrabi from the stem end, leaving the shell about ½ inch [1 cm.] thick, chop the scooped-out vegetable flesh and stir it into the bread mixture. Fill the kohlrabi with the mixture and put them in a buttered baking dish. Top the kohlrabi with the bread crumbs fried in butter, then melt the remaining 3 tablespoons [45 ml.] of butter and sprinkle it on the crumbs. Pour the remaining sour cream over the kohlrabi. Put the dish in an oven, preheated to 425° F. [220° C.], and bake for about 10 minutes. Serve with the sauce.

ELEK MAGYAR
KOCHBUCH FÜR FEINSCHMECKER

Kohlrabi in Cream and Dill Sauce

Kohlrabi à l'Aneth

	To serve 6	
8	kohlrabi heads, sliced ¼ inch [6 mm.] thick and cut into julienne ¼ inch [6 mm.] wide	8
	salt	
2 tbsp.	butter	30 ml.
½ cup	heavy cream	125 ml.
	pepper	
1 tbsp.	chopped dill	15 ml.
1 tbsp.	fresh lemon juice (optional)	15 ml.

Blanch the kohlrabi in a large pan of salted boiling water for 2 to 3 minutes. Drain.

Heat the butter in another saucepan, add the kohlrabi and toss well. Add the cream, salt and pepper. Allow to cook for a few minutes, or until the cream coats the vegetables. Add the dill and the lemon juice, if needed, and serve.

MADELEINE KAMMAN
WHEN FRENCH WOMEN COOK

Roots and Tubers

Grated Beets, Russian-Style

This recipe is of Polish origin, but most Russians think of it as one of their own national ways of serving beets.

	To serve 6	
4 cups	coarsely grated raw beets	1 liter
2 tbsp.	butter	30 ml.
3 to 4 tbsp.	fresh lemon juice	45 to 60 ml.
1½ tsp.	salt	7 ml.
	pepper	
1 tbsp.	flour	15 ml.
½ cup	water	125 ml.

Heat the butter in a skillet. Add the beets, lemon juice, salt and a little pepper. Cover the skillet and cook for 25 minutes over very low heat, stirring from time to time. Sift the flour on top of the beets. Do not stir. Cover the skillet again and continue cooking for 15 minutes, then stir and add the water. Bring to a boil and serve.

ALEXANDRA KROPOTKIN
THE BEST OF RUSSIAN COOKING

Braised Beet Slices

Betterave à la Poitevine

	To serve 2 or 3	
3	large fresh beets, peeled and sliced	3
2 tbsp.	lard or butter	30 ml.
2	onions, thinly sliced	2
1	garlic clove, thinly sliced	1
2 tsp.	flour	10 ml.
1 tbsp.	wine vinegar	15 ml.
¾ cup	chicken or veal stock	175 ml.
	salt and pepper	

Melt the fat in a fireproof earthenware casserole, and brown the onions and garlic over low heat. Add the beet slices, cook until golden brown, then sprinkle the slices on both sides with the flour. Stir with a wooden spoon until the flour browns, then add the vinegar and the stock to the casserole.

Season with salt and pepper, cover the casserole and simmer gently over low heat for about 25 minutes, or until the beet slices are cooked thoroughly. Serve hot.

JEAN MERCIER AND IRENE LABARRE
LA CUISINE DU POITOU ET DE LA VENDÉE

Carrots in Cream

Carottes Nouvelles à la Crème

This recipe is especially suited to the first new carrots of spring. If older carrots are used, they should be thinly sliced or cut into julienne.

	To serve 4	
1 lb.	carrots, left whole if small, but cut into julienne 1 inch [2½ cm.] long if large	½ kg.
¼ cup	water	50 ml.
1 tbsp.	butter	15 ml.
	salt and pepper	
2 tbsp.	fines herbes	30 ml.
½ cup	heavy cream	125 ml.
2 or 3	egg yolks, lightly beaten	2 or 3

Put the carrots, water and butter in a saucepan. Season with salt and pepper and add the fines herbes. Cook, uncovered, over low heat. After 10 to 15 minutes, or when the carrots are about half-cooked, stir in the cream. Continue to cook the carrots very gently, uncovered, until they are tender. Remove the pan from the heat, stir a spoonful of the hot sauce into the egg yolks and add them to the pan. Mix thoroughly, but gently, and reheat the carrots for a moment without boiling them. Serve immediately.

JULES BRETEUIL
LE CUISINIER EUROPÉEN

Fried Carrots

Havuc Kizartmasi

	To serve 4	
5 or 6	medium-sized carrots (about 1 lb. [½ kg.]), sliced into ¼-inch [6-mm.] rounds	5 or 6
	salt	
2 tbsp.	olive oil	30 ml.
1 tbsp.	flour, seasoned with salt and pepper	15 ml.
1 cup	unflavored yogurt, heated to lukewarm	¼ liter
½ tsp.	caraway seeds	2 ml.

Parboil the carrots in salty water. When they are almost soft, drain and cool them a little. Heat the oil in a skillet, toss the carrots in the seasoned flour, and then fry them in the oil until they are brown. Arrange the carrots in a warmed serving dish, pour over them the heated yogurt, and sprinkle with the caraway seeds.

VENICE LAMB
THE HOME BOOK OF TURKISH COOKERY

Carrots Cooked with Marsala

Carote al Marsala

	To serve 4	
10 to 12	medium-sized carrots, thinly sliced	10 to 12
2 tbsp.	butter	30 ml.
	salt and freshly ground pepper	
⅓ cup	dry Marsala	75 ml.

In a heavy saucepan with a close-fitting lid, heat the butter. Add the carrots and cook over medium heat, stirring constantly, for about 2 minutes. Season lightly with salt and pepper. Add the Marsala, cover tightly and simmer over very low heat for 10 to 15 minutes, or until tender.

NIKA STANDEN HAZELTON
THE REGIONAL ITALIAN KITCHEN

Celeriac and Potato Purée

Purée de Céleri-rave

	To serve 6	
1¼ lb.	celeriac, sliced	⅔ kg.
	salt	
2	medium-sized potatoes, halved	2
4 tbsp.	butter	60 ml.
½ cup	hot (not boiling) milk	125 ml.
	sugar	

Bring a pan of salted water to a boil. Add the celeriac and cook, covered, at a light boil for 30 minutes. Add the potatoes to the pan, cover, and cook for another 20 to 25 minutes, or until the potatoes and the celeriac are tender.

Drain the vegetables and put them through a sieve or food mill to make a smooth purée. Transfer the purée to a sauté pan, add the butter and cook, stirring, over brisk heat. Gradually add the milk, stirring constantly. Season with salt and a pinch of sugar. Serve very hot.

MADAME SAINT-ANGE
LA BONNE CUISINE DE MADAME SAINT-ANGE

Celeriac Gratin

Céleri-rave au Gratin

To serve 2

1 lb.	celeriac, peeled and quartered	½ kg.
6 tbsp.	butter	90 ml.
	salt	
3 oz.	water	75 ml.
½ cup	freshly grated Parmesan or Gruyère cheese	125 ml.

Spread 2 tablespoons [30 ml.] of butter in a stainless-steel sauté pan and arrange the celeriac quarters in it. Season with salt and add the water. Cook, covered, over low heat for 45 minutes, turning the quarters once or twice.

Drain the celeriac, reserving the liquid. Butter a shallow gratin dish with another 2 tablespoons of butter and put in the celeriac. Reduce the cooking liquid a little over high heat and pour it over the celeriac. Melt the remaining butter. Sprinkle the cheese and melted butter over the celeriac and put in an oven, preheated to 425° F. [220° C.], for about 10 minutes or until the top is lightly colored.

PROSPER MONTAGNÉ
MON MENU

Purée of Celeriac Gratin

Selleriepüree, Überbacken

To serve 4

3	celeriac, diced	3
2	small potatoes (about ¼ lb. [125 g.] each), diced	2
	salt	
5 tbsp.	butter	75 ml.
½ cup	milk	125 ml.
2 tbsp.	freshly grated Parmesan cheese	30 ml.
1 tbsp.	dry bread crumbs	15 ml.

Boil the celeriac and potatoes in slightly salted water until they are tender. Drain the vegetables and mash them, reserving the cooking liquid. Melt 4 tablespoons [60 ml.] of the butter in a saucepan; add the mashed vegetables and cook over low heat for a few minutes, stirring. Then, add the milk and enough of the reserved cooking liquid to form a thin purée. Grease a shallow ovenproof dish and put the purée in it. Sprinkle the purée with the cheese, the bread crumbs and the remaining butter cut into small pieces. Put the dish in an oven, preheated to 400° F. [200° C.], and leave it there until the surface of the purée is lightly browned—about 15 minutes. Serve with fried sausages.

HERMINE KIEHNLE AND MARIA HÄDECKE
DAS NEUE KIEHNLE KOCHBUCH

Jerusalem Artichoke Daube

Topinambours en Daube

To serve 3 or 4

1½ lb.	Jerusalem artichokes, coarsely diced	¾ kg.
1	medium-sized onion, finely chopped	1
2 tbsp.	olive oil	30 ml.
	salt and pepper	
	freshly grated nutmeg	
2	garlic cloves, chopped	2
1	bouquet garni	1
½ cup	dry red wine	125 ml.
½ cup	water	125 ml.

In a fireproof earthenware or enameled casserole, fry the onion in the olive oil until slightly colored. Add the artichokes, salt and pepper, nutmeg, garlic and bouquet garni. Cover and allow to stew gently for 15 minutes, shaking the casserole from time to time. Moisten with the wine and water. Cook over high heat, uncovered, until almost all of the liquid has evaporated. Then cover and continue cooking, over very low heat, for 1 hour.

C. CHANOT-BULLIER
VIEILLES RECETTES DE CUISINE PROVENÇALE

Crisped Parsnips

To serve 4

6	medium-sized parsnips	6
	salt	
½ cup	butter	125 ml.
1 cup	flour	¼ liter

Split the parsnips in half lengthwise and cook them gently in boiling salted water until tender. Drain and cool, then cut them once again lengthwise. (Each parsnip has been divided into fourths.) Roll the parsnips in 4 tablespoons [60 ml.] melted butter; set them aside on a plate to chill. When chilled, dredge the parsnips with flour and sauté them lightly in 4 tablespoons butter until crisp. This is a delicious vegetable; so good that my family forgets manners and eats them with their fingers, like candy.

ESTHER B. ARESTY
THE DELECTABLE PAST

Parsnip Fritters

To serve 4

5	large parsnips	5
	salt	
1 tbsp.	flour	15 ml.
1 tsp.	brown sugar	5 ml.
1 tbsp.	butter	15 ml.
	black pepper, salt to taste	
2	eggs	2
4 tbsp.	butter	60 ml.

Scrape and cut the parsnips, put them into a saucepan with a teaspoon [5 ml.] of salt and 2 quarts [2 liters] of boiling water. Boil until perfectly tender, drain, then mash until smooth; add the other ingredients, lastly the eggs. Make the mix into round cakes and fry to a nice brown on both sides.

MRS. PETER A. WHITE
THE KENTUCKY HOUSEWIFE

New Potatoes with Chopped Mushrooms

Krielaardappels Duxelles

To serve 4

1½ lb.	small new potatoes, peeled	¾ kg.
3 tbsp.	butter	45 ml.
1	scallion, including 2 inches [5 cm.] of the green top, finely chopped	1
1½ cups	finely chopped fresh mushrooms	375 ml.
2 tbsp.	flour	30 ml.
1½ cups	veal or chicken stock	375 ml.
1	bay leaf	1
2 tsp.	finely chopped fresh parsley or mint	10 ml.

Boil the potatoes in salted water until tender—about 15 minutes. Drain and set them aside.

Melt the butter in a heavy saucepan. Sauté the scallion in it for 2 to 3 minutes, then stir in the mushrooms and sauté for 3 to 4 minutes. Add the flour and stir until smoothly mixed. Gradually add the stock, stirring all the time until smooth. Add the bay leaf and bring the mixture to a boil, then reduce the heat and simmer, uncovered, for 8 minutes.

Add the cooked potatoes to the sauce and, stirring occasionally, heat through over low heat. Taste and adjust the seasoning. Sprinkle with the parsley or mint and serve.

This dish goes well with broiled veal chops.

HUGH JANS
VRIJ NEDERLANDS KOOKBOEK

Parsnip and Mushroom Soufflé

For instructions on how to prepare a collar for a soufflé dish, see the recipe for Turnip Soufflé on page 127.

To serve 6

9	medium-sized parsnips (about 1½ lb. [¾ kg.])	9
¼ lb.	fresh mushrooms, sliced (about 1½ cups [375 ml.])	125 g.
1	garlic clove, crushed	1
8 tbsp.	butter	120 ml.
3 tbsp.	heavy cream	45 ml.
4	egg yolks	4
	salt and pepper	
4	egg whites, beaten until stiff	4

Boil the parsnips until tender. Meanwhile, cook the mushrooms and garlic together gently in 2 tablespoons [30 ml.] of the butter. Peel the parsnips when cooked and put them through a food mill. Stir in the mushroom mixture, the remaining butter, the cream and the egg yolks. Season well and gently fold in the egg whites with a metal spoon.

Pour the mixture into a 1-quart [1-liter] collared soufflé dish. Bake at 450° F. [230° C.] until the soufflé has risen and is brown on top—about 20 minutes. Serve immediately.

JANE GRIGSON
GOOD THINGS

Smothered Potatoes

Patata Fgata

To serve 4

4 to 6	medium-sized potatoes, peeled and cut into irregular shapes	4 to 6
2	medium-sized onions, sliced	2
2 or 3	garlic cloves, chopped	2 or 3
½ tsp.	finely chopped marjoram, oregano or thyme	2 ml.
½ cup	water	125 ml.
3 or 4 tbsp.	olive oil	45 or 60 ml.
	salt and pepper	

Place the onions and the potatoes in a saucepan. Add the garlic (as much as you like) and herbs. Now add the water and pour the oil over the potatoes. Season and cover. Cook over fierce heat until the mixture begins to bubble, then lower the heat as much as possible and leave to simmer. The dish should be ready in about 20 minutes.

ANNE AND HELEN CARUANA GALIZIA
RECIPES FROM MALTA

Mashed Potatoes and Turnips
Stwns

It is a custom in Wales to combine mashed potatoes with other cooked vegetables to make *stwns*—named after the *stwnsher,* or specially carved wooden tool traditionally used to mash the vegetables. Peas, broad beans and rutabagas as well as turnips are used, and the mixture is usually served with fried liver and onions.

	To serve 6 to 8	
3	medium-sized potatoes (about 1 lb. [½ kg.]), boiled and mashed	3
5 or 6	young turnips (about 1 lb. [½ kg.]), boiled and mashed with the potatoes	5 or 6
6 tbsp.	butter	90 ml.
	salt and pepper	
	buttermilk	

In a saucepan, mix the potatoes, turnips and butter. Season with salt and pepper, and add enough buttermilk to give the mixture a creamy consistency. Heat through and serve.

LIZZIE BOYD (EDITOR)
BRITISH COOKERY

Potatoes in White Caper Sauce
Pommes de Terre à la Polonaise

	To serve 4	
7	medium-sized potatoes (about 2 lb. [1 kg.])	7
1 tbsp.	olive oil or butter	15 ml.
2	large onions, quartered	2
1 tsp.	crumbled dried thyme	5 ml.
1 tsp.	crumbled bay leaf	5 ml.
1 tsp.	crumbled dried basil	5 ml.
2	whole cloves	2
	salt and coarsely ground pepper	
	White caper sauce	
1	shallot, finely chopped	1
2 tbsp.	olive oil	30 ml.
1 tbsp.	flour	15 ml.
1½ cups	beef or veal stock	375 ml.
1 tbsp.	capers, rinsed and drained well	15 ml.
	salt and pepper	

First, make the white caper sauce. Gently cook the shallot in the oil for about 5 minutes until softened. Add the flour and stir over low heat for 2 minutes, without browning. Gradual-ly stir in the stock. Add the capers, season with salt and pepper, and cook until thickened, about 20 minutes.

Boil the potatoes, unpeeled, in water with the oil or butter, the onions, thyme, bay leaf, basil, cloves, salt and pepper. Let the potatoes boil until they are soft to the touch; turn them into a colander to drain; peel them while they are still hot. Cut each potato into not more than two or three pieces and pour the white caper sauce over them.

OFFRAY AÎNÉ
LE CUISINIER MÉRIDIONAL

Potatoes in Sour Cream

	To serve 4	
2 lb.	small new potatoes	1 kg.
1 cup	sour cream	¼ liter
	salt	
4	scallions, including 2 inches [5 cm.] of the green tops, finely chopped	4
⅓ cup	finely chopped fresh dill	75 ml.

Drop the potatoes into boiling water, cover, and cook them for about 20 minutes, or until tender. Drain and peel them while they are hot. Combine them with the sour cream, add salt to taste, and toss gently. Sprinkle them with the scallions and dill, and serve.

As a variation, use melted butter instead of sour cream.

SONIA UVEZIAN
THE BEST FOODS OF RUSSIA

Aromatic Potatoes
Pommes de Terre à la Barigoule

	To serve 4 to 6	
1 lb.	small new potatoes	½ kg.
1 cup	chicken or veal stock	¼ liter
1 cup	water	¼ liter
¼ cup	olive oil	50 ml.
	salt and pepper	
1	medium-sized onion, chopped	1
2	small turnips or parsnips, diced	2
1	bouquet garni	1

Put the potatoes in the stock and water with the olive oil, a little salt and pepper, the onion, the turnips or parsnips and the bouquet garni. Boil them, uncovered, until the liquid evaporates. When the vegetables are tender and there is no stock or water left, discard the bouquet garni. Let the vegetables fry for a few minutes in the oil, stirring constantly. When they are a nice color, serve the vegetables accompanied by olive oil, vinegar, salt and pepper.

MERIGOT
LA CUISINIÈRE RÉPUBLICAINE

Potatoes with Salt Pork and Cheese
La Truffado

The tome called for in this recipe is the fresh, unfermented cheese of Cantal. If unavailable, substitute Port-Salut.

To serve 4

5	medium-sized potatoes (about 1½ lb. [¾ kg.]), cut into slices ⅛ inch [3 mm.] thick	5
¼ lb.	lean salt pork with the rind removed, blanched in boiling water for 5 minutes, drained and diced	125 g.
2 tbsp.	oil or butter	30 ml.
	salt and pepper	
2	garlic cloves, finely chopped	2
½ lb.	*tome* cheese, cut into small dice	¼ kg.

In a skillet, lightly fry the salt pork in the oil or butter, then add the potatoes; shake the pan frequently so the potatoes do not stick. Season with salt, pepper and the chopped garlic.

When the potatoes are cooked—after about 10 minutes—drain off any excess fat and add the fresh *tome*, distributing it as well as you can by turning over the potatoes two or three times. Cover and set aside for about 5 minutes so that the cheese will melt with the heat from the potatoes. The *tome* must melt and become "thready" but should never become oily. Serve immediately.

AUSTIN DE CROZE
LES PLATS RÉGIONAUX DE FRANCE

Potato Floddies

To serve 6

4	medium-sized potatoes, grated	4
2	medium-sized onions, finely chopped	2
½ cup	flour	125 ml.
1	egg	1
	milk	
	salt and pepper	
4 tbsp.	lard	60 ml.

Mix the potatoes and onions, blend with the flour and egg, and beat with enough milk to give a stiff batter. Season with salt and pepper. Fry tablespoons of the mixture in the lard until they are golden.

Grated cheese, fried sausage meat or chopped herbs may be added to the batter mixture, and the floddies served as a complete supper dish.

LIZZIE BOYD (EDITOR)
BRITISH COOKERY

Potato Croquettes

To serve 4 or 5

4 or 5	medium-sized potatoes (about 1½ lb. [¾ kg.]), boiled and mashed	4 or 5
2	egg yolks	2
	salt and black pepper	
	grated nutmeg	
1	egg, beaten	1
6 tbsp.	fine dry bread crumbs	90 ml.
1 quart	peanut oil or a mixture of peanut oil and butter	1 liter

Beat the egg yolks into the potatoes. Season with salt, pepper and a little grated nutmeg. Spread out the mixture on a floured board. When the mixture is cool, divide it into 15 or 16 equal parts and form these into rolls, or croquettes. Coat each croquette first with the beaten egg, and then with the bread crumbs. Heat the peanut oil, or butter and oil, and fry the croquettes until golden on all sides. Drain on paper towels. Serve as soon as possible.

ARABELLA BOXER
NATURE'S HARVEST: THE VEGETABLE COOKBOOK

French Potato Pancake
Pommes de terre Darphin

For best results, cover the skillet for the first half of the cooking time but leave it uncovered for the second half. Whenever the lid is lifted, it should be held horizontally so that none of the water that has condensed on its undersurface drips back into the skillet.

To serve 4

6	medium-sized potatoes, cut into julienne or coarsely grated	6
	salt	
7 tbsp.	butter	105 ml.
1 tbsp.	oil	15 ml.

Dry the potatoes in a towel, spread them out on a large plate and sprinkle them lightly with salt. Heat the butter with the oil in a large, heavy skillet. Cook the potatoes over low-to-medium heat for about 20 minutes or until they are golden brown on one side, then turn them over like a pancake and do the same to the other side. Place the potato pancake on a warmed platter and serve very hot.

RAYMOND OLIVER
LA CUISINE

Hash-brown Potatoes

To serve 3 or 4

8	medium-sized (or 10 small) waxy potatoes, boiled, peeled and coarsely chopped	8
10 tbsp.	butter, beef drippings or rendered bacon fat	150 ml.
	salt and freshly ground pepper	

Melt 6 tablespoons [90 ml.] of the butter, beef drippings or bacon fat in a heavy iron or aluminum skillet. Add the potatoes, forming them into a flat cake and pressing them down. Let them cook over medium heat for about 5 or 6 minutes until a crust forms on the bottom. Run a spatula around the edge to keep the cake loose and shake the pan gently from time to time. Add another 2 tablespoons [30 ml.] of fat on top and let it trickle through the potatoes. Salt them and give them a few grinds of pepper.

Off the heat, place a large plate or pan over the skillet for a moment or two and let the cake steam. Invert the cake quickly onto the plate. Melt the remaining fat in the skillet and slide the cake back into it to brown the other side. Slide it out onto a warmed platter.

JAMES BEARD
JAMES BEARD'S AMERICAN COOKERY

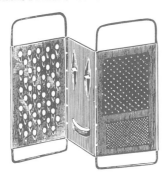

Potato Patties

Côtelettes de Pommes de Terre

To serve 6 to 8

8	medium-sized potatoes (about 2 lb. [1 kg.])	8
1 cup	flour	¼ liter
¼ cup	chopped fines herbes	50 ml.
	salt and pepper	
	grated nutmeg	
2	eggs, lightly beaten	2
2 cups	oil for deep frying	½ liter

Grate the peeled potatoes and put them in a colander lined with cheesecloth and set over a bowl. Allow the potatoes to drain for an hour. In a bowl, mix the potatoes thoroughly with the flour. Add the fines herbes, and season well with salt, pepper and nutmeg. Blend in the eggs.

Heat the oil. With a tablespoon, drop spoonfuls of the mixture into the hot oil. Fry until nicely browned all over. Drain on paper towels, and serve the potato patties very hot.

GINETTE MATHIOT
À TABLE AVEC EDOUARD DE POMIANE

Ringed Potatoes

Instructions for shaving potatoes are given on page 57.

To serve 4

3	medium-sized potatoes (about 1 lb. [½ kg.])	3
8 tbsp.	lard	120 ml.
	salt	

After peeling the potatoes, use your knife or potato peeler to shave them round and round in rings, as you would pare an apple. In a large skillet, heat the lard until very hot, and add the potato rings. Fry over moderately high heat, stirring so that they brown evenly without sticking.

When the potato rings are cooked and crisp, drain them. Then place them on a warmed platter and sprinkle with salt. Serve immediately.

THE BUCKEYE COOKBOOK

Stuffed Potatoes

Gefüllte Kartoffeln

To serve 4

4	large potatoes, peeled	4
	salt and pepper	
8 tbsp.	butter	120 ml.
¾ cup	grated Gruyère cheese	175 ml.
1	egg yolk	1
¼ cup	sour cream	50 ml.

Trim off the ends of the potatoes, keeping four of the end pieces for lids. Hollow out each potato and stand it upright. Grate the scooped-out potato, season it with salt and pepper, and mix it with 4 tablespoons [60 ml.] of the butter, ¼ cup [50 ml.] of the cheese, the egg yolk and the sour cream. Fill the potatoes with this mixture and cover with the potato lids. Stand the potatoes in an ovenproof dish. Melt the remaining butter and pour it over the potatoes. Bake in a moderate oven, preheated to 350° F. [180° C.], for 45 minutes to 1 hour, basting from time to time. Before serving, sprinkle with the remaining cheese.

ELEK MAGYAR
KOCHBUCH FÜR FEINSCHMECKER

Baked Potatoes with Cream and Chives

Pommes de Terre Rôties Fermière

To serve 4

4	large potatoes (about 6 oz. [175 g.] each), baked in their skins and halved lengthwise	4
4 tbsp.	butter	60 ml.
⅓ cup	cream	75 ml.
2 tbsp.	finely cut fresh chives	30 ml.
	salt and pepper	
⅓ cup	fine, freshly grated Parmesan or Gruyère-type cheese	75 ml.

Scoop out the pulp of the baked potatoes into a bowl. Break it up with a fork or whisk, and mix in the butter, cream, chives and seasoning. Beat until smooth. Refill the potato skins with this mixture, scatter the cheese over the top, and put under the broiler for about 5 minutes, or until brown.

A. BAUTTE
239 MANIÈRES D'ACCOMMODER LES POMMES DE TERRE

Baked Potatoes Stuffed with Mushrooms

To serve 6

6	large baking potatoes, approximately ½ lb. [¼ kg.] each	6
1	small piece pork fat	1
1	leek, white part only, chopped, or 1 onion, chopped	1
3 tbsp.	butter	45 ml.
4 cups	finely chopped fresh mushrooms (about ¾ lb. [⅓ kg.])	1 liter
1	egg yolk, lightly beaten	1
	salt	
	pepper	
	grated nutmeg	
1 tbsp.	cream or milk (optional)	15 ml.

Rub the outsides of the potatoes with the pork fat, and bake them in a 425° F. [220° C.] oven for about 1 hour.

Meanwhile, in a large skillet, cook the leek or the onion—leek tastes a little better if you can get one—in 2 tablespoons [30 ml.] of hot butter for 10 minutes, without browning. Add the chopped mushrooms to the pan with the leek or onion and cook slowly for 10 minutes. Season with salt, pep-

per and a small pinch of nutmeg. Add the egg yolk. Remove the pan from the heat.

When the potatoes are baked, cut off and discard a lengthwise slice and scoop out a little more than half of the pulp. Mix the scooped-out potato pulp with the mushrooms, adding the cream or milk if the mixture seems too thick.

Stuff the potato shells with the mushroom mixture, rounding off the tops to neat mounds. Melt the remaining tablespoon [15 ml.] of butter and sprinkle it over the potatoes. Return them to the oven for 15 minutes.

ALEXANDRA KROPOTKIN
THE BEST OF RUSSIAN COOKING

Potato Pancakes with Applesauce

Kartoffelpuffer mit Apfelmus

To serve 6 as a vegetable

6	medium-sized potatoes (about 2 lb. [1 kg.]), preferably baking potatoes	6
2	eggs	2
¼ cup	finely grated onion	50 ml.
⅓ cup	flour	75 ml.
1 tsp.	salt	5 ml.
	rendered bacon fat or lard	
	applesauce or imported lingonberry (*Preiselbeeren*) preserves	

Peel the potatoes and, as you proceed, drop them into cold water to prevent their discoloring. In a large mixing bowl, beat the eggs enough to break them up, add the onion and gradually beat in the flour and salt. One at a time, pat the potatoes dry and grate them coarsely into a sieve or colander. Press down each potato firmly into the sieve to squeeze out as much moisture as possible, then immediately stir the potato into the egg and onion batter.

Preheat the oven to 250° F. [120° C.]. In a heavy 8- to 10-inch [20- to 25-cm.] skillet, melt 8 tablespoons [120 ml.] of bacon fat or lard over high heat until it splutters. Pour in ⅓ cup [75 ml.] of the potato mixture and, with a large spatula, flatten it into a pancake about 5 inches [13 cm.] in diameter. Fry it over moderate heat for about 2 minutes on each side. When the pancake is golden brown on both sides and crisp around the edges, transfer it to a heated, ovenproof plate and keep it warm in the oven. Continue making similar pancakes with the remaining batter, adding more fat to the pan when necessary to keep it at a depth of ¼ inch [6 mm.]. Serve the pancakes as soon as possible with applesauce or lingonberry preserves.

FOODS OF THE WORLD/THE COOKING OF GERMANY

Curnonsky's Potato Gratin

Gratin Dauphinois

To serve 6 to 8

15	medium-sized waxy potatoes (about 4 lb. [2 kg.]), finely sliced	15
	salt and pepper	
	grated nutmeg (optional)	
16 tbsp.	butter	240 ml.
1	garlic clove (optional)	1
6 cups	light cream	1½ liters

Wash the potato slices, dry them in a towel, then season them with salt and pepper. (One may add a suspicion of nutmeg, but that is not to all tastes.)

Butter a large gratin dish (in the country, they rub the interior of the dish with a clove of garlic before buttering it). Layer the potatoes in the dish up to ½ inch [1 cm.] from the top, in order that they can be covered with the light cream. Place a few pieces of butter here and there. Set the potatoes to cook gently in an oven, preheated to 325° F. [160° C.], for 1½ to 2 hours. Serve immediately.

Above all, do not put in eggs or cheese. Eggs deprive the gratin of all its smoothness by leaving lumps of more or less scrambled egg inside it; cheese distorts the flavor.

CURNONSKY
CUISINE ET VINS DE FRANCE

Lithuanian Potato Pudding

To serve 4 to 6

10	large potatoes (about 2½ lb. [2 kg.])	10
1	medium-sized onion	1
5	slices bacon	5
½ cup	milk, warmed	125 ml.
3	eggs, beaten	3
¼ tsp.	pepper	1 ml.
	salt and pepper to taste	

Finely grate the potatoes and onion into a bowl. Cut the bacon crosswise into narrow strips, and fry until crisp. Pour the fat and the bacon over the potatoes. Add the hot milk. Add the beaten eggs, a little at a time, and the salt and pepper. Pour the mixture into a greased 12-by-18-inch [30-by-45-cm.] roasting pan. Bake in an oven, which has been preheated to 400° F. [200° C.], for 15 minutes. Reduce the heat to 375° F. [190° C.] and bake for 45 minutes longer, or until the top is nicely browned. Cut the pudding into squares and serve hot with sour cream.

GLADYS TABER
MY OWN COOK BOOK: FROM STILLMEADOW & CAPE COD

Potatoes Cooked in Milk

To serve 3 or 4

1 lb.	potatoes, thickly sliced, or whole, small new potatoes	½ kg.
2 cups	milk	½ liter
	salt	
	grated nutmeg	
	dried thyme or basil	

Pour the cold, uncooked milk over the potatoes in a sauce-pan, add a very little salt and simmer (if you let the milk boil, it will spill over and the potatoes will stick, so look out) until the potatoes are just tender but not breaking up. Strain off the milk—it makes good vegetable-soup stock—and transfer the potatoes to a shallow ovenproof dish. Sprinkle them very lightly with nutmeg and a little thyme or basil, add 3 to 4 tablespoons [45 to 60 ml.] of the milk and leave them uncovered in an oven, preheated to 300° to 350° F. [150° to 180° C.], for about 15 minutes.

ELIZABETH DAVID
SPICES, SALT AND AROMATICS IN THE ENGLISH KITCHEN

Fernand Point's Potato Gratin

Véritable Gratin Dauphinois

To serve 4 to 6

6 or 7	waxy potatoes (about 2 lb. [1 kg.]), peeled, wiped dry and thinly sliced	6 or 7
1	garlic clove	1
	salt and pepper	
8 tbsp.	butter	120 ml.
2	eggs, lightly beaten	2
1¾ cups	milk, boiled and cooled	400 ml.
1 tbsp.	heavy cream	15 ml.

Take a large baking dish of enameled ironware or fireproof earthenware, and rub it lightly with garlic and then with salt. Butter it and spread the potatoes (overlapping) in a single layer. Salt and pepper the potatoes lightly. Mix the beaten eggs, milk and cream—no suggestion of any cheese. Coat the potatoes with this mixture and dot the top with pieces of butter. Start cooking the potatoes on top of the stove, over very low heat for about 15 minutes, and finish cooking in a moderate oven, preheated to 350° F. [180° C.], for about 40 minutes. Scatter some pieces of butter on top and serve from the cooking dish, while it is very hot.

FERNAND POINT
MA GASTRONOMIE

Potatoes Languedoc-Style

Pommes de Terre à la Languedocienne

To serve 4

2 to 2½ lb.	large, long potatoes	1 kg.
¼ cup	chopped onion	50 ml.
1 tbsp.	butter	15 ml.
1 tbsp.	oil	15 ml.
2	large tomatoes peeled, chopped and lightly sautéed in 2 tbsp. [30 ml.] olive oil	2
	salt and pepper	
1 tsp.	ground thyme	5 ml.
1 tsp.	crumbled bay leaf	5 ml.
1 cup	veal or chicken stock, or water	¼ liter
1	small garlic clove, crushed	1

In a fireproof casserole sauté the onion in the butter and oil. Lay the potatoes on top and cover them with the tomatoes. Season with salt, pepper, thyme and bay leaf. Moisten with the stock or water and add the garlic. Cover and cook in an oven, preheated to 325° F. [160° C.], for 50 minutes to 1 hour, basting regularly with the cooking liquid.

PROSPER MONTAGNÉ
MON MENU

Potato Kugel

To serve 6 to 8

3 to 4	medium-sized potatoes, peeled, grated and drained (about 3 cups [¾ liter])	3 to 4
3	eggs	3
⅓ cup	potato flour	75 ml.
½ tsp.	baking powder	2 ml.
1½ tsp.	salt	7 ml.
⅛ tsp.	pepper	½ ml.
3 tbsp.	grated onion	45 ml.
4 tbsp.	butter, melted	60 ml.

In a large bowl, beat the eggs until they are thick. Stir in the potatoes, potato flour, baking powder, salt, pepper, onion and melted butter. Turn the mixture into a greased 1½-quart [1½-liter] baking dish. Bake the kugel in an oven, preheated to 350° F. [180° C.], for about an hour, or until browned. Serve the kugel hot.

JENNIE GROSSINGER
THE ART OF JEWISH COOKING

Jansson's Temptation

Jansson's Frestelse

To serve 4 to 6

7	medium-sized boiling potatoes, peeled, sliced ¼ inch [6 mm.] thick and cut into strips 2 inches [5 cm.] long	7
4½ tbsp.	butter with 2 tbsp. [30 ml.] cut into bits	75 ml.
2 tbsp.	vegetable oil	30 ml.
2 to 3	large yellow onions, thinly sliced	2 to 3
16	anchovy fillets, soaked in cold water for 10 minutes, patted dry and finely chopped	16
	white pepper	
2 tbsp.	fine dry bread crumbs	30 ml.
½ cup	milk	125 ml.
1 cup	heavy cream	¼ liter

Preheat the oven to 400° F. [200° C.]. Place the potato strips in cold water to keep them from discoloring. Heat 2 tablespoons [30 ml.] of the butter with the oil in a 10- to 12-inch [25- to 30-cm.] skillet. When the foam subsides, add the onions and cook for 10 minutes, stirring frequently, until they are soft but not brown.

With a pastry brush or paper towel, spread a 1½- to 2-quart [1½- to 2-liter] soufflé dish or baking dish with ½ tablespoon [7 ml.] of butter. Drain the potatoes and pat them dry with paper towels. Arrange a layer of potatoes on the bottom of the dish and then alternate layers of onions, anchovies and potatoes, ending with a layer of potatoes. Sprinkle each layer with a little white pepper. Scatter bread crumbs over the top layer of potatoes and dot the crumbs with the butter bits.

In a small saucepan, heat the milk and cream until the mixture just simmers, then pour it slowly down the sides of the dish. Bake in the center of the oven for 45 minutes, or until the potatoes are tender when pierced with the tip of a sharp knife and the liquid is nearly absorbed.

FOODS OF THE WORLD/THE COOKING OF SCANDINAVIA

Seethed Potatoes

This simple, but almost forgotten, traditional recipe for cooking potatoes comes from a book published in 1916.

To serve 2 to 4

1 lb.	small new potatoes, unpeeled	½ kg.
	salt	
1 tbsp.	butter (optional)	15 ml.

Put the potatoes in a cast-iron pot with a sprinkling of salt and very little water. A small piece of butter may also be added. Cook, uncovered, over low heat for 40 minutes, or until the potatoes are tender. No person who has not eaten potatoes thus prepared can conceive how delicious they are.

MAY BYRON
MAY BYRON'S VEGETABLE BOOK

Creamed Potatoes, Spanish-Style

Patatas a la Crema

To serve 4 to 6

2 to 2½ lb.	potatoes, cut into ½-inch [1-cm.] slices	1 kg.
2 tbsp.	olive oil	30 ml.
1 tbsp.	flour	15 ml.
	salt	
2	garlic cloves, chopped	2
2 tbsp.	chopped fresh parsley	30 ml.
1 tbsp.	fresh lemon juice	15 ml.
1	egg, lightly beaten	1

Heat the olive oil in a saucepan, blend in the flour, cook for a moment, then immediately add the potatoes. Cook for a few minutes, turning over the potatoes, then pour in just enough water to cover. Season with salt, add the garlic and 1 tablespoon [15 ml.] of the chopped parsley, and leave to cook, stirring from time to time with great care so as not to break the potatoes. When the potatoes are tender, after about 20 minutes, remove them from the heat, and add the lemon juice and egg. Mix well, but very carefully, turn onto a warmed dish and sprinkle with the rest of the parsley.

VICTORIA SERRA, TRANSLATED BY ELIZABETH GILI
TIA VICTORIA'S SPANISH KITCHEN

Sweet Potato Tipsy

To serve 8

8	medium-sized sweet potatoes (about 2½ lb.[1 kg.])	8
5 tbsp.	butter	75 ml.
2 tbsp.	brown sugar	30 ml.
⅓ cup	light cream	75 ml.
2 tbsp.	sweet sherry	30 ml.

Boil the sweet potatoes until tender (about 25 to 30 minutes). Peel, mash, then whip them, adding the butter, brown sugar, cream and sherry. Turn the potatoes into a buttered casserole. Bake in an oven, preheated to 350° F. [180° C.], for about 25 minutes or until the top is browned.

CLEMENTINE PADDLEFORD
THE BEST IN AMERICAN COOKING

Potato with Salt Pork and Onion

Matahami

To serve 4

8 to 10	medium-sized potatoes (about 2 to 2½ lb. [1 kg.]), washed but not peeled	8 to 10
½ lb.	salt pork without the rind, blanched in boiling water for 5 minutes, drained and sliced	¼ kg.
	salt and pepper	
2	large onions, coarsely chopped	2

Boil the potatoes in their skins. When they are cooked, peel them and cut them into fairly thick rounds. Line an oven-proof dish or casserole with a tight-fitting lid with half of the salt pork. Put in a layer of potatoes, season lightly with salt and pepper, then add a layer of onions and so on until all the potatoes and onions are used up. Cover the top with the remaining slices of salt pork and cook, covered, in an oven, preheated to 375° F. [190° C.], for about 30 minutes.

SIMIN PALAY
LA CUISINE DU PAYS

Sweet Potato and Apple

To serve 10

6	medium-sized sweet potatoes	6
½ cup	molasses	125 ml.
8 tbsp.	butter	120 ml.
4	medium-sized apples, cored and cut into ½-inch [1-cm.] slices	4
¼ cup	fresh orange juice	50 ml.
1 tbsp.	grated orange peel	15 ml.
½ tsp.	salt	2 ml.

Scrub the sweet potatoes, submerge them in boiling salted water, cover and simmer for 30 minutes, or until the potatoes are tender.

Meanwhile, in a skillet, heat ¼ cup [50 ml.] of the molasses with 4 tablespoons [60 ml.] of the butter. Add the apple slices and turn them to coat with the mixture. Simmer the apple slices very gently for about 10 minutes, or until barely tender, turning them twice during the cooking.

Drain the sweet potatoes, peel, and mash them or purée them in a food mill. Add the remaining molasses, the orange juice, orange peel and salt. Beat the mixture until it is light and fluffy. Mound the mixture on top of the apple slices and serve immediately.

JEAN HEWITT
THE NEW YORK TIMES NATURAL FOODS COOKBOOK

Sweet Potatoes Congolese

Beignets de Patates Douces

To serve 4

4	medium-sized sweet potatoes	4
¼ cup	honey	50 ml.
¼ cup	brandy	50 ml.
1 tsp.	grated lemon peel	5 ml.
	fat for deep frying	
	Beer batter	
2 cups	flour	½ liter
2 cups	light beer	½ liter

Blend the flour and the beer until a smooth batter is obtained. Set the batter aside.

Blanch the sweet potatoes for 5 minutes in boiling water. Peel and slice them. Marinate them for 1 hour in the honey, brandy and lemon peel mixture. Without drying the slices, dip them in the batter. Fry them in the deep fat heated to 390° F. [195° C.] until golden brown. Serve very hot. These fritters are excellent with roast turkey.

JULIETTE ELKON
A BELGIAN COOKBOOK

Stuffed Yams

To serve 6

6	yams, 4 to 5 inches [12 cm.] long	6
2 tbsp.	butter	30 ml.
½ tsp.	salt	2 ml.
	heavy cream	

Bake the yams in an oven, preheated to 400° F. [200° C.], for about 50 minutes. Scoop out the flesh of the yams and mix it with butter, salt and enough cream to make a soft purée. Refill the skins with the purée and bake for about 5 minutes.

JIM HARWOOD AND ED CALLAHAN
SOUL FOOD COOK BOOK

Baked Sweet Potatoes

To serve 8

6	large sweet potatoes	6
2 to 3 tbsp.	sugar	30 to 45 ml.
2 to 3 tbsp.	butter	30 to 45 ml.
2 tbsp.	water	30 ml.

Boil the sweet potatoes in lightly salted water; when done, peel and slice them lengthwise into two or three pieces. Put a layer of potatoes in a deep baking dish, sprinkle them with 1 tablespoon [15 ml.] of sugar, and scatter 1 tablespoon of butter, cut in small pieces, over the potatoes. Then make another layer of potatoes, sugar, and butter pieces; lastly, add some thin slices of butter and sprinkle sugar freely over them. Bake the potatoes for about 20 minutes in an oven preheated to 375° F. [190° C.]. Before serving, sprinkle about 2 tablespoons [30 ml.] of hot water over the potatoes, then add some more sugar.

MRS. PETER A. WHITE
THE KENTUCKY HOUSEWIFE

Baked Sweet Potatoes with Apples

To serve 6

3	large sweet potatoes, boiled	3
3	large apples, peeled, cored and sliced	3
5 tbsp.	butter	75 ml.
1 tsp.	salt	5 ml.
½ cup	maple syrup	125 ml.

Fry the apples in 3 tablespoons [45 ml.] of the butter until they are light brown. Slice the potatoes. Arrange the apples and potatoes in alternate layers in a buttered 1½-quart [1½-liter] baking dish. Add the salt. Pour the syrup over this and dot the layers with small pieces of the remaining butter. Bake in a moderate oven, preheated to 350° F. [180° C.], for about 30 minutes or until the syrup has been absorbed and the top is lightly browned.

MARY PEARL
VERMONT MAPLE RECIPES

Candied Sweet Potatoes

Camotes Garapiñados

To serve 6

6	medium-sized sweet potatoes, quartered	6
4 tbsp.	butter	60 ml.
½ cup	sugar	125 ml.
¼ cup	hot water	50 ml.
¼ cup	dry white wine	50 ml.
1½ tbsp.	ground cinnamon	22 ml.
⅛ tsp.	salt	½ ml.

In a skillet, fry the potatoes in the butter until brown. Add the rest of the ingredients and stir well. Cover and simmer until all the liquid has been absorbed or the potatoes are tender, about 20 minutes. Serve the potatoes with ham.

DON CARLOS
SPANISH-MEXICAN COOKBOOK

Old-fashioned Sweet Potato Pone

To serve 6

6	medium-sized sweet potatoes	6
2 cups	sugar	½ liter
¼ cup	butter, cut into small pieces	50 ml.
3	eggs, lightly beaten	3
1 tsp.	ground cinnamon	5 ml.
1 tsp.	ground allspice	5 ml.
1 tsp.	grated nutmeg	5 ml.
1 tsp.	ground cloves	5 ml.
1½ cups	white raisins	375 ml.

Boil the potatoes until tender. Peel, and place them in a single layer in a baking dish. In a bowl, blend the sugar and butter. Mix in the remaining ingredients. Pour this mixture over the potatoes. Bake in a preheated 250° F. [120° C.] oven for 1 hour or until the potato pone has caramelized.

CLEMENTINE PADDLEFORD
THE BEST IN AMERICAN COOKING

Mashed Rutabagas

To serve 4

2 lb.	rutabagas, sliced 1 inch [2½ cm.] thick and cut into 1-inch cubes	1 kg.
4 to 6 tbsp.	butter	60 to 90 ml.
¼ cup	chicken or beef stock	50 ml.
	salt	
	freshly ground pepper	
	ground mace	
¼ cup	dry sherry	50 ml.

Cook the rutabagas in boiling salted water for 10 minutes, or until very tender. Drain and put them through a ricer. Return the rutabagas to the saucepan. Over low heat, stir in 4 tablespoons [60 ml.] of the butter. Stir in the stock, and season the mixture with salt, pepper and a pinch of mace. Beat as you would mashed potatoes; if the rutabagas are too dry, beat in all or part of the remaining butter. Beat in the sherry. Cook, beating constantly, for 2 or 3 more minutes. Serve very hot.

NIKA HAZELTON
THE UNABRIDGED VEGETABLE COOKBOOK

Salsify in Butter and Onion Sauce

Schwarzwurzeln in Buttersosse

To serve 6 to 8

2 to 2½ lb.	salsify	1 kg.
1 tbsp.	flour	15 ml.
2 tbsp.	wine vinegar	30 ml.
1 cup	milk	¼ liter
1 quart	water, lightly salted	1 liter
	Butter and onion sauce	
3 tbsp.	butter	45 ml.
1	medium-sized onion, chopped	1
⅓ cup	flour	75 ml.
1 cup	meat or vegetable stock	¼ liter
2 cups	milk	½ liter
	salt	
⅛ tsp.	grated nutmeg	½ ml.
1 tbsp.	fresh lemon juice	15 ml.
2 tbsp.	heavy cream	30 ml.
1	egg yolk	1

Have ready a bowl of cold water containing the flour and vinegar. Peel the salsify and cut it, crosswise, into 1¼-inch [3-cm.] rounds, putting them straight into the bowl; this will keep them from turning black. Put the milk and salted water in a large pot, bring to a boil and add the salsify, cooking until it is slightly softened—about 15 minutes. Drain, place the salsify in a saucepan, and cover to keep it warm.

In another saucepan, prepare the sauce. Cook the onion in the butter, add the flour, stir in the stock and milk and bring to a boil, stirring all the time. Then lower the heat and cook until the sauce is thickened, still stirring. Add salt, the nutmeg and the lemon juice.

Put the sauce through a sieve and pour it over the salsify. Cover the pan and simmer the salsify until done—about 40 minutes. Just before serving, mix the cream and egg yolk and stir them into the sauce without letting it boil.

HERMINE KIEHNLE AND MARIA HÄDECKE
DAS NEUE KIEHNLE-KOCHBUCH

Fried Salsify

This recipe is adapted from the 1865 edition of Eliza Acton's classic cookbook.

	To serve 4	
1½ lb.	salsify, washed	¾ kg.
	salt	
1 tbsp.	butter	15 ml.
2 tbsp.	white vinegar or fresh lemon juice	30 ml.
	oil for deep frying	
	batter for deep frying *(recipe, page 167)*	

Gently scrape the dark outside skin off the salsify roots and throw them into cold water as they are done, to prevent them from turning black. Cut the salsify into lengths of 3 to 4 inches [8 to 10 cm.] and, when all are ready, put them to cook in plenty of boiling water with a little salt and the butter and vinegar or lemon juice. If the roots are thick, they may take 45 minutes to 1 hour; try them with a fork after about 30 minutes and when they are perfectly tender, drain them. Dry them by pressing them lightly in a soft cloth.

Heat the oil for deep frying. Throw the bits of salsify into the batter. Take them out separately and fry them to a light brown, then drain them well. Place them in a dish, sprinkle a little salt over them and serve them quickly.

ELIZA ACTON
MODERN COOKERY

Deep-fried Marinated Salsify

Salsifis en Marinade

	To serve 4	
1½ lb.	salsify, cut into 2- to 3-inch [5- to 8-cm.] pieces	¾ kg.
3 to 4 quarts	cold water, mixed with ½ cup [125 ml.] white wine vinegar	3 to 4 liters
1 tbsp.	butter	15 ml.
	salt and peppercorns	
1 tbsp.	fresh lemon juice or white wine vinegar	15 ml.
	batter for deep frying *(recipe, page 167)*	
	oil for deep frying	
	Vinegar marinade	
¼ cup	white wine vinegar	50 ml.
	salt and pepper	

Peel the salsify and, to stop discoloring, immediately plunge them into the water-vinegar bath. Drain the salsify, place in an enameled or stainless-steel saucepan, cover with water and add the butter, seasoning and lemon juice or vinegar. Simmer for 1 hour, then drain.

Sprinkle the marinade over the salsify and leave to marinate for 2 to 3 hours. Meanwhile, make the batter.

Heat the oil. Dip the salsify in the batter and fry in the oil until golden brown. Drain well and serve immediately.

OFFRAY AINÉ
LE CUISINIER MÉRIDIONAL

Turnips in Cider

Navets au Cidre

	To serve 6	
2 lb.	young turnips	1 kg.
4 tbsp.	butter	60 ml.
1 cup	veal, duck or goose stock	¼ liter
1 cup	hard cider	¼ liter
1	egg yolk	1
	salt	
	Pork and bacon stuffing	
½ lb.	lean pork, finely chopped	¼ kg.
5	slices bacon, finely chopped	5
1	shallot, finely chopped	1
2 tbsp.	chopped, mixed fresh tarragon, parsley and thyme, and a crumbled bay leaf	30 ml.
	pepper	
	mixed spices	
1	egg	1

Peel the turnips; hollow out the pulp with an apple corer if they are the long type, or use a potato baller or knife if they are the round type. Blanch the hollow turnips and the pulp in boiling water for a few minutes. Drain thoroughly.

Prepare the stuffing by mixing together the pork, bacon, shallot and herbs. Season it with pepper and a pinch of mixed spices, and bind the mixture with the egg.

Firmly pack the stuffing mixture into the hollow turnips. Brown them in the butter in a fireproof casserole or heavy saucepan. Add the stock and cider, cover, and simmer for about 1 hour. Fifteen minutes before serving, purée the turnip pulp and add it to the liquid in the casserole.

Arrange the turnips on a warmed platter. Over high heat reduce the cooking liquid to half its volume, then bind it with the egg yolk, and strain the resulting sauce. Taste and add salt if necessary. Coat the turnips with the sauce and serve.

ALI-BAB
ENCYCLOPEDIA OF PRACTICAL GASTRONOMY

Shredded Turnip Gratin

To serve 4

6 or 7	medium-sized turnips (1½ lb. [¾ kg.]), peeled and shredded or grated	6 or 7
8 tbsp.	butter	120 ml.
	salt	
⅔ cup	heavy cream	150 ml.
	pepper	
⅓ cup	fresh bread crumbs	75 ml.

Give the gratings of turnip a good salting and leave them to drain for 30 minutes. Place a large sieve over the sink and repeatedly squeeze the turnips over it until the mass feels dry and weightless.

Melt 4 tablespoons [60 ml.] of the butter in a skillet. Add the turnips, season with salt and, stirring frequently, cook over low heat for 10 minutes. Place the turnips in a buttered gratin dish, pour cream over them and season generously with pepper. Melt the remaining butter, stir in the bread crumbs and cook until lightly browned. Sprinkle the crumbs over the turnips and bake in an oven, preheated to 375° F. [190° C.], for 30 minutes or until a golden gratin has formed.

JUDITH OLNEY
SUMMER FOOD

Turnip Soufflé

To serve 4

2	medium-sized turnips, grated	2
3 tbsp.	butter	45 ml.
2 to 3 tbsp.	bread crumbs, browned in butter	30 to 45 ml.
1	medium-sized onion, finely chopped	1
1 tbsp.	flour	15 ml.
2 tsp.	dry mustard	10 ml.
2 tsp.	freshly grated horseradish	10 ml.
1 cup	milk	¼ liter
4	eggs, yolks separated from the whites	4
	salt and pepper	
1	extra egg white (optional)	1

Preheat the oven to 375° F. [190° C.]. Butter a 6-cup [1½-liter] soufflé dish and sprinkle in about 1 tablespoon [15 ml.] of the bread crumbs. Tip the dish backward and forward so the crumbs stick to the butter, then tip out any loose crumbs.

To support the sides of the soufflé as it rises in the oven, cut a double thickness of wax paper a little longer than the circumference of the soufflé dish plus about twice its depth. Wrap the paper around the outside of the rim of the dish and tie the paper on with cotton string (nylon disintegrates in the oven). Butter the inside of the paper projecting above the dish and sprinkle it with a tablespoon of the bread crumbs.

Melt 2 tablespoons [30 ml.] of butter in a saucepan over low heat. Add the turnip and onion, and cook them gently, stirring occasionally, until they are just beginning to brown. Stir in the flour, mustard and horseradish. Remove from the heat and blend in the milk. Return the pan to the heat, bring the mixture to a boil, stirring, and cook until it is thick. Allow the mixture to cool, then put it into a mixing bowl. Beat in the egg yolks and seasoning. Whip the egg whites until stiff and fold them into the mixture. Quickly pile the mixture into the soufflé dish and dust the top with the remaining bread crumbs. Cook the soufflé in the center of the oven for 35 minutes. Remove the paper collar before serving.

GAIL DUFF
FRESH ALL THE YEAR

Turnip Custard

To serve 4

1½ cups	grated turnip	375 ml.
3	eggs, lightly beaten	3
3 cups	milk, scalded	¾ liter
	salt and pepper	
	freshly grated nutmeg	
1 tsp.	grated onion	5 ml.
1 tsp.	finely chopped fresh parsley	5 ml.
1 tsp.	finely chopped green pepper	5 ml.
3 tbsp.	butter, melted	45 ml.
½ tsp.	sugar	2 ml.

Stir the turnip and the milk into the eggs, then season to taste with salt, pepper and nutmeg. Beat the custard mixture very briskly until foamy, then stir in the onion, parsley, green pepper and, finally, the melted butter. Pour the mixture into a buttered 1½-quart [1½-liter] baking dish, dust the surface with the sugar and bake in a moderately slow oven, preheated to 325° F. [160° C.], for 40 to 45 minutes, or until set. Serve at once from the baking dish.

LOUIS P. DE GOUY
THE GOLD COOK BOOK

Pods and Seeds

Sautéed Bean Sprouts

To serve 4 to 6

1 quart	mung-bean, soybean or chick-pea sprouts or sprouted wheat berries	1 liter
3 tbsp.	oil	45 ml.
1	scallion, including 2 inches [5 cm.] of the green top, finely chopped	1
½ inch	slice fresh ginger root, finely chopped	1 cm.
1 tbsp.	soy sauce	15 ml.
⅓ cup	sliced water chestnuts	75 ml.

Heat the oil in a wok or heavy skillet. Add the scallion and cook for 30 seconds. Add the sprouts and cook for 1 minute. Add the ginger, soy sauce and water chestnuts. Cover and cook for 4 minutes. Serve hot.

JEAN HEWITT
THE NEW YORK TIMES NATURAL FOODS COOKBOOK

Broad Beans, Maltese-Style

Ful Imgiddem

If broad beans are not available, unpeeled lima beans may be used as a substitute.

This dish should be made toward the end of the broad-bean season, when the beans are large and coarse.

To serve 4

3½ lb.	broad beans, shelled and skins removed	1½ to 2 kg.
2 tbsp.	olive oil	30 ml.
2	large garlic cloves	2
	salt and pepper	
1 tbsp.	puréed tomato (optional)	15 ml.
½ cup	fine fresh bread crumbs	125 ml.
1 tbsp.	chopped fresh parsley	15 ml.

Heat the oil in a skillet, add the garlic, the beans and enough water to cover them. (See that there is sufficient water as the beans, which should remain whole, ought not to be stirred while cooking.) Add the salt and pepper and puréed tomato. Cover and simmer for about 30 minutes, or until the beans are tender. Drain the beans, discarding the garlic cloves, then stir in the bread crumbs and parsley. Serve hot or cold.

ANNE AND HELEN CARUANA GALIZIA
RECIPES FROM MALTA

Purée of Broad Beans

Purée de Fèves au Maigre

If broad beans are not available, unpeeled lima beans may be used as a substitute.

To serve 4

5 lb.	large broad beans, shelled and peeled	2½ kg.
4 tbsp.	butter	60 ml.
½ cup	milk	125 ml.
1	sprig savory	1
	salt	
½ tsp.	sugar	2 ml.
2 to 3 tbsp.	heavy cream	30 to 45 ml.
2	slices bread with the crusts removed, cut into 8 triangles and fried in 2 tbsp. [30 ml.] butter	2

Melt 2 tablespoons [30 ml.] of the butter in a heavy saucepan and sauté the beans for a few minutes. Moisten with the milk; add the savory, salt and sugar. Cover and cook over low heat for 20 minutes. When the beans are tender, press them through a sieve. Put the purée in a fireproof casserole and reheat, stirring to prevent sticking. When the purée is hot, remove the casserole from the heat and stir in the cream and the remaining 2 tablespoons of butter. Serve garnished with the fried bread.

ARISTIDE QUILLET
LA CUISINE MODERNE

Broad Beans with Savory

Les Fèves Nouvelles à la Sarriette

Winter savory is a traditional herb for seasoning boiled beans. The creators of this recipe, Dumont and Lespine, also recommend adding a tablespoon [15 ml.] of chopped savory to the beans before serving. If the broad beans are very young they may not need to be skinned after shelling. If they are mature, the outer skins should be removed (page 15); skins can make broad beans tough and spoil their delicate flavor. If broad beans are not available, lima beans may be used as a substitute; lima beans do not require skinning.

To serve 4 to 6

4 lb.	young broad beans, shelled and skinned	2 kg.
1	bunch winter savory, tied together	1
4 tbsp.	butter, cut into small pieces	60 ml.
1 tbsp.	chopped winter savory	15 ml.

Cook the beans in boiling salted water with the bunch of savory. When the beans are tender, after 2 to 10 minutes, depending on their size, drain off the water and remove the savory. Toss the beans over high heat for a moment to evaporate any remaining moisture. Take off the heat, add the butter and mix carefully, without breaking the beans. Serve in a warmed vegetable dish, garnished with the chopped savory.

AUSTIN DE CROZE
LES PLATS RÉGIONAUX DE FRANCE

❖

Lima Bean Purée

To serve 6

1½ lb.	lima beans, shelled	¾ kg.
½ tsp.	salt	2 ml.
1	medium-sized onion, thinly sliced	1
¾ cup	heavy cream	175 ml.
2 tbsp.	butter	30 ml.
2 tbsp.	grated horseradish	30 ml.
1 tsp.	Worcestershire sauce	5 ml.
	salt and pepper	

Bring 2 cups [½ liter] of water to a boil. Add the salt and the onion, and simmer over low heat for 5 minutes. Add the lima beans and cook them for 10 minutes once the water returns to a boil. Drain the beans and the onion.

Pour the cream into a blender. Add the drained beans and onions, cover and purée. Do not overblend; the beans should not be completely smooth. Put the purée in a pot.

Add the butter, horseradish, Worcestershire sauce, salt and pepper. Reheat gently. If you feel that the purée is too thick, thin it with a little more cream.

CAROL CUTLER
THE SIX-MINUTE SOUFFLÉ AND OTHER CULINARY DELIGHTS

❖

Green Beans in Egg Sauce

Haricots Verts Quercynoise

To serve 4

1 lb.	green beans	½ kg.
	salt	
2	eggs	2
1 tbsp.	vinegar	15 ml.
2	shallots, finely chopped	2
1	garlic clove, finely chopped	1
	pepper	
½ tbsp.	chopped fresh parsley	7 ml.

In a saucepan, boil the beans in salted water until just tender. Drain off the water, but reserve 1 tablespoon [15 ml.]

of it in a bowl. Add the eggs and the vinegar to the reserved water, and beat together. Pour the mixture over the beans, add the shallots and garlic, season with salt and pepper, and stir over very low heat until the beans are covered with a thick creamy sauce. Serve with a little chopped parsley scattered over the top.

ANNE-MARIE PENTON
CUSTOMS AND COOKERY IN THE PÉRIGORD AND QUERCY

Green Beans in Sour Cream and Tomato Sauce

To serve 6

1 lb.	green beans, trimmed and halved crosswise (about 3 cups [¾ liter])	½ kg.
	salt	
4 tbsp.	butter	60 ml.
1	large onion, halved lengthwise and thinly sliced	1
1	medium-sized green pepper, seeded, deribbed and chopped	1
2	large tomatoes, peeled, seeded and chopped	2
2 tbsp.	finely chopped fresh basil	30 ml.
¾ cup	sour cream	175 ml.
	freshly ground black pepper	

Drop the beans into lightly salted boiling water. Boil uncovered for about 10 minutes, or until tender but still somewhat firm to the bite. Drain and set the beans aside.

In a heavy skillet, melt the butter over moderate heat. Add the onion and green pepper, and cook until soft but not browned, stirring frequently. Add the tomatoes and basil, and cook for 2 minutes, stirring often. Add the beans, mix well, lower the heat and simmer for 2 minutes. Beat the sour cream with salt and pepper, and stir it into the vegetables gently but thoroughly. Taste for seasoning. Transfer to a warmed serving bowl and serve the beans immediately.

SONIA UVEZIAN
THE BEST FOODS OF RUSSIA

Pears, Beans and Bacon

Birnen, Bohnen und Speck

To serve 6

1 lb.	green beans, trimmed and broken into pieces	½ kg.
6	firm ripe pears, peeled, cored and sliced	6
½ cup	water	125 ml.
1	thin sliver lemon peel	1
1 tsp.	salt	5 ml.
6	slices bacon	6
¼ cup	sugar	50 ml.
2 tbsp.	vinegar	30 ml.
1 tsp.	fresh lemon juice	5 ml.

Place the pear slices in a saucepan with the water and lemon peel, bring to a boil, lower the heat, and simmer uncovered for 5 minutes. Then stir in the green beans and the salt, and continue cooking.

Meanwhile, fry the bacon in a skillet. When the bacon is crisp, remove it to a paper towel to drain. Pour off all but about 2 tablespoons [30 ml.] of the fat remaining in the skillet. Add the sugar, vinegar and lemon juice to the bacon fat in the pan. Simmer for 3 minutes. Pour this sauce over the pears and beans and cook until tender. Crumble the bacon and add it to the beans just before serving.

BETTY WASON
THE ART OF GERMAN COOKING

Steamed Green Beans

Phali Dum

To serve 2 to 4

¾ lb.	green beans	⅓ kg.
1	small onion	1
2 tsp.	chopped ginger root	10 ml.
½ to 1 tbsp.	butter	7 to 15 ml.
½ tsp.	salt	2 ml.
	ground fennel seed	

Slice the beans slantwise into ½-inch [1-cm.] slivers. Cut the onion into pieces the same size. Bring to a boil a few tablespoons of water mixed with the butter. Add the beans, onions and ginger root, season with salt and a good pinch of ground fennel seed. Mix well. Cover tightly and let the beans steam

for 5 to 7 minutes. The moisture should have dried off; if not, raise the heat briefly and shake well. Serve very hot. Do not overcook the beans—they should be *al dente*.

DHARAMJIT SINGH
INDIAN COOKERY

Green Beans with Anchovies

Haricots Verts

This recipe is from a book published anonymously in 1922, but thought to be by the writer and gastronome Leo Larguier.

To serve 4

1 lb.	green beans, trimmed, parboiled for 5 to 6 minutes and drained	½ kg.
3 tbsp.	olive oil	45 ml.
4	anchovy fillets, soaked in cold water for 10 minutes and patted dry	4
1	garlic clove, crushed	1
1 tbsp.	vinegar	15 ml.

Heat the oil slightly in a sauté pan. Add the anchovies and garlic and, with a fork, crush and soften them in the oil over low heat. Then add the green beans and sauté them over fairly high heat until they are heated through, adding the vinegar at the last moment.

CLARISSE OU LA VIEILLE CUISINIÈRE

Green Beans with Garlic

Les Haricots Verts à l'Ail

To serve 6

1¼ lb.	green beans, trimmed and cut into 1¼-inch [3-cm.] pieces	⅔ kg.
6 tbsp.	olive oil	90 ml.
6	garlic cloves, crushed with the side of a knife blade	6
3 cups	fresh bread crumbs	¾ liter
	salt and pepper	

Heat the olive oil in a large skillet and, when hot, throw in the garlic cloves. When the garlic begins to turn transparent, add the green beans and stir with a wooden spoon.

Keep the oil very hot. When the beans start to turn dark green, add the bread crumbs and stir very briskly so that they do not burn or stick to the bottom of the pan. Turn the mixture immediately onto a warmed platter. Add salt and pepper to taste, and serve at once.

JACQUES MÉDECIN
LA CUISINE DU COMTÉ DE NICE

Piquant Wax Beans

To serve 6

1½ lb.	yellow beans, cut into julienne	¾ kg.
4	slices bacon	4
2 tbsp.	chopped pimiento	30 ml.
2 tbsp.	vinegar	30 ml.
½ tsp.	sugar	2 ml.
1 tbsp.	Worcestershire sauce	15 ml.
¼ tsp.	dry mustard	1 ml.
	Tabasco	

Boil the wax beans and keep them warm. Dice the bacon and sauté it in a skillet until crisp. Drain the bacon on paper towels and reserve 2 tablespoons [30 ml.] of the grease. Add the bacon to the hot beans. Add the remaining ingredients to the bacon fat and cook, stirring constantly, for 2 to 3 minutes. Pour the mixture over the beans and toss. Serve at once. Yellow beans particularly complement baked ham.

BERYL M. MARTON
OUT OF THE GARDEN INTO THE KITCHEN

Corn on the Cob

To serve 3 or 4

6 to 8	ears of corn	6 to 8
1 tsp.	sugar	5 ml.

In a large skillet with a tight-fitting lid, bring 1 inch [2½ cm.] of water to a boil. Shuck the corn and remove the silks, using a small knife or stiff brush if it is helpful. Arrange the corn in a single layer in the boiling water and sprinkle it lightly with the sugar. Cover, bring again to a boil, and immediately remove from the heat. Let the corn stand covered, for 8 to 10 minutes. (Corn cooked by this method can stand for up to 30 minutes in hot water without overcooking.) Serve the corn hot, with butter, salt and pepper.

JEANNE A. VOLTZ
THE FLAVOR OF THE SOUTH

Stuffed Cornhusks

Humita en Chala

Instructions for stuffing cornhusks are given on page 68.

To serve 8 to 10

12	ears of corn, shucked, with the husks washed and reserved	12
2 tbsp.	oil	30 ml.
1	medium-sized onion, finely chopped	1
3	medium-sized tomatoes, peeled and chopped	3
	salt and pepper to taste	
½ cup	freshly grated Muenster cheese	125 ml.

In a large bowl, mix together the oil, onion, tomatoes, and salt and pepper. Scrape the corn off the cobs, and add the kernels and the cheese to the tomato mixture.

Put two of the husks on top of each other to form a cross and place about 4 tablespoons [60 ml.] of the corn mixture on top. Fold the husks up into a package, and tie the packages securely with strings torn from the husks. Braise the stuffed husks in boiling water for about 15 minutes, or until the packages feel firm to the touch. Serve the stuffed husks hot, letting each diner open his own.

JOSEFINA VELILLA DE AQUINO
TEMBI'U PARAGUAI COMIDA PARAGUAYA

Indonesian Fried Corn

Frikadel Djagung

To serve 4

1 cup	corn kernels, cut from 1 or 2 freshly cooked ears	¼ liter
1	small onion, finely chopped	1
1	rib celery, finely chopped	1
2 tbsp.	chopped coriander leaves	30 ml.
½ tsp.	salt	2 ml.
1	egg, lightly beaten	1
1 tbsp.	flour	15 ml.
3 tbsp.	peanut oil	45 ml.

Combine all the ingredients except the oil in a large bowl. Mix thoroughly.

Heat the oil in a 12-inch [30-cm.] wok or in a large skillet. Add the vegetable mixture and stir fry over high heat for about 5 minutes, or until the vegetables are golden.

LAROUSSE TREASURY OF COUNTRY COOKING

Corn Timbales

To serve 4

1 cup	uncooked corn kernels, cut from 2 large ears	¼ liter
4	eggs	4
1 tsp.	grated onion	5 ml.
1 tsp.	salt	5 ml.
	Tabasco sauce	
1 cup	heavy cream	¼ liter

Mushroom sauce

1¼ cups	finely chopped fresh mushrooms	300 ml.
½ cup	sour cream	125 ml.
½ cup	beef stock	125 ml.
2 tbsp.	flour	30 ml.
2 tbsp.	butter	30 ml.
	salt and pepper	

Combine the corn with the eggs, onion, salt and Tabasco. Whip the cream and fold it into the corn mixture. Butter individual custard cups. Fill each cup two-thirds full and place it on top of a rack, or on several thicknesses of paper, in a pan of hot water. Bake the timbales in an oven, preheated to 325° F. [160° C.], for 20 to 30 minutes or until the custard is set. Turn out and serve with the mushroom sauce, made by first whirling all the ingredients in a blender until the sauce is smooth, then heating in a pan until the sauce is thick.

MARJORIE PAGE BLANCHARD
HOME GARDENER'S COOKBOOK

Green Corn Pudding

To serve 4

4	large ears of corn	4
1 quart	milk	1 liter
3	eggs, lightly beaten	3
1 oz.	beef suet, finely chopped	50 g.
	sugar	
2 tbsp.	butter, cut into small chunks	30 ml.

Draw a sharp knife through each row of corn kernels lengthwise, then scrape the pulp into a heavy saucepan. Add the milk, eggs, suet, sugar to taste, and a few chunks of butter. Cook the mixture over low heat, stirring occasionally, until it thickens. Transfer the mixture to a buttered ovenproof dish and bake in a 300° F. [150° C.] oven for about 2 hours. The pudding is done when a knife inserted into the center of the pudding comes out clean.

THE BUCKEYE COOKBOOK

Corn Fritters

To serve 4 to 6

2 cups	cooked corn kernels, cut from 4 large ears	½ liter
1¼ cups	flour	300 ml.
2¼ tsp.	baking powder	11 ml.
1 tsp.	salt	5 ml.
1	egg, yolk separated from white	1
¾ cup	milk	175 ml.
1½ tsp.	corn oil	7 ml.
	fat for deep frying	
	pancake syrup (optional)	

Sift the dry ingredients together. Beat the egg yolk, milk and corn oil together. Gradually add the flour mixture. Beat the egg white until stiff, and fold it into the batter. Gently stir in the corn. Drop by the spoonful into deep-frying fat preheated to 375° F. [190° C.]. Fry until the fritters are puffed and brown, turning once. This should take approximately 5 minutes. Drain the fritters on paper toweling and serve at once, with pancake syrup, if desired, or sprinkled with sugar. Corn fritters are a wonderful accompaniment for barbecued or broiled chicken.

BERYL M. MARTON
OUT OF THE GARDEN INTO THE KITCHEN

Grated Corn Pudding

To serve 8

3 to 4 cups	uncooked corn kernels, cut from 8 ears	¾ to 1 liter
2¼ cups	milk	550 ml.
8 tbsp.	butter, melted	120 ml.
4	eggs, beaten	4
1 to 2 tbsp.	sugar	15 to 30 ml.
2 tsp.	salt	10 ml.
½ tsp.	white pepper	2 ml.
2 drops	Tabasco	2 drops

Scald the milk in a heavy saucepan. Remove it from the heat and add the rest of the ingredients. Mix well and pour into a buttered 2-quart [2-liter] baking dish. Place the baking dish in a pan half-filled with warm water and bake in an oven, preheated to 325° F. [160° C.], for approximately 1 hour and 15 minutes. The pudding is done when a knife inserted into the center of it comes out clean.

THE JUNIOR LEAGUE OF NEW ORLEANS
THE PLANTATION COOKBOOK

Purée of Fresh Green Peas

To serve 4 or 5

1 cup	shelled peas	¼ liter
1 tbsp.	chopped fresh parsley	15 ml.
3 tbsp.	butter	45 ml.
½ tsp.	salt	2 ml.
¼ tsp.	pepper	1 ml.
1	egg yolk	1
½ cup	light cream	125 ml.

Cook the peas in salted water. Drain. Rub the peas through a strainer into a saucepan. Fry the parsley in the butter and combine it with the puréed peas. Add the salt and pepper. Bring the purée to a boil. Beat the egg yolk and cream together, and blend in before serving.

FLORENCE SCHWARTZ (EDITOR)
VEGETABLE COOKING OF ALL NATIONS

Peas and Cucumbers in Sour Cream

To serve 6

3 cups	freshly shelled peas (about 3 lb. [1½ kg.])	¾ liter
2	medium-sized cucumbers	2
1 cup	sour cream at room temperature	¼ liter
3 tbsp.	finely chopped fresh dill	45 ml.
	salt and pepper	

Cook the peas in boiling salted water until barely tender. Drain. Peel the cucumber, quarter it and scoop out the seeds, then dice it. Cook the diced cucumber quickly for about 2 minutes in just enough boiling water to cover. Do not overcook: the cucumber should remain crisp. Drain immediately.

Just before serving, combine the cooked cucumber and peas in the top of a double boiler, then mix in the sour cream, dill, and salt and pepper to taste. Heat slowly over hot—not boiling—water until the vegetables are warm. Serve.

BARBARA R. FRIED
THE FOUR-SEASON COOKBOOK

Jugged Peas

An 18th Century recipe from Surrey, England.

	To serve 4	
2 cups	freshly shelled peas	½ liter
1 tbsp.	butter	15 ml.
1 tsp.	confectioners' sugar	5 ml.
¼ tsp.	salt	1 ml.
12	fresh mint leaves	12
	black pepper	

Put the peas into a clean, 2-pound [1-kg.] jar with a close-fitting top, adding the butter, sugar, salt, mint and a very little black pepper. Cover the jar tightly and immerse it to half its height in a pan of boiling water. Set the latter over high heat and boil briskly, uncovered. Check the peas periodically to make sure the water does not boil away. Examine the peas in 30 minutes: if very young, the peas should be done by then; if old, they will of course take longer.

MARIE STONE
THE COVENT GARDEN COOKBOOK

Peas with Prosciutto

Piselli al Prosciutto

	To serve 4	
3 lb.	peas, shelled (about 3 cups [¾ liter])	1½ kg.
4 tbsp.	butter	60 ml.
1	small onion, finely chopped	1
	salt and pepper	
⅔ cup	hot chicken, beef or veal stock, or water	150 ml.
	sugar (optional)	
¼ lb.	thinly sliced prosciutto, cut into strips	125 g.
4	firm-textured white bread slices with the crusts removed, cut into triangles and fried in butter (optional)	4

In a saucepan, melt the butter and sauté the onion over low heat until it begins to change color. Add the peas, season with salt and pepper, and moisten with the stock or water. Cook, uncovered, over brisk heat for 10 minutes or until the peas are tender, adding a pinch of sugar if the peas are not young and sweet. Two minutes before the peas are ready, add the ham and stir gently.

Served in a decorative vegetable dish, the color combination of peas and ham is very attractive. Garnish with the triangles of fried bread, if desired, and serve very hot.

ADA BONI
ITALIAN REGIONAL COOKING

Green Peas, Poitou-Style

Petits Pois à la Poitevine

To serve 4

2 cups	freshly shelled green peas, preferably small young peas (about 2 lb. [1 kg.])	½ liter
4 tbsp.	butter	60 ml.
3	medium-sized onions, finely sliced	3
2 tbsp.	chopped fresh parsley	30 ml.
1	sprig thyme	1
1	sprig savory	1
1 tsp.	chopped fresh hyssop	5 ml.
1 or 2 tsp.	sugar	5 or 10 ml.
1	lettuce heart, shredded	1
	salt and pepper	

Melt the butter in a heavy saucepan and put in the peas, the onions, and the parsley, thyme, savory and hyssop. Sauté for several minutes, then add the sugar and the lettuce. Pour in enough boiling water to cover the peas, season with salt and pepper and simmer gently, covered, for 30 minutes or until the peas are tender.

JEAN MERCIER AND IRENE LABARRE
LA CUISINE DE POITOU ET DE LA VENDÉE

Family-Style Peas

Petits Pois à la demi Bourgeoise

To serve 4

4 lb.	young peas, shelled (about 4 cups [1 liter] after shelling)	2 kg.
4 tbsp.	butter	60 ml.
5 or 6	parsley sprigs, tied together with 1 scallion	5 or 6
1	head lettuce, trimmed and quartered	1
1 tsp.	sugar	5 ml.
	salt	
2	egg yolks, lightly beaten	2
1 cup	heavy cream	¼ liter

Put the peas in a saucepan with the butter, parsley and scallion, and the lettuce. Cook, covered, over very low heat for about 40 minutes until there is almost no liquid left in the pan; then add the sugar and salt to taste. Mix the egg yolks with the cream and stir into the peas, still over low heat. Simmer for a few minutes, then serve.

MENON
LA CUISINIÈRE BOURGEOISE

Snow Peas with Mushrooms

To serve 4

1 lb.	snow peas	½ kg.
1 lb.	mushrooms	½ kg.
2 tbsp.	peanut or soy oil	30 ml.
1 to 3 tsp.	Japanese soy sauce	5 to 15 ml.

Soak the snow peas briefly in cold water; trim the ends from the pods. Drain the pods and refrigerate them until ready to use. Cut the mushroom caps and stems into thin slices. Heat the oil in a wok or large shallow skillet and, over high heat, stir fry the mushrooms for 2 minutes. Add the whole pea pods and stir fry for a minute or so more. The snow peas must be very crisp-textured when served—scarcely cooked at all, just heated through. Add the soy sauce, mix through, and serve at once. Marvelous!

ALEX D. HAWKES
COOKING WITH VEGETABLES

Mushrooms

Mushrooms in Butter with Anchovies, Mint and Lemon Juice

Funghi alla Casalinga

To serve 4 to 6

2 lb.	small mushrooms	1 kg.
8 tbsp.	butter	120 ml.
1 tbsp.	olive oil	15 ml.
	salt and coarsely ground pepper	
4	anchovy fillets, soaked in water for 10 minutes, patted dry and chopped	4
2	sprigs mint, chopped	2
3 to 4 tbsp.	fresh lemon juice	45 to 60 ml.
2 tbsp.	chopped fresh parsley	30 ml.

Heat the butter and oil in a deep skillet and fry the mushrooms over high heat, tossing them constantly. After about 5 minutes, add the salt and pepper, anchovies and mint. Mix together and then add the lemon juice. Fry for a moment longer. Sprinkle with parsley and serve.

JANET ROSS AND MICHAEL WATERFIELD
LEAVES FROM OUR TUSCAN KITCHEN

Mushrooms Polonaise

To serve 6

1 ½ lb.	mushrooms, sliced	¾ kg.
1	onion, chopped	1
12 tbsp.	butter	180 ml.
2 tbsp.	flour	30 ml.
1 cup	sour cream	¼ liter
1 cup	heavy cream	¼ liter
½ tsp.	grated nutmeg	2 ml.
	salt and pepper	
¼ cup	chopped fresh parsley	50 ml.
¼ cup	fresh white bread crumbs	50 ml.

Place the sliced mushrooms and chopped onion in a heavy skillet without any fat. Cover the skillet and allow the vegetables to steam in their own juices over medium heat for about 15 to 20 minutes, until they almost stick to the pan. Add 8 tablespoons [120 ml.] of butter. When the butter has melted, stir in the flour. Cook, stirring, for 5 minutes over very low heat. Blend in the sour cream and the heavy cream. Season with nutmeg, salt and pepper. Continue to cook, uncovered, until the mixture thickens. Stir in the parsley.

Pour the mixture into a buttered, shallow casserole. Sauté the bread crumbs in the remaining butter until lightly colored and sprinkle them on top. Bake in a moderate oven, preheated to 350° F. [180° C.], until the mixture has set and the bread crumbs have browned a little more.

PAULA PECK
PAULA PECK'S ART OF GOOD COOKING

Baked Mushrooms and Pine Nuts

Funghi Arrosto con Pignoli

To serve 4 to 6

2 lb.	extra-large mushrooms, stems removed	1 kg.
1	lemon, halved	1
2 tbsp.	olive oil	30 ml.
2	garlic cloves, very finely chopped	2
¼ to ⅓ cup	pine nuts	50 to 75 ml.
	freshly ground sea salt and black pepper	

Rub the outside skins of the mushroom caps with the lemon. Place the mushroom caps, insides facing upward, in an oiled, shallow baking pan. Sprinkle with the garlic and pine nuts and season with sea salt and pepper to taste. Bake in an oven, preheated to 400° F. [200° C.], for 10 minutes. Remove the pan and place it under a hot broiler for 2 minutes. Serve.

ANNA MUFFOLETTO
THE ART OF SICILIAN COOKING

Baked Mushrooms

Champignons au Four

To serve 3 or 4

1 lb.	small mushrooms	½ kg.
¼ lb.	salt pork with the rind removed, diced, blanched in boiling water for 5 minutes and drained	125 g.
2 tbsp.	butter	30 ml.
2 tbsp.	chopped fresh parsley	30 ml.
6 to 8	whole scallions, including 2 inches [5 cm.] of the green tops	6 to 8
	salt and pepper	
	grated nutmeg	
6 to 8	sprigs parsley, main stems removed	6 to 8
2 to 3 tbsp.	oil	30 to 45 ml.

Mix the mushrooms, salt pork, butter, chopped parsley, scallions and seasonings together, and put the mixture into an ovenproof earthenware dish. Cook uncovered in a moderate oven, preheated to 350° F. [180° C.], for 30 to 40 minutes, or until the salt pork and scallions are lightly browned. Just before serving, fry the parsley sprigs in the oil and use them to garnish the dish.

BUC'HOZ
MANUEL ALIMENTAIRE DES PLANTES

Vegetable Fruits

Fried Cucumbers

To serve 4 or 5

2	6- to 7-inch [15- to 18-cm.] cucumbers	2
2	eggs, beaten	2
	salt and pepper	
1 cup	bread crumbs	¼ liter
	fat for frying	

Peel and slice the cucumbers into rounds ¼ inch [6 mm.] thick, and let the slices soak in salted water for 20 minutes. Drain the cucumbers and squeeze them dry; dip each cucumber slice into the beaten egg seasoned with salt and pepper, then into the bread crumbs. In a large skillet, heat the fat, and fry the coated slices in it until they are golden. Serve them immediately on a warmed platter.

MRS. W. H. WILSON AND MISS MOLLIE HUGGINS
GOOD THINGS TO EAT

Creamed Cucumbers

Concombres à la Poulette

To serve 4

2	large cucumbers (12 inches [30 cm.] long, or 4 or 5 medium-sized), peeled, quartered lengthwise, and seeded	2
	salt	
4 tbsp.	butter	60 ml.
	pepper	
1 cup	light cream	¼ liter
3	egg yolks, lightly beaten	3
1 tsp.	wine vinegar	5 ml.

Cut the cucumber quarters into finger-length pieces. Blanch them in lightly salted boiling water for 2 or 3 minutes. Drain. In a saucepan, melt the butter, add the cucumber pieces and sauté them over medium heat for 5 minutes. Season with salt and pepper. Stir in the cream and simmer uncovered to allow it to reduce slightly. Just before serving, mix the egg yolks with the vinegar. Stir in a spoonful of the hot sauce, and then add the yolk mixture to the cucumbers. Reheat without boiling to thicken the sauce slightly.

JULES BRETEUIL
LE CUISINIER EUROPÉEN

Stewed Cucumbers with Sour Cream and Dill

Schmorgurken mit Saurem Rahm und Dill

To serve 6

6	medium-sized cucumbers (about 3 lb. [1½ kg.]), peeled, halved lengthwise, seeded and cut into 1-inch [2½-cm.] pieces	6
2 tsp.	salt	10 ml.
2 tbsp.	butter	30 ml.
½ cup	finely chopped onions	125 ml.
2 tbsp.	flour	30 ml.
2 cups	milk	½ liter
2 tbsp.	sour cream	30 ml.
1 tbsp.	finely chopped fresh parsley	15 ml.
1 tbsp.	finely chopped fresh dill (or substitute 1 tsp. [5 ml.] dried dill weed)	15 ml.
	pepper	

Place the cucumbers in a large bowl and sprinkle them with salt, tossing them with a spoon to spread the salt evenly. Let the cucumbers stand at room temperature for 30 minutes, then drain off the liquid and pat them dry with paper towels.

In a heavy 10- to 12-inch [25- to 30-cm.] skillet, melt the butter over moderate heat. Add the onions and cook, stirring frequently, for 8 to 10 minutes, or until it colors slightly. Add the flour and cook, stirring constantly, until the flour turns golden brown. Watch for any sign of burning and regulate the heat accordingly. Pour in the milk and, stirring constantly, bring to a boil. Reduce the heat to low and simmer for 1 or 2 minutes, until the mixture thickens slightly. Add the cucumbers and simmer, uncovered, for 15 minutes. When the cucumbers are tender but still slightly firm, add the sour cream, parsley and dill. Taste for seasoning. Serve in a warmed bowl.

FOODS OF THE WORLD/THE COOKING OF GERMANY

Stuffed Cucumbers

Gefüllte Gurken

To serve 2

2	medium-sized cucumbers, peeled, halved lengthwise and seeded	2
2 tbsp.	butter	30 ml.
4	slices bacon	4
½ cup	dry white wine (optional)	125 ml.
Beef and bread-crumb stuffing		
10 oz.	ground beef	350 g.
3 tbsp.	fresh bread crumbs, soaked in a little milk	45 ml.
1	egg	1
1	medium-sized onion, chopped	1
3 tbsp.	chopped fresh parsley	45 ml.
	salt and white pepper	

Make the stuffing by mixing together the ground beef, bread crumbs, egg, onion, parsley and seasoning. Fill each of the cucumber halves with this mixture, then put the halves together again and tie them with cotton thread so they resemble whole cucumbers.

Butter a baking dish and put the cucumbers into it. Cover each cucumber with two slices of bacon. Cook in a moderate oven, preheated to 350° F. [180° C.], for 30 minutes or until the cucumbers are tender and translucent. If, after 15 minutes, the cucumbers are already browned, pour the wine over them and cover the dish with a lid or with foil. Serve the stuffed cucumbers with a potato purée.

GRETE WILLINSKY
KOCHBUCH DER BÜCHERGILDE

Eggplant Purée

Kahrmus

To serve 4

2 to 2½ lb.	eggplant, peeled, sliced 1 inch [2½ cm.] thick and cut into 1-inch cubes (about 3 cups [¾ liter])	1 kg.
¼ cup	olive oil	50 ml.
2	garlic cloves, finely chopped	2
½ tsp.	salt	2 ml.
½ tsp.	black pepper	2 ml.
1 tsp.	Hungarian paprika	5 ml.

Steam the eggplant cubes in a colander over boiling water for 30 minutes. Heat the oil in a wide saucepan and add the eggplant along with the remaining ingredients. Stir constantly over medium heat for 10 minutes, or until the eggplant becomes a purée. Serve hot, immediately.

IRENE DAY
THE MOROCCAN COOKBOOK

Fried Eggplant

Melanzane Fritte

To serve 2

1	medium-sized eggplant, peeled and cut crosswise into ½-inch [1-cm.] slices	1
	flour	
1	egg, lightly beaten	1
½ to ¾ cup	olive oil	125 to 175 ml.

Dredge the eggplant slices with flour and dip them in the beaten egg. Heat the oil in a large skillet and fry the eggplant slices slowly over medium heat until they are golden brown (about 5 to 6 minutes each side).

BERYL GOULD-MARKS
THE HOME BOOK OF ITALIAN COOKERY

Eggplant Fans

Aubergines en Eventail

The technique for assembling eggplant fans is demonstrated on pages 80-81. The method for paring artichoke hearts is demonstrated on page 25.

To serve 6

3	medium-sized eggplants (about 1 to 1¼ lb. [½ to ⅔ kg.] each), ends trimmed	3
2	large, firm tomatoes (about 1 lb. [½ kg.]), halved lengthwise, cored and thinly sliced	2
⅓ to ½ cup	olive oil	75 to 125 ml.
1	large onion, finely chopped	1
4	garlic cloves, thinly sliced	4
4	tender artichokes	4
½ cup	small pitted black olives, rinsed	125 ml.
2	bay leaves, crumbled	2
1 tsp.	mixed dried thyme, oregano and savory	5 ml.
	salt and pepper	
	fresh parsley or basil leaves (optional)	

Split the eggplants lengthwise. Place the halves, split side down, on a chopping board, and cut each half lengthwise into ½-inch [1-cm.] thicknesses, leaving the slices attached at the stem end to form fans. Slip tomato slices into the slits of the eggplant halves. Oil a large gratin dish with 2 tablespoons [30 ml.] of the olive oil, and scatter half the onion and garlic over the bottom. Arrange the eggplant halves, gently forced together, side by side in the dish.

Pour the remaining olive oil into a bowl. Pare the artichokes to the hearts and quarter them, removing the chokes; place the hearts immediately in the oil, turning them around to coat them completely and protect them from contact with air. Force the quartered artichoke hearts and the olives into the crevices around the eggplant fans. Fit in the bay leaf fragments here and there, scatter the remaining onion and garlic over the surface, and sprinkle with the herbs, salt and pepper. Press everything into place to form as regular a surface as possible. Dribble the oil left over from the artichokes over the entire surface, adding a bit more if necessary. Place a sheet of aluminum foil loosely over the surface and bake for about 1½ hours, starting with a very hot oven, preheated to 450° F. [230° C.], and turning the heat down to about 350° F. [180° C.] after 10 minutes or so.

When done, the stem ends of the eggplants should be soft to the touch. Serve as an hors d'oeuvre, either tepid or cold (but not chilled), sprinkled, if you like, with chopped parsley or fresh basil leaves torn into small fragments.

RICHARD OLNEY
SIMPLE FRENCH FOOD

Roasted Eggplant

Aubergines en Gigot

This is a recipe from the Catalan Coast of France.

To serve 4

4	small eggplants (about 10 oz. [¼ to ⅓ kg.] each)	4
4	slices bacon, cut into small pieces	4
12	garlic cloves	12
	salt and pepper	
	marjoram or basil	
¼ cup	olive oil	50 ml.

In each whole, unpeeled eggplant, make two lengthwise rows of small incisions about ½ inch [1 cm.] apart; into these put, alternately, small pieces of bacon and garlic cloves that have been rolled in salt, pepper and herbs—either marjoram or basil. Put the eggplants in an earthenware casserole with a little oil poured over them. Cover the casserole and roast the eggplants in an oven, preheated to 300° F. [150° C.], for about 1 hour.

These should be served as a separate course. They are also very good cold, split open, salted, and with a little fresh oil poured over.

ELIZABETH DAVID
FRENCH COUNTRY COOKING

Eggplant and Tomato Gratin

Bohémienne

The ratatouille Niçoise has become internationally famous but, in the rest of Provence, the Bohémienne—using equal quantities of eggplants and tomatoes—is preferred.

To serve 6 to 8

3	large eggplants (about 3 lb. [1½ kg.]), peeled and cut into small pieces	3
9	medium-sized tomatoes (about 3 lb. [1½ kg.]), peeled, seeded and cut into small pieces	9
½ cup	olive oil	125 ml.
1	garlic clove, crushed	1
2	anchovy fillets	2
1 tbsp.	flour	15 ml.
½ cup	milk	125 ml.
	salt and pepper	
¼ cup	fresh bread crumbs	50 ml.

Heat 4 tablespoons [60 ml.] of the oil in a large sauté pan, add the eggplant, tomatoes and garlic, and cook, uncovered, over medium heat until the mixture has softened and can be crushed with a fork.

Meanwhile, soften the anchovy fillets in 3 tablespoons [45 ml.] of the oil, in a small saucepan standing in boiling water or set over very low heat. When the fillets have melted in the oil, add them to the vegetables. Blend the flour with the milk and stir into the vegetables. Season with salt and pepper, bearing in mind that the anchovies are quite salty. Mix everything together well and turn into an oiled gratin dish. Sprinkle on the bread crumbs and the remaining oil. Bake in an oven, preheated to 375° F. [190° C.], for 20 to 30 minutes, until a crust has formed on top.

LOUIS GINIÉS
LA CUISINE PROVENÇALE

Eggplant Gratin

To prepare the aromatic pepper and allspice mixture called for in this recipe, combine about 3 parts of freshly ground black pepper with 2 parts of freshly ground white pepper and 1 part of finely pulverized allspice berries. Store the mixture in a tightly closed jar.

To serve 4

1	medium-sized eggplant (about 1½ lb. [¾ kg.]), peeled and cut lengthwise into ½-inch [1-cm.] slices	1
about 1 cup	olive oil	about ¼ liter
1	medium-sized onion, finely chopped	1
1	garlic clove, finely chopped	1
3	medium-sized tomatoes (about 1 lb. [½ kg.]), peeled, seeded and coarsely chopped	3
	sugar	
	cayenne pepper	
	salt	
½ cup	brousse or ricotta cheese	125 ml.
1	egg	1
⅓ cup	freshly grated Parmesan cheese	75 ml.
½ cup	heavy cream	125 ml.
	freshly ground mixed pepper and allspice	
2 to 3 tbsp.	torn-up basil leaves	30 to 45 ml.

In a large skillet, fry the eggplant slices in olive oil over medium heat until they are golden on both sides and the stem ends, which take longer to cook than the remainder of the eggplant, offer no resistance to the point of a knife. The frying will have to be done in several batches, with more oil being added as needed. As each slice is ready, remove it and put it to drain on paper towels.

In a small skillet, cook the chopped onion and garlic in 1 tablespoon [15 ml.] of olive oil over medium heat until they have softened and become golden. Add the tomatoes; season with a pinch of sugar, cayenne pepper to taste, and salt. Toss briefly over high heat, then lower the heat and simmer, uncovered, for 15 to 20 minutes, or until nearly all of the tomato liquid has disappeared.

Meanwhile, put the *brousse* or ricotta into a bowl with the egg and blend with a fork until smooth. Mix in enough grated Parmesan to form a stiff paste, then gradually add heavy cream until the mixture has a thick pouring consistency. Taste for salt.

Arrange half the eggplant slices in the bottom of a gratin dish, salt lightly, and add a few pinches of the mixed pepper and allspice. Spread the sautéed tomato mixture over the eggplant slices, sprinkle with the basil and season with the pepper mixture. Make another layer with the remaining eggplant slices, season lightly with salt and the pepper mixture, and pour on the cheese-and-cream mixture. Sprinkle the remaining Parmesan over the top and bake in a very hot oven, preheated to 450° F. [230° C.], for 10 minutes, then reduce the heat to 375° F. [190° C.] and bake for a further 20 minutes, or until the surface has swelled to a golden-brown dome that is firm to the touch at the center.

NATHAN D'AULNAY
PETITS PROPOS CULINAIRES

Breaded Eggplant Sandwiches

Fette di Melanzane Ripiene

The mortadella called for in this recipe is a mild-flavored sausage, similar to bologna, obtainable wherever Italian foods are sold.

	To serve 4 to 6	
1	large eggplant (about 2 lb. [1 kg.]), unpeeled but cut crosswise into ½-inch [1-cm.] slices	1
	salt	
1½ cups	dry bread crumbs	375 ml.
⅓ cup	freshly grated Parmesan cheese	75 ml.
⅓ cup	chopped fresh parsley	75 ml.
½ lb.	mortadella, thinly sliced	¼ kg.
½ lb.	provolone cheese, thinly sliced	¼ kg.
2	eggs, slightly beaten	2
¼ cup	olive oil	50 ml.

Place the eggplant slices in a bowl, salting each layer of slices liberally. Weight them down with a heavy plate and leave them for 1 hour to draw out their excess moisture.

Rinse off the salt and dry the slices with paper towels. Set aside. Preheat the oven to 350° F. [180° C.].

Combine the bread crumbs, Parmesan cheese, ¼ teaspoon [1 ml.] of salt and the parsley. Set aside.

Sandwich one or two slices of mortadella and one slice of provolone between each pair of eggplant slices. Dip these eggplant sandwiches into the beaten eggs, then into the bread-crumb mixture.

Pour the olive oil into a large, shallow baking pan; heat it in the oven for 5 minutes. Place the eggplant sandwiches in the pan and bake for 15 minutes on each side. Serve hot or at room temperature.

ANNA MUFFOLETTO
THE ART OF SICILIAN COOKING

Eggplant with Yogurt Stuffing

Aubergines Farcies

	To serve 2	
2	large eggplants	2
4 tbsp.	chopped scallions, including 2 inches [5 cm.] of the green tops	60 ml.
½ cup	sliced fresh mushrooms	125 ml.
¼ cup	grated carrots	50 ml.
5 tbsp.	butter	75 ml.
3 tbsp.	flour	45 ml.
1 cup	unflavored yogurt	¼ liter
	salt and pepper	
¾ cup	bread crumbs, fried in 3 tbsp. [45 ml.] butter	175 ml.

Cut off a thick, lengthwise slice from each eggplant. Cook the eggplant in boiling salted water for about 15 minutes, or until tender. Remove the eggplant pulp, leaving the shells about ¼ inch [6 mm.] thick. Chop the pulp and set it aside; reserve the shells.

Sauté the scallions, mushrooms and carrots in the butter for 4 to 5 minutes. Blend in the flour and the yogurt, stirring continuously until the mixture boils. Add the eggplant pulp and season the mixture with salt and pepper. Do not boil again. Fill the eggplant shells with the mixture, and top them with the bread crumbs. Put the shells in an oiled baking dish and bake them, uncovered, for 25 minutes in a moderate oven, preheated to 350° F. [180° C.]. Serve very hot.

IRFAN ORGA
COOKING WITH YOGURT

Okra Pudding, Barbados-Style

Coo-coo

To serve 6

12	small young okra, trimmed and cut crosswise into ¼-inch [6-mm.] slices	12
1½ quarts	water	1½ liters
	salt	
2 cups	yellow cornmeal	½ liter
3 tbsp.	unsalted butter	45 ml.

Bring the water to a boil in a saucepan. Add the salt and okra. Cook, covered, for 10 minutes. Then add the cornmeal to the water and okra, pouring it in a slow, steady stream and stirring constantly with a wooden spoon. Cook, still stirring constantly, over medium heat for about 5 to 8 minutes, or until the mixture is very thick and smooth.

To mold the mixture, pour it into a buttered 1½-quart [1½-liter] heatproof bowl. Pat the mixture down into the bowl, let it stand a minute or two, then turn it onto a warmed serving platter and spread the butter on top of it. Alternatively, the mixture may be turned directly onto a warmed platter without molding. Serve hot.

ELISABETH LAMBERT ORTIZ
THE COMPLETE BOOK OF CARIBBEAN COOKING

Italian Peppers and Onions

To serve 4

8	Italian peppers, seeded, deribbed, and cut lengthwise into thin strips	8
3 tbsp.	olive oil	45 ml.
1	medium-sized onion, thinly sliced	1
1	garlic clove, crushed	1
½ tsp.	salt	2 ml.
	pepper	

Heat the oil in a large, heavy skillet over moderate heat. Add the peppers, onion and garlic, and stir fry for 8 minutes until the onion is golden. Cover, turn the heat to low and simmer for 5 minutes, shaking the pan occasionally. Uncover the skillet and cook the mixture, stirring for 1 to 2 minutes to drive off excess moisture. Add the salt and a pinch of pepper, and serve. This is especially good with veal or chicken.

JEAN ANDERSON AND ELAINE HANNA
THE DOUBLEDAY COOKBOOK

Jarvis Stuffed Peppers

To serve 6

6	green peppers	6
2	medium-sized tomatoes	2
	salt and pepper	
½ cup	hot cooked rice	125 ml.
1	calf's sweetbread, parboiled for 5 minutes, trimmed and finely diced	1
⅛ tsp.	paprika	½ ml.
¼ cup	bread crumbs, mixed with 2 tbsp. [30 ml.] softened butter	50 ml.
6	slices firm white bread, cut into circles the diameter of the peppers and sautéed in butter	6

Littleton sauce		
1 tsp.	flour	5 ml.
1 tsp.	prepared mustard	5 ml.
1 tbsp.	butter, melted	15 ml.
1 tbsp.	vinegar	15 ml.
½ cup	boiling water	125 ml.
3	egg yolks, beaten	3
¼ tsp.	salt	1 ml.
⅛ tsp.	pepper	½ ml.
⅛ tsp.	cayenne pepper	½ ml.
1 tbsp.	red currant jelly	15 ml.

Cut a slice from the stem end of each pepper, then remove the seeds and parboil the peppers for 3 minutes in boiling water; remove and drain.

Bring the tomatoes to the boiling point and let them simmer for 20 minutes. Rub them through a sieve and continue simmering until you have about ½ cup [125 ml.] of purée. Season with salt and pepper, and add the rice. Allow the mixture to stand until the rice has absorbed the tomato; then add the sweetbread. Season with the paprika.

Fill the peppers with the mixture, arrange them in a casserole with 2 to 3 tablespoons [30 to 45 ml.] of water in the bottom. Sprinkle the tops with the bread crumbs and bake in an oven, preheated to 350° F. [180° C.], for 30 to 40 minutes, or until the crumbs are brown.

Meanwhile, make the Littleton sauce. Mix the flour and mustard and, when thoroughly blended, add the melted butter, vinegar, boiling water and eggs. Cook in a double boiler, stirring constantly until the mixture thickens. Add the seasonings. Just before serving, add the red currant jelly. To serve, arrange the peppers on the sautéed bread circles and pour the sauce over them.

FANNIE MERRITT FARMER
THE BOSTON COOKING SCHOOL COOKBOOK, 1924 EDITION

Stewed Peppers with Tomatoes

Peperonata

To serve 4 to 6

6 or 7	red, yellow or green peppers (about 2 lb. [1 kg.]), seeded, deribbed and cut into small pieces	6 or 7
½ cup	oil	125 ml.
2	medium-sized onions, diced	2
2 or 3	garlic cloves, thinly sliced	2 or 3
6	small bay leaves	6
	salt and freshly ground pepper	
4	medium-sized tomatoes (about 1 lb. [½ kg.]), peeled, seeded and cut into strips	4

Pour the oil into a skillet, add the onions, garlic and bay leaves. Sauté over moderate heat until the onions are golden, stirring constantly. Add the peppers, then season with salt and pepper. Cook over brisk heat for about 10 minutes, stirring frequently. Add the tomatoes to the skillet and cook for another 15 minutes.

LUIGI CARNACINA AND LUIGI VERONELLI
LA BUONA VERA CUCINA ITALIANA

Fried Green Tomatoes with Cornmeal

For best results, use only stone-ground cornmeal for this recipe. Its texture is floury, so that the meal will adhere more firmly to the tomatoes than will a more granular cornmeal. Firm, ripe tomatoes may also be fried the same way. Soft, ripe tomatoes will be reduced to mush.

To serve 4 to 6

4	medium-sized green tomatoes	4
⅔ cup	yellow or white stone-ground cornmeal	150 ml.
1½ tsp.	salt	7 ml.
½ tsp.	pepper	2 ml.
3 to 4 tbsp.	rendered bacon fat	45 to 60 ml.

Do not peel or core the tomatoes. Slice each about ½ inch [1 cm.] thick, then pat the cut surfaces dry with paper toweling. In a pie plate, combine the cornmeal, salt and pepper. Dredge the tomato slices in the seasoned cornmeal, making sure each slice is well coated.

In a large heavy skillet over moderately high heat, fry the tomatoes quickly in the sizzling-hot bacon fat. You need only brown the slices on each side—1 to 1½ minutes to a side should do it. Serve straight away.

JEAN ANDERSON
THE GRASS ROOTS COOKBOOK

Fried Green Tomatoes with Bacon

To serve 2

2	medium-to-large green (or half-ripe) tomatoes	2
4	thick slices lean bacon	4
1	egg, beaten with 1 tsp. [5 ml.] water	1
	flour	
	salt and pepper	
¼ cup	light cream	50 ml.
2 or 3	scallions, finely chopped	2 or 3

Slowly fry the bacon in a heavy skillet until lightly crisped. Drain the bacon on paper towels and keep it warm. Reserve the fat in the skillet. Slice the tomatoes vertically, from bottom to blossom end (this keeps the seeds in), about ¼ inch [6 mm.] thick. Discard the two outer slices. Dip the slices first in egg, then in flour. Fry over medium heat in the bacon fat, and season with salt and pepper. Turn the slices once so that both sides are golden brown and crisp.

Put the slices on a hot platter, pour off any remaining fat from the skillet, deglaze the pan with the cream and pour the sauce over the tomatoes. Scatter the scallions on top and put the bacon around the tomatoes.

MIRIAM UNGERER
GOOD CHEAP FOOD

Sautéed Cherry Tomatoes

Here is a quick vegetable garnish that looks beautiful on a meat platter.

To serve 6 to 8

1 quart	cherry tomatoes, stems removed	1 liter
4 tbsp.	butter	60 ml.
½ tsp.	sugar	2 ml.
½ tsp.	salt	2 ml.
¼ tsp.	freshly cracked black pepper	1 ml.
2 tbsp.	chopped fresh parsley	30 ml.

Heat the butter in a large sauté pan. When the butter is foaming, add the tomatoes. Toss them over high heat, shaking the pan back and forth for about 3 minutes and sprinkling the tomatoes with the sugar (this gives them a shiny glaze). Do not overcook, or the skins will split and the tomatoes will be too soft. Season with salt and pepper, and garnish with chopped parsley.

JULIE DANNENBAUM
JULIE DANNENBAUM'S CREATIVE COOKING SCHOOL

Fried Tomatoes

Tomates Frites

Use only the firmest ripe tomatoes—or underripe ones.

	To serve 6 to 8	
8	medium-sized, very firm tomatoes (about 2 lb. [1 kg.])	8
	salt and pepper	
	batter for deep frying (recipe, page 167)	
	oil for deep frying	

Immerse the tomatoes in boiling water for a second, then peel them. Cut them in slices about ½ inch [1 cm.] thick and remove the seeds. Season the slices with salt and pepper; dip each slice, one after another, into the batter and plunge it into very hot oil until golden, about 2 to 3 minutes. Drain on paper towels. Arrange on a warmed platter and serve.

AUGUSTE ESCOFFIER
MA CUISINE

Stuffed Tomatoes, Calabria-Style

Pomodori Ripieni alla Calabrese

	To serve 4	
8	firm tomatoes	8
	salt	
4	thin slices stale French or Italian bread	4
2	garlic cloves, crushed	2
⅓ cup	olive oil	75 ml.
8	anchovy fillets, soaked in cold water for 10 minutes, patted dry and finely chopped	8
¼ cup	pine nuts	50 ml.
2 tbsp.	yellow raisins, soaked in warm water for 10 to 15 minutes and drained	30 ml.
2 tbsp.	chopped fresh parsley	30 ml.
	freshly ground black pepper	

Preheat the oven to 375° F. [190° C.]. Cut a slice off the top of each tomato, scoop out and discard the pulp and seeds. Reserve the top slices. Sprinkle the interior of the shells with salt and set them upside down to drain. Rub the bread slices with garlic and cut them into ¼-inch [6-mm.] cubes. Brown the cubes lightly in the oil and drain them on paper towels.

In a bowl, mix the anchovies with the bread cubes, nuts, raisins and parsley. Season the mixture with pepper and very little salt. Stuff the tomatoes with the mixture, cover them with their tops, arrange in an oiled, shallow baking dish and bake in the oven for 20 to 25 minutes. Serve hot.

PAULA WOLFERT
MEDITERRANEAN COOKING

Tomatoes Baked with Garlic

Tomates à la Provençale

	To serve 4	
8	tomatoes	8
1½ cups	fresh bread crumbs	375 ml.
6 tbsp.	chopped fresh parsley	90 ml.
4	garlic cloves, roughly chopped	4
	salt and pepper	
⅓ cup	olive oil	75 ml.

Remove the hard cores from the tomatoes with the tip of a knife and cut the top off each tomato. Scoop out the seeds and juice, and arrange the tomatoes in a shallow baking dish.

Mix the bread crumbs with the parsley, garlic and seasonings, then stuff the tomatoes loosely with this mixture.

Sprinkle with the olive oil, then cook in an oven, preheated to 400° F. [200° C.], for 15 to 20 minutes, or until the tops are golden brown.

H. HEYRAUD
LA CUISINE À NICE

Scalloped Tomatoes

Brown Tom

	To serve 4	
3 or 4	medium-sized tomatoes (about 1 lb. [½ kg.]), peeled and sliced	3 or 4
2	slices lean bacon, preferably Canadian bacon	2
1	large onion, chopped	1
1 tbsp.	chopped fresh parsley	15 ml.
½ tsp.	dried basil (or substitute 2 tsp. [10 ml.] chopped fresh basil)	2 ml.
1½ cups	fresh whole-grain bread crumbs	375 ml.
	salt and freshly ground pepper	
½ tsp.	sugar (optional)	2 ml.
3 tbsp.	butter	45 ml.

Mince together the bacon and onion, and mix with the parsley, basil and bread crumbs. Put a layer of this mixture into a lightly buttered, shallow ovenproof dish, and add a layer of the tomatoes. Season with the salt, pepper, and the sugar, if you like. Layer again, finishing with crumbs, and dot the top layer with the remaining butter. Bake in an oven, preheated to 400° F. [200° C.], for about 30 minutes, or until well browned and bubbling.

MARGARET COSTA
MARGARET COSTA'S FOUR SEASONS COOKERY BOOK

Baked Tomatoes with Soubise

Soubise is a purée of onion and rice, normally used as an accompaniment to meat.

To serve 6 to 8

6 to 8	medium-sized tomatoes, sliced ½ inch [1 cm.] thick	6 to 8
1 tsp.	salt	5 ml.
½ tsp.	freshly ground black pepper	2 ml.
¼ cup	freshly grated Parmesan cheese	50 ml.
	Soubise filling	
4 tbsp.	butter	60 ml.
4 cups	chopped onions	1 liter
6 tbsp.	raw unprocessed rice	90 ml.
⅔ cup	chicken stock	150 ml.
¼ cup	heavy cream	50 ml.
2	egg yolks	2
1 tbsp.	fresh lemon juice	15 ml.
1 tsp.	salt	5 ml.
½ tsp.	pepper	2 ml.

First make the soubise filling. Melt the butter in a heavy ovenproof saucepan. Stir in the onions and rice, and cook for a minute over high heat, stirring to coat them well with the butter. Add the chicken stock and bring the mixture to a boil. Cover the pan tightly and set it in a moderately slow oven preheated to 325° F. [160° C.]. Look at the mixture in 20 minutes; if it is dry, add a little hot chicken stock. Continue cooking for about 20 minutes longer, or until the onions and rice are tender. Purée the mixture through a food mill and stir in the cream, egg yolks and lemon juice. Add more cream if necessary; the sauce should fall lazily from a spoon. Season with salt and pepper to taste.

Sprinkle the tomato slices with salt and pepper, and lay them on an oiled baking sheet. Put 1 tablespoon [15 ml.] of the soubise filling on each tomato slice and top with about a teaspoon [5 ml.] of Parmesan cheese. (The recipe may be prepared ahead to this point.) Bake in an oven, preheated to 350° F. [180° C.], for about 15 to 20 minutes, or at 425° F. [220° C.] for about 10 minutes, until the tops are bubbly.

JULIE DANNENBAUM
MENUS FOR ALL OCCASIONS

Tomatoes Stuffed with Potato Purée

To serve 6

3	medium-sized tomatoes	3
1 tbsp.	finely chopped fresh parsley	15 ml.
	Potato purée	
6	medium-sized potatoes (about 2 lb. [1 kg.])	6
1 tbsp.	unsalted butter	15 ml.
1 cup	milk, heated to lukewarm	¼ liter
	salt and pepper	

To prepare the purée, first boil the potatoes in salted water until tender. Drain. Force the potatoes through a sieve or food mill. Beat in the butter and gradually add the hot milk. Whip the potatoes until light, then season with the salt and pepper. (I find a wire whisk produces the best results.)

Preheat the oven to 350° F. [180° C.]. Halve the tomatoes crosswise and, with a spoon, scoop out the centers, being careful not to break the skins. Discard the pulp.

Using a pastry bag fitted with a large star tube, fill the tomato halves with purée, mounding the purée. Bake the tomatoes for approximately 20 minutes, or until the halves are tender and the purée is browned. Sprinkle the tomatoes with the parsley before serving.

MAURICE MOORE-BETTY
COOKING FOR OCCASIONS

Squashes

Squash Puff

To serve 6

3 cups	puréed cooked acorn squash	¾ liter
½ cup	molasses	125 ml.
3 tbsp.	whole-wheat flour	45 ml.
1 tsp.	salt	5 ml.
¼ tsp.	grated nutmeg	1 ml.
¼ tsp.	ground ginger	1 ml.
3	eggs, yolks separated from whites	3
¼ cup	finely chopped pecans or walnuts	50 ml.

Preheat the oven to 350° F. [180° C.]. In a large bowl, blend together the squash, molasses, flour, salt, nutmeg, ginger and egg yolks. Beat the egg whites until stiff, but not dry. Fold the whites into the squash mixture. Turn the mixture into an oiled 1½-quart [1½-liter] baking dish. Sprinkle the nuts around the outside edge, and bake the mixture for 1 hour, or until golden and crusty.

JEAN HEWITT
THE NEW YORK TIMES NATURAL FOODS COOKBOOK

Baked Butternut Squash

To serve 4

1	large butternut squash (about 1 lb. [½ kg.])	1
	salt	
	freshly ground pepper	
2 tsp.	anise seed, crushed	10 ml.
⅛ tsp.	ground cardamom	½ ml.
2 to 3 tbsp.	light or dark brown sugar	30 to 45 ml.
8 tbsp.	butter, melted	120 ml.
2 tbsp.	fresh lemon juice	30 ml.

Peel and cut open the squash. Remove and discard the seeds and the fibers. Cut the squash into 1-inch [2½-cm.] cubes. Turn the squash into a buttered 2-quart [2-liter] baking dish. Sprinkle with the salt and pepper, anise seed, cardamom and brown sugar. Drizzle the butter and lemon juice over the top. Bake the squash, uncovered, in a preheated 350° F. [180° C.] oven for about 30 minutes, or until tender.

NIKA HAZELTON
THE UNABRIDGED VEGETABLE COOKBOOK

Chayotes with Cheese and Onion Stuffing

Christophene au Gratin

This recipe comes from the French West Indian island of Martinique, where boiled chayote is also popular in salads.

To serve 6

3	chayotes (about ¾ lb. [⅓ kg.] each)	3
5 tbsp.	unsalted butter	75 ml.
1	large onion, finely chopped	1
	salt and freshly ground pepper	
1¼ cups	freshly grated Parmesan cheese	⅓ liter

Boil the whole chayotes in salted water for about 30 minutes, or until tender. Remove them from the saucepan and, when they are cool enough to handle, cut them into halves lengthwise. Scoop out the pulp, including the edible seeds, mash the pulp and set it aside. Reserve the shells.

Heat 3 tablespoons [45 ml.] of the butter in a skillet and sauté the onions until they are tender but not browned. Add the mashed chayote pulp, salt and pepper to taste, and cook, stirring, for a few minutes to dry out the mixture a little. Off the heat, add 1 cup [¼ liter] of the cheese, stirring to mix well. Stuff the shells with the mixture, dot with the remaining butter and sprinkle with the extra cheese. Place the chayotes on a baking sheet and bake in an oven, preheated to 350° F. [180° C.], for 15 minutes, or until the tops are lightly browned. Serve as a luncheon or supper dish.

ELISABETH LAMBERT ORTIZ
THE COMPLETE BOOK OF CARIBBEAN COOKING

Stuffed Crookneck Squash

To serve 6

6	medium-sized crooknecks	6
2 tbsp.	butter	30 ml.
½ cup	chopped onion	125 ml.
1½ cups	soft bread crumbs	375 ml.
¼ cup	chopped fresh parsley	50 ml.
¼ cup	freshly grated Parmesan cheese	50 ml.
	salt and freshly ground pepper	
6 tbsp.	butter	90 ml.

Parboil the squash for 5 minutes in salted water. Drain and cool. Melt the butter in a skillet. Sauté the onion over medium heat for 5 to 6 minutes. Meanwhile, cut a lengthwise slice off each squash, removing the top third, and chop the slices finely. Add the chopped slices to the onion. Scoop out the seeds from the squash and discard. Scoop out the flesh, leaving shells ¼ inch [6 mm.] thick. Chop this scooped-out flesh, add it to the onion mixture and cook for 5 to 6 minutes. Add the bread crumbs, parsley, Parmesan cheese, salt and pepper to the onion and squash mixture. Toss well. Pile the mixture into the squash shells, dot with the butter, and bake in a preheated 375° F. [190° C.] oven for about 20 minutes.

BERYL M. MARTON
OUT OF THE GARDEN INTO THE KITCHEN

Scalloped Pattypan

To serve 4

4	medium-sized pattypan squash	4
4 tbsp.	butter	60 ml.
¼ cup	flour	50 ml.
2 cups	milk	½ liter
1 tsp.	salt	5 ml.
	Tabasco	
½ tsp.	dry mustard	2 ml.
½ cup	freshly grated Gruyère cheese mixed with ½ cup bread crumbs	125 ml.

Parboil the squash in boiling salted water until just tender. Drain the squash and cut them into crosswise slices. Melt the butter in a saucepan. Stir in the flour and cook until the roux is golden and bubbly. Pour in the milk and cook until the sauce is thick and smooth. Season it with the salt, Tabasco and mustard. Layer the squash slices and sauce in a buttered baking dish. Sprinkle the top with the cheese and crumbs. Reheat the squash in an oven, preheated to 350° F. [180° C.], for 10 minutes and run under a broiler to brown.

MARJORIE PAGE BLANCHARD
THE HOME GARDENER'S COOKBOOK

Stuffed Pattypan Squash

To serve 6

6	pattypan squash	6
6	slices lean bacon	6
½ cup	finely chopped onions	125 ml.
½ tsp.	salt	2 ml.
½ tsp.	freshly ground pepper	2 ml.
½ tsp.	basil	2 ml.
1 tbsp.	finely chopped fresh parsley	15 ml.
	butter	
½ cup	sauterne	125 ml.

Cut off the tops of the squash and carefully scoop out the centers, leaving a firm shell. Discard the pith and seeds or, if desired, roast the seeds for snacking later on. Coarsely chop the squash flesh. In a skillet, fry the bacon until crisp, then drain and crumble it. Pour off all but about 2 tablespoons [30 ml.] of bacon fat from the skillet, and sauté the onion until soft, stirring often. Add the squash flesh and cook for about 3 minutes, stirring often. Mix in the crumbled bacon, salt, pepper, basil and parsley. Spoon this stuffing into the squash shells, top them rather liberally with butter and arrange them in a shallow greased baking pan. Pour the wine over the stuffed squash, cover the pan with foil and bake in a preheated 350° F. [180° C.] oven until the squash is tender, usually about 30 minutes. Remove the foil for the last 5 minutes or so to allow the topping to brown.

ALEX D. HAWKES
COOKING WITH VEGETABLES

Pumpkin or Squash Gratin

Le Gratin de Courge

To serve 4

2 to 2½ lb.	pumpkin or other winter squash, halved, seeded, peeled, and cut into ½-inch [1-cm.] cubes	1 kg.
¼ cup	flour	50 ml.
⅓ cup	olive oil	75 ml.
7 or 8	garlic cloves, finely chopped	7 or 8
2 tbsp.	finely chopped fresh parsley	30 ml.
	salt and pepper	

Toss the cubes of pumpkin or squash in the flour until they are evenly coated. Generously oil the bottom and sides of an ovenproof earthenware casserole. Fill it with the pumpkin or squash, and scatter the garlic and parsley over it. Season with salt and pepper, and sprinkle the remaining oil over the surface. Cook in an oven, preheated to 325° F. [160° C.], for 2

to 2½ hours or until the top has formed a rich dark crust. (It is not necessary to add any water during cooking, because the squash produces enough liquid of its own.)

RENÉ JOUVEAU
LA CUISINE PROVENÇALE

Pumpkin and Apples

To serve 6

2 lb.	pumpkin, peeled, seeded and cut into 1-inch [2½-cm.] squares	1 kg.
2	medium-sized tart apples, cored, peeled and chopped	2
⅓ cup	sugar	75 ml.
½ cup	water	125 ml.
4 tbsp.	butter	60 ml.
	salt	
⅓ cup	blanched almonds or hazelnuts, toasted in a 300° F. [150° C.] oven for 20 minutes (turning occasionally) and chopped	75 ml.

Cinnamon yogurt sauce

1 cup	unflavored yogurt	¼ liter
	sugar (optional)	
1 tsp.	ground cinnamon	5 ml.

To make the sauce, combine the yogurt and the sugar, if you are using it, in a small bowl. Blend thoroughly. Sprinkle with the cinnamon. Cover and set aside.

Combine the pumpkin and apples in a heavy saucepan. Sprinkle with the sugar, and pour in the water. Dot with the butter, season with a pinch of salt and bring to a boil over high heat. Reduce the heat, cover, and cook gently for about 20 minutes or until the pumpkin is tender, stirring several times and adding more water if needed. Transfer the mixture to a warmed serving dish. Sprinkle with the nuts and serve at once with the cinnamon yogurt sauce.

This is a great accompaniment to roast turkey.

SONIA UVEZIAN
THE BOOK OF YOGURT

Baked Pumpkin and Tomatoes

Gratin de Potiron et Tomates

To serve 4

2 to 2½ lb.	pumpkin, peeled and cut into pieces ½ inch [1 cm.] wide and 3 inches [7½ cm.] long	1 kg.
⅓ cup	olive oil	75 ml.
3	medium-sized tomatoes (about 1 lb. [½ kg.]), sliced crosswise	3
2	garlic cloves, crushed	2
2 tbsp.	chopped fresh parsley	30 ml.
	salt and pepper	
¼ cup	dry bread crumbs	50 ml.
1 tbsp.	butter	15 ml.

Blanch the pumpkin pieces for 5 minutes in boiling salted water, then drain and dry them with a cloth. Heat 3 tablespoons [45 ml.] of the oil in a large skillet, add the pumpkin and fry over low heat until the pieces begin to look transparent. Transfer them to a shallow ovenproof dish.

Add the rest of the oil to the skillet, together with the sliced tomatoes, the garlic and 1 tablespoon [15 ml.] of the parsley. Season with salt and pepper. Fry this mixture until the tomatoes begin to form a purée and some of the moisture has evaporated.

Spread the tomatoes on top of the pumpkin. Mix the rest of the parsley with the bread crumbs and sprinkle over the tomatoes. Dot with the butter and bake for 20 minutes in an oven preheated to 400° F. [200° C.].

ANNE-MARIE PENTON
CUSTOMS AND COOKERY IN THE PÉRIGORD AND QUERCY

Zucchini with Walnuts

To serve 4

6 to 8	small zucchini (about 1 lb. [½ kg.])	6 to 8
4 tbsp.	butter	60 ml.
½ cup	walnuts, coarsely chopped	125 ml.
1 tbsp.	butter	15 ml.
	salt and freshly ground black pepper	

Remove the ends and cut the zucchini into slices 1 inch [2½ cm.] thick. Heat 3 tablespoons [45 ml.] of the butter in a skillet and sauté the zucchini until it just begins to soften.

Meanwhile, brown the walnuts in the remaining butter. Combine the walnuts with the zucchini; season with salt and pepper, and cook until the zucchini is tender.

MARIAN BURROS
PURE AND SIMPLE

Sautéed Summer Squash

To serve 4 to 6

1½ lb.	summer squash (do not peel if tender), thinly sliced	¾ kg.
3 tbsp.	olive oil	45 ml.
2	garlic cloves	2
	salt	
	freshly ground pepper	
1 tbsp.	cider vinegar	15 ml.
¼ cup	finely chopped fresh basil or parsley	50 ml.

Heat the olive oil in a deep skillet. Cook the garlic cloves until they begin to turn golden. Discard the garlic. Add the squash and season it with salt and pepper. Cook the squash over medium heat, stirring with a fork, for 3 to 5 minutes, or until it is tender but still crisp. Stir in the vinegar and the basil, and cook 30 seconds longer.

NIKA HAZELTON
THE UNABRIDGED VEGETABLE COOKBOOK

Zucchini with Cream

Calabacitas con Crema

Chili serranos are tapered, bright green, smooth peppers, 1 to 2 inches long. They are available in cans and can be found in markets that sell Latin American foods.

In Mexico, there are hundreds of ways to cook squash, and every cook has a personal method and concept of seasoning. This dish has an exotic flavor and can be prepared well in advance. It is perhaps even better heated up the next day.

To serve 6

1½ lb.	zucchini, diced	¾ kg.
2	medium-sized tomatoes (about ¾ lb. [⅓ kg.]), peeled, seeded and chopped	2
6	peppercorns	6
4	sprigs coriander	4
2	sprigs mint	2
½ inch	stick cinnamon	1 cm.
4	whole cloves	4
2	whole chili serranos	2
½ cup	light cream	125 ml.
	salt	

Put all the ingredients into a saucepan. Cover the pan with a tightly fitting lid and cook over low heat for about 30 minutes. From time to time stir the mixture and scrape the bottom of the pan to prevent sticking. If the vegetables are drying up too much, add a little water. When cooked, the zucchini should be very soft, the cream completely absorbed and no liquid should remain in the pan. The chilies should remain whole and just flavor the zucchini; the dish should not be spicily hot.

DIANA KENNEDY
THE CUISINES OF MEXICO

Baked Zucchini

Firinda Kabak

	To serve 6 to 8	
6	small zucchini	6
3	eggs	3
5	scallions, white and green parts, chopped	5
½ cup	chopped fresh dill	125 ml.
½ cup	chopped fresh mint	125 ml.
½ cup	chopped fresh parsley	125 ml.
1 cup	freshly grated Gruyère cheese	¼ liter
½ cup	grated feta or ricotta cheese	125 ml.
1½ cups	flour	375 ml.
	salt and pepper	
	cayenne pepper	
4 tbsp.	butter	60 ml.
10	pitted black olives (optional)	10

Preheat the oven to 350° F. [180° C.]. Grate the zucchini coarsely into a large bowl. Add the eggs, scallions, dill, mint, parsley and both cheeses. Mix well. Add the flour, a little at a time, mixing continually. Season to taste with salt, pepper and cayenne pepper.

Grease a 9-inch [23-cm.] square baking dish with 2 tablespoons [30 ml.] of the butter. Pour in the zucchini mixture, spreading it evenly. Decorate with the olives, if you are using them. Dot the top with the rest of the butter.

Bake in the oven for 45 to 55 minutes, or until well browned. Cut into squares, and serve hot or cold.

NESET EREN
THE ART OF TURKISH COOKING

Zucchini Stewed in Butter

Zucchini al Burro

	To serve 4	
2 to 2½ lb.	small zucchini, trimmed but not peeled	1 kg.
¼ cup	water	50 ml.
8 tbsp.	butter	120 ml.
	salt and ground pepper	
2 tbsp.	chopped fresh parsley	30 ml.
2 tsp.	fresh lemon juice	10 ml.

Put the zucchini in a heavy saucepan with the water, butter, salt and pepper. Cover with a lid and place on low heat. Shake the pan frequently until the zucchini are very nearly soft *(al dente)*. Serve in a hot dish, sprinkled with the parsley and lemon juice.

JANET ROSS AND MICHAEL WATERFIELD
LEAVES FROM OUR TUSCAN KITCHEN

Zucchini Mold

	To serve 4	
6 to 7	small zucchini (about 1 lb. [½ kg.]), thinly sliced	6 to 7
1	carrot, finely chopped	1
1	onion, finely chopped	1
¼ cup	finely chopped fresh parsley	50 ml.
3 tbsp.	butter	45 ml.
	salt and pepper	
⅓ cup	freshly grated Parmesan cheese	75 ml.
3	eggs, lightly beaten	3
1 cup	béchamel sauce *(recipe, page 165)*	¼ liter

In a skillet, cook the carrot, onion and parsley in the butter until the onion has browned. Add the zucchini and seasoning, then cook gently for 10 to 15 minutes until the zucchini are tender. Remove the pan from the heat and add the cheese, eggs and béchamel sauce.

Put the mixture into a buttered ovenproof mold and cover the mold with a sheet of wax paper. Place the mold in a large baking pan, pour in enough hot water to reach halfway up the sides of the mold, and cook in a 300° F. [150° C.] oven for 45 minutes. Serve hot.

THE COOK TO A FLORENTINE FAMILY
NOT ONLY SPAGHETTI!

Zucchini Pudding Soufflé

Pudding Soufflé aux Courgettes

To serve 4

5 or 6	small zucchini (about 1 lb. [½ kg.]), coarsely shredded, salted for 30 minutes, rinsed well and squeezed almost dry	5 or 6
4 tbsp.	butter	60 ml.
3	eggs, yolks separated from whites	3
½ cup	freshly grated Parmesan cheese	125 ml.
Thick white sauce		
2 tbsp.	butter	30 ml.
3 tbsp.	flour	45 ml.
¾ cup	milk	175 ml.
	salt and pepper	
Tomato and cream sauce		
½ cup	puréed tomato (or substitute 1½ cups [375 ml.] drained canned tomatoes)	125 ml.
1 cup	heavy cream	¼ liter
	salt and pepper	
⅛ tsp.	cayenne pepper	½ ml.

Heat 2 tablespoons [30 ml.] of the butter in a sauté pan and sauté the zucchini over medium heat for 7 to 8 minutes, tossing often and spreading the mass out again with a wooden spoon, until well dried and lightly colored.

To prepare the thick white sauce, melt the butter in a saucepan, stir in the flour and cook, stirring over low heat for 2 to 5 minutes. Whisk in the milk, raise the heat, and whisk until the sauce comes to a boil. Remove the sauce from the heat as soon as it is stiff. Allow it to cool for a couple of minutes before adding the egg yolks, one at a time, stirring well after each addition. Add salt and pepper to taste and stir in the zucchini. In a bowl, beat the egg whites until they stand in peaks, incorporate about one third of the whites into the zucchini mixture, turning and folding gently with your hands or a spatula to render the mixture more supple. Then carefully fold in the remaining beaten whites. (If you have beaten the egg whites in a large bowl, you may find it easier to add the white sauce mixture to the egg whites. Gently pour the mixture around the sides of the bowl and fold it into the whites with your hands.)

Pour the mixture into a generously buttered, quart [1-liter] ring mold (filling it no more than two-thirds to three-quarters full), smooth the surface with the back of a spoon

and tap the mold lightly against the tabletop to settle the contents. Stand the mold in a bain-marie; that is, place the mold in a large pan, installing it at the entry to the oven, and then pour in enough hot but not boiling water to come two thirds of the way up the sides of the mold. Bake in a moderate oven, preheated to 350° F. [180° C.], for 20 to 25 minutes, or until the surface of the soufflé is firm and springy.

Remove the mold from the bain-marie and leave to cool for 10 minutes or so before unmolding the pudding soufflé onto a large, round, shallow baking dish (a ceramic quiche dish, for instance—something ovenproof and presentable for serving). Turn up the oven to 450° F. [230° C.].

Whisk together the puréed tomato and the cream, season to taste, and pour the sauce slowly and evenly over the unmolded soufflé, masking it entirely (but permitting only as much as is necessary to coat the inner sides of the soufflé to run down into the well). Sprinkle the cheese over the surface and return the soufflé to the oven for 20 minutes, or until the surface is richly colored and the sauce bubbling. Serve on heated plates, spooning the sauce to the side of the soufflé so as not to mask the gratin.

RICHARD OLNEY
SIMPLE FRENCH FOOD

Stalks

Minute Asparagus

To serve 4

2 lb.	asparagus, peeled	1 kg.
	salt	
8 tbsp.	butter	120 ml.
3 tbsp.	soy sauce	45 ml.
1 tbsp.	fresh lemon juice	15 ml.
	freshly ground pepper	

Cut the asparagus into very thin diagonal slices, not more than ¼ inch [6 mm.] thick—thinner if possible. Place the slices in a colander or cooking basket. Pour enough water into a saucepan to cover the colander or cooking basket, add the salt and bring the water to a boil. Heat the butter in a large skillet and have the soy sauce, lemon juice and pepper at hand. When the water boils, dip the asparagus in, bring to a second boil and cook for just 1 full minute. Remove, drain, and toss the asparagus into the skillet with the butter. Add the other ingredients and toss well over medium heat until the butter has browned and the asparagus is crisp and deliciously flavored.

JAMES BEARD
JAMES BEARD'S AMERICAN COOKERY

Asparagus Pie

Tourte d'Asperges

To serve 4

2 to 2½ lb.	asparagus, peeled and tough ends removed	1 kg.
	short-crust or rough puff pastry (recipe, page 167, but double the quantities called for)	
2 tbsp.	butter, melted	30 ml.
	fines herbes	
2 or 3	scallions, white parts only, finely chopped	2 or 3
	salt and pepper	
	grated nutmeg	
½ cup	heavy cream or *crème fraîche*	125 ml.
1	egg yolk	1

Blanch and drain the asparagus. Line an 8-inch [20-cm.] piepan with pastry dough, reserving some dough for the lid. Arrange the asparagus on the pastry. Sprinkle with the butter, fines herbes, scallions, salt, pepper and nutmeg. Cover with the reserved pastry, dampen the edges of the dough and press them together. Crimp the edges and make a 1-inch [2½-cm.] hole in the center of the lid. Bake in an oven, preheated to 400° F. [200° C.], for 30 to 35 minutes. Mix the cream with the egg yolk and pour this mixture through a funnel into the pie. Return the pie to the oven for 5 minutes.

L'ESCOLE PARFAITE DES OFFICIERS DE BOUCHE

Asparagus Gratin

Les Asperges au Gratin

To serve 2

1 lb.	asparagus, trimmed, peeled, and tied together in a bundle	½ kg.
	salt	
8 tbsp.	butter, melted	120 ml.
¼ to ⅓ cup	grated Gruyère cheese	50 to 75 ml.
	pepper	

Cook the asparagus, uncovered, in boiling salted water for about 10 minutes, or until tender. Drain the asparagus on a kitchen towel and remove the tie.

Just before serving, dip each asparagus tip in the melted butter. Place the asparagus in layers in a buttered gratin dish, and sprinkle the grated cheese over the tips of each layer. Season with a little pepper and brown the asparagus under a preheated broiler.

LA MÈRE BESSON
MA CUISINE PROVENÇALE

Fried Asparagus

To serve 4 to 6

2 to 2½ lb.	asparagus, peeled	1 kg.
	batter for deep frying (recipe, page 167)	
	oil for deep frying	
	salt	

Blanch the asparagus in boiling salted water for 2 to 3 minutes. Drain and dry the stalks. Dip the stalks, one by one, into the batter and deep fry in hot oil at 375° F. [190° C.] until the batter is golden and crisp. When done, drain, sprinkle the asparagus with salt and serve hot.

THE BUCKEYE COOKBOOK

Gratin of Asparagus

For instructions on how to cook asparagus, see page 39.

To serve 4 to 6

1 to 2 lb.	asparagus	½ to 1 kg.
4 tbsp.	butter	60 ml.
2 tbsp.	flour	30 ml.
1 cup	milk, heated	¼ liter
¼ cup	heavy cream	50 ml.
2	slices cooked ham, chopped (optional)	2
	salt and pepper	
	grated nutmeg	
4 to 6	eggs, hard-boiled and sliced	4 to 6
¼ cup	freshly grated cheese, preferably Gruyère	50 ml.
1 tbsp.	fresh bread crumbs	15 ml.

Cook and drain the asparagus in the usual way, reserving 1 cup [¼ liter] of the water. In a heavy pan, melt half the butter, stir in the flour and leave to bubble for a moment or two. Add the milk and reserved asparagus water gradually to make a smooth sauce. Simmer for 15 minutes or more, until the sauce is thick. Add the cream, and the ham if you are using it. Season with salt, pepper and nutmeg to taste.

Arrange the asparagus in an oval gratin dish, with the sliced hard-boiled eggs on top. Pour the sauce over the asparagus, leaving a clear ¼ inch [6 mm.] at the top of the dish so that the sauce does not boil over and make a mess. Mix the cheese and bread crumbs, and scatter them on top of the sauce. Melt the remaining butter and dribble it evenly over the top. Put into an oven, preheated to 425° F. [220° C.], for about 20 minutes until the dish is bubbling and brown. (This browning can also be done under the broiler.)

JANE GRIGSON
GOOD THINGS

Natural Asparagus

If the asparagus is young and tender, it need not be peeled.

To serve 4		
1 to 1½ lb.	asparagus, trimmed and peeled	½ to ¾ kg.
	salt and pepper	
3 tbsp.	butter, cut into small bits	45 ml.

Preheat the oven to 300° F. [150° C.].

Place the asparagus in one or two layers in a buttered, shallow baking dish just large enough to hold them. Season with salt and pepper to taste, then dot with butter bits. Cover the dish tightly and bake in the oven for 30 minutes. The asparagus will be crunchy and will not lose their color.

THE JUNIOR LEAGUE OF WINSTON-SALEM, NORTH CAROLINA
WINSTON-SALEM'S HERITAGE OF HOSPITALITY

Baked Celery with Herb Sauce

To serve 6		
2	bunches celery, root ends and leafy tops removed, cut into 2½-inch [6-cm.] lengths	2
2 tsp.	salt	10 ml.
5 tbsp.	butter	75 ml.
½ cup	fresh bread crumbs	125 ml.
Herb sauce		
1½ cups	dry white wine	375 ml.
2 tbsp.	chopped fresh parsley	30 ml.
2 tbsp.	chopped fresh basil	30 ml.
¾ cup	chicken stock	175 ml.
	salt and pepper	

Preheat the oven to 400° F. [200° C.].

To make the herb sauce, first combine the wine, chopped parsley and basil in a small enameled or stainless-steel saucepan and simmer, uncovered, for about 20 minutes. Add the stock, and salt and pepper to taste. Simmer this herb sauce for another 3 minutes.

Meanwhile bring a large quantity of salted water to a boil. Add the celery pieces and cook for about 15 minutes until they are almost tender. Drain at once.

Grease a baking dish with 1 tablespoon [15 ml.] of the butter and place the celery pieces in the dish. Pour the sauce over the celery. Cover the top completely with the bread crumbs and dot with the remaining butter. Bake in the oven for about 30 minutes or until the top is nicely browned. Serve directly from the dish.

CAROL CUTLER
THE SIX-MINUTE SOUFFLÉ AND OTHER CULINARY DELIGHTS

Braised Celery Stalks

Lu Api Broustoulit

To serve 6		
6	medium-sized bunches celery, trimmed to within 6 inches [15 cm.] of the bases	6
2 tbsp.	olive oil	30 ml.
2 oz.	salt pork with the rind removed, blanched in boiling water for 5 minutes, drained and diced	75 g.
1	carrot, thinly sliced	1
1	onion, thinly sliced	1
1	garlic clove, thinly sliced	1
¼	bay leaf	¼
1 cup	beef or veal stock	¼ liter
	salt and pepper	

Blanch the celery in boiling water for 5 minutes. Put the olive oil into a fireproof earthenware pot and add the salt pork, carrot, onion, garlic and piece of bay leaf. When the onion has colored, moisten with the stock, season with salt and pepper, and add the celery.

Cover the pot and cook in an oven, preheated to 325° F. [160° C.], for 40 minutes.

Take the celery out of the pot, cut each bunch lengthwise into halves or quarters, depending on how thick it is. Arrange the celery on a dish and pour over the cooking juices.

JACQUES MÉDECIN
LA CUISINE DU COMTÉ DE NICE

Stewed Celery, Michigan-Style

To serve 6		
2	large bunches celery	2
	salt	
3 tbsp.	butter	45 ml.
6	scallions, trimmed and most of the green parts removed	6
1	small garlic clove, chopped	1
1½ cups	chicken or beef stock	375 ml.
	pepper	

Separate the celery ribs, then remove the tops. Wash the ribs thoroughly and cut them into 3-inch [8-cm.] lengths. Throw the celery into boiling salted water and cook, uncovered, for

3 minutes. Drain. Bring the stock to a boil. Melt the butter in a saucepan, and add the scallions, garlic and celery. Pour in the stock and cook, covered, over low heat until the vegetables are quite tender (about 30 minutes), adding more stock, if necessary. When done, the stock should have cooked away entirely. Season to taste before serving.

SHEILA HIBBEN
AMERICAN REGIONAL COOKERY

Braised Celery with Yogurt

To serve 3

1	small bunch celery (about ¾ lb. [⅓ kg.]), separated into ribs and cut into small pieces	1
2	sprigs parsley	2
1 tsp.	chopped marjoram	5 ml.
1	onion, thinly sliced	1
½ cup	beef stock	125 ml.
¼ cup	unflavored yogurt	50 ml.
	salt and pepper	
½ cup	fresh bread crumbs, mixed with 4 tbsp. [60 ml.] melted butter	125 ml.

Put the celery, herbs and onion into a well-buttered baking dish. Combine the stock and yogurt, beat well and pour over the vegetables. Season, and sprinkle the top with the bread crumbs. Bake in an oven, preheated to 350° F. [180° C.], for 30 to 35 minutes, or until the celery pieces are tender but not soft. Serve hot.

IRFAN ORGA
COOKING WITH YOGURT

Celery Amandine

A distinctive yet subtle combination of flavors, this dish is excellent with roast poultry or fried fish.

To serve 4

2	medium-sized bunches celery (about 1¼ lb. [⅔ kg.]), trimmed	2
4 tbsp.	butter	60 ml.
½ cup	slivered, blanched almonds	125 ml.
2	shallots, finely chopped	2
	salt and freshly ground black pepper	
½ cup	light cream	125 ml.

Take apart the bunches of celery and cut the ribs into 1-inch [2½-cm.] pieces, splitting them lengthwise into two or three sections if they are very thick.

Heat the butter in a heavy saucepan with a tight-fitting lid. Add the almonds and sauté them until they are crisp and

a rich golden color, taking care not to let them burn. Lift out the almonds with a slotted spoon and set them aside.

Add the celery and shallots to the pan, mix well with the hot butter, and season generously with salt and pepper. Cover the pan tightly and cook over low heat for 15 minutes, stirring frequently.

Stir in the cream. Replace the lid and continue to cook gently for 20 minutes more, or until the celery is tender and the cream is reduced slightly.

Mix in the sautéed almonds. Correct the seasoning and cook gently over low heat for 5 minutes before serving, to allow the flavors to blend.

GEORGE SEDDON AND HELENA RADECKA
YOUR KITCHEN GARDEN

Celery-Leaf Casserole

Feuilles de Céleris à la Ménagère

To serve 4

1 lb.	small celery ribs with leaves (about 3 cups [¾ liter])	½ kg.
	salt	
4 tbsp.	butter	60 ml.
	pepper	
2	anchovy fillets, soaked in cold water for 10 minutes, patted dry and very finely chopped	2
1 cup	fresh bread crumbs	¼ liter
1 cup	beef, veal or chicken stock, salted water or milk	¼ liter
3	egg yolks, lightly beaten	3
¼ cup	freshly grated Parmesan cheese (optional)	50 ml.

Bring a large pan of salted water to a boil and parboil the celery leaves and ribs for 5 minutes. Drain, squeeze dry, then chop the celery. Melt the butter in a saucepan, add the celery, season lightly with salt and pepper, and stir in the anchovy. Cover and simmer for several minutes over low heat.

Meanwhile, add the bread crumbs to the stock, water or milk and bring to a boil. Drain the crumbs, reserving the liquid. Stir the bread crumbs into the celery mixture, and add enough of the cooking liquid to make a creamy sauce. Simmer a few minutes more to blend and thicken. Stir a few spoonfuls of the sauce into the egg yolks, and—off the heat—stir the egg yolks back into the celery mixture.

The celery can be reheated over low heat, without boiling, and served directly from the pan. Or you can turn it into a buttered gratin dish, sprinkle it with the grated cheese, and brown in a hot oven, preheated to 400° F. [200° C.], or under a broiler.

CHARLES DURAND
LE CUISINIER DURAND

Saffroned Chard Ribs

Côtes de Blettes au Safran

Instructions on how to separate the chard ribs from the leaves appear on page 21. Use the leaves for another dish.

	To serve 2 to 4	
2 to 2½ lb.	chard, leaves and strings removed, ribs cut into strips 1 inch [2½ cm.] wide and 4 inches [10 cm.] long	1 kg.
2 quarts	water	2 liters
1	large onion, thinly sliced	1
2	bay leaves	2
1	large sprig thyme	1
1 tbsp.	wine vinegar	15 ml.
	salt and pepper	
2	anchovy fillets, soaked in cold water for 10 minutes, drained and patted dry	2
2	large garlic cloves	2
1 tbsp.	olive oil	15 ml.
1 tbsp.	flour	15 ml.
3 to 4 tbsp.	chopped fresh parsley	45 to 60 ml.
	cayenne pepper	
¼ tsp.	ground saffron	1 ml.

Bring the water to a boil. Add the onion, bay leaves, thyme, vinegar and a little salt, and cook, covered, at a light boil for 30 minutes. Strain the liquid, discarding the solids. Cook the chard ribs in the liquid, covered, at a light boil for about 12 minutes, or until tender. With a large wire skimming spoon, transfer the chard ribs to an ovenproof gratin dish, reserving the cooking liquid. Grind pepper over the surface.

In a mortar, pound the anchovy fillets and garlic to a paste. Cook the olive oil and the flour together for a minute or two over low heat, stirring. Add the anchovy-garlic paste, the parsley, a pinch of cayenne pepper and the saffron. Stir well together and gradually add about 1½ cups [375 ml.] of the chard cooking liquor, stirring the while to avoid lumping. Continue stirring until a boil is reached. With the pan half off the heat, leave to simmer for 20 minutes—skimming the skin off the surface two or three times. Taste for salt. Pour the sauce evenly over the chard ribs and bake in an oven, preheated to 450° F. [230° C.], for 20 minutes. This dish can be served as the main course of a light supper, accompanied by a rice pilaf.

RICHARD OLNEY
SIMPLE FRENCH FOOD

Chard with Anchovies

Blettes aux Anchois

For this recipe, only the ribs of the chard are used. The leaves can be added to soups or stuffings, or they can be blanched and sautéed in butter.

	To serve 4	
2 to 2½ lb.	chard, stripped of leaves, ribs cut into 1½-inch [4-cm.] pieces	1 kg.
6	garlic cloves, unpeeled	6
	salt	
¼ cup	olive oil	50 ml.
1	onion, very finely chopped	1
12	salted anchovy fillets, soaked in cold water for 10 minutes and patted dry (or substitute 12 oil-packed anchovy fillets, similarly soaked and dried, plus 1½ tbsp. [22 ml.] anchovy paste)	12
¼ cup	finely chopped fresh parsley	50 ml.
	pepper	

Parboil the chard ribs and garlic cloves in salted water for 15 minutes. Drain in a colander. Remove the garlic cloves, squeeze out the pulp from the skins and reserve this purée.

Heat the olive oil in a saucepan or fireproof casserole. Add the onion and soften it without allowing it to color. Add the garlic purée and the anchovy fillets. Stir with a wooden spoon over low heat until the anchovies have disintegrated. Finally, add the chard and simmer for about 15 minutes. Sprinkle with the parsley, season with pepper and continue cooking for 10 minutes. Serve immediately.

HENRI PHILIPPON
CUISINE DE PROVENCE

Fennel Braised in a Skillet

	To serve 4	
6	small fennel bulbs, trimmed and quartered	6
1	garlic clove, sliced	1
2 tbsp.	olive oil	30 ml.
½ tsp.	salt	2 ml.
½ tsp.	pepper	2 ml.
½ cup	stock or water	125 ml.

Place the fennel in a skillet with the garlic, oil and seasoning, and cook over moderate heat for 10 minutes, stirring frequently. Add the stock or water, cover the skillet and cook slowly for 20 minutes, or until tender.

ADA BONI
THE TALISMAN ITALIAN COOK BOOK

Fennel with Tomatoes and Garlic

Finocchi al Forno

To serve 4

4	fennel bulbs, trimmed, halved lengthwise, and cut into julienne	4
½ cup	olive oil	125 ml.
1	onion, thinly sliced	1
2	garlic cloves, chopped	2
2 or 3	medium-sized tomatoes, peeled and coarsely chopped (or substitute 12 oz. [⅓ kg.] canned Italian tomatoes, drained and chopped)	2 or 3
	salt and freshly ground pepper	
Lemony crumb topping		
½ cup	coarse bread crumbs	125 ml.
½ cup	freshly grated Parmesan cheese	125 ml.
1 tsp.	grated lemon peel	5 ml.
1	garlic clove, finely chopped	1

Heat the olive oil in a large skillet and fry the onion and garlic for a minute or two. Add the fennel and continue frying, stirring occasionally with a wooden spoon. When the fennel is beginning to brown and is almost cooked, add the tomatoes and seasoning. Lower the heat and cook gently for 5 minutes. This initial cooking can be done in advance.

Transfer the fennel and tomato mixture to a heavy, shallow gratin dish. Mix the topping ingredients together and sprinkle over the fennel in the gratin dish. Bake in an oven, preheated to 425° F. [220° C.], for about 15 minutes, or until the topping is crisp.

JANET ROSS AND MICHAEL WATERFIELD
LEAVES FROM OUR TUSCAN KITCHEN

The Onion Family

Garlic Roasted in Ashes

Ail Cuit sous la Cendre

This is an excellent way of cooking garlic if you have an open fire or a barbecue. If not, you can wrap whole garlic bulbs in foil and roast them in the oven (page 77).

To serve 4

8 to 12	garlic bulbs	8 to 12

Cover the whole bulbs of garlic with hot wood ashes and incandescent embers. Cook until the outside cloves are superficially charred and the inside cloves thoroughly softened. Serve very hot and eat with bread and butter. For each bite take a clove of garlic and squeeze out its pulp onto the bread like a fragrant cream. The slightly burnt cloves have a different, but equally delicious, taste.

GASTON DERYS
L'ART D'ÊTRE GOURMAND

Leek and Potato Hash

Porrosalda

To serve 4

10 to 12	medium-sized leeks (about 2 lb. [1 kg.]), trimmed, sliced and separated into rings	10 to 12
3	medium-sized potatoes, diced	3
2	slices lean salt pork with the rind removed, blanched in boiling water for 5 minutes, drained and diced	2
1 tbsp.	lard or rendered goose fat	15 ml.
1 tbsp.	flour	15 ml.
¾ cup	water	175 ml.
1	bouquet garni	1
2	garlic cloves, crushed	2
	salt and pepper	

In a large skillet over medium heat, brown the salt pork in the lard or goose fat. Add the leeks and potatoes. Cook, stirring, until they turn golden, about 10 minutes, then sprinkle in the flour. Brown for a few moments, while stirring with a wooden spoon, then moisten with the water. Add the bouquet garni and garlic, then season with salt and pepper. Cover and simmer over low heat for about 30 minutes. At the end of the cooking time, the sauce should be fairly thick.

IRENE LABARRE
LA CUISINE DES TROIS B

Stewed Leeks, Turkish-Style

Prasa Yahnisi

To serve 4

8 to 10	leeks (about 2 lb. [1 kg.]), including 2 inches [5 cm.] of the green leaves, halved crosswise	8 to 10
2	large onions, sliced and separated into rings	2
½ cup	olive oil	125 ml.
1	large tomato, peeled, seeded and chopped	1
	salt and pepper	
1 cup	veal stock	¼ liter
2 tsp.	chopped dill	10 ml.

Fry the onions in the oil over moderate heat until they are soft. Add the leeks; turn them over several times in the oil, then add the tomato. Season the vegetables with salt and pepper, and cover with the stock. Simmer gently for half an hour. Serve hot or cold, with chopped dill sprinkled on top.

VENICE LAMB
THE HOME BOOK OF TURKISH COOKERY

Leeks Deviled

To serve 4 to 6

12	medium-sized leeks (about 2 to 2½ lb. [1 kg.]), trimmed to 1 inch [2½ cm.] above the white part	12
2	sprigs parsley	2
1	sprig chervil	1
1	bay leaf	1
1	sprig thyme	1
1	whole clove	1
1 tbsp.	butter	15 ml.
⅓ cup	dry white wine	75 ml.
½ cup	chicken or veal stock	125 ml.
½ tsp.	salt	2 ml.
½ tsp.	pepper	2 ml.
6	slices firm white bread, toasted	6
1 tbsp.	Dijon-style prepared mustard	15 ml.
3 tbsp.	dry bread crumbs	45 ml.

Place the leeks in a fireproof earthenware or enameled-iron casserole with the herbs, clove and butter. Moisten with the

wine and stock, and season with the salt and pepper. Cover the casserole, boil briskly over high heat for 5 minutes, then cook in an oven, preheated to 350° F. [180° C.], for 30 minutes. With a slotted spoon, lift out the leeks. Split them open lengthwise. Place the slices of toast in a baking dish, arrange the leeks on top of the toast and strain the cooking liquid through dampened muslin or a fine strainer into the baking dish. Spread the mustard over the leeks and sprinkle the bread crumbs on top of them. Bake at 400° F. [200° C.] for 15 minutes and serve.

MAY BYRON
MAY BYRON'S VEGETABLE BOOK

Onions with Cream

Oignons à la Crème

To serve 4

16	small onions, peeled	16
	salt	
½ cup	heavy cream, whipped	125 ml.
2 tbsp.	finely chopped fresh parsley	30 ml.

Soak the onions in cold water for 4 to 5 hours, being careful to change the water several times. Parboil the onions for 15 to 20 minutes in salted water, making sure that they do not disintegrate. Remove the onions, plunge them into cold water, then drain them.

Place the onions side by side in a baking dish, and place in a 250° F. [120° C.] oven to dry for 30 minutes. After removing the dish from the oven, cover each onion with about ½ tablespoon [7 ml.] of cream, then sprinkle the onions with a little salt and chopped parsley. Serve immediately.

CURNONSKY
CUISINE ET VINS DE FRANCE

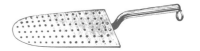

Crisp Onion Rings

To serve 3 or 4

1	large onion, thickly sliced	1
⅔ cup	milk	150 ml.
	flour seasoned with salt and pepper	
	oil or fat for deep frying	

Separate the onion slices into rings. Dip them first in milk, then in seasoned flour. Heat the oil or fat to 375° F. [190° C.] and deep fry the onion rings for about 3 minutes. Drain on paper towels and serve with broiled or fried chops or steaks.

TERENCE CONRAN AND MARIA KROLL
THE VEGETABLE BOOK

Baked Onions

To serve 4

4	large onions, unpeeled	4
	salt and pepper	
	butter pats	

Put the onions in a baking dish with about 1 inch [2 cm.] of water, not more. Bake in a very slow oven, 250° F. [120° C.], for 2 hours, or until the onions are soft when you squeeze them. When they are cooked, pull back the brown skins and cut them off at the roots. Serve the onions with salt and pepper and pats of butter.

THEODORA FITZGIBBON
A TASTE OF IRELAND

Onion Tart with Cheese

To serve 8

4	medium-sized onions, thinly sliced (about 3 cups [¾ liter])	4
1¼ cups	cracker crumbs or crumbled water biscuits	300 ml.
10 tbsp.	butter, softened	150 ml.
¼ cup	flour	50 ml.
1 cup	hot milk	¼ liter
½ cup	hot chicken stock	125 ml.
½ cup	sour cream	125 ml.
1	egg yolk, beaten	1
	salt and pepper	
1 to 1½ cups	freshly grated mild Cheddar cheese	250 to 375 ml.

With your fingers, mix the cracker or water biscuit crumbs with 4 tablespoons [60 ml.] of the butter. Press the mixture into the bottom and sides of a 9-inch [23-cm.] pie plate.

In a heavy-bottomed pan, sauté the onions in 2 tablespoons [30 ml.] of the butter until tender.

In another pan, prepare the sauce by first melting the rest of the butter. Stir in the flour and cook for 1 minute. Take the pan off the heat and stir in the hot milk and chicken stock. Return the pan to the heat and stir the sauce until thickened. Add the sour cream mixed with the egg yolk. Season to taste with salt and pepper.

Mix the sauce with the onions and pour them into the lined pie plate. Spread the cheese over the top of the tart and bake in an oven, preheated to 350° F. [180° C.], for about 25 to 30 minutes or until golden brown.

THE JUNIOR LEAGUE OF DALLAS INC.
THE DALLAS JUNIOR LEAGUE COOKBOOK

Cornish Onion and Apple Pie

To serve 4

4	medium-sized onions (about 1 lb. [½ kg.]), chopped	4
	short-crust pastry (recipe, page 167, but double the quantities called for)	
3 or 4	cooking apples (about 1 lb. [½ kg.]), peeled, cored and thinly sliced	3 or 4
2 tsp.	finely chopped sage	10 ml.
	salt and pepper	
¼ tsp.	mixed spices	1 ml.
3 tbsp.	butter	45 ml.

Line a 7-inch [18-cm.] flan dish or piepan with thinly rolled pastry, and cover the bottom with a layer of apple. Then add a layer of onion. Sprinkle with some of the sage, seasonings and spices. Go on with alternate layers till the top is reached.

Moisten the edge of the pastry; put scraps of butter on top of the onions. Cover with a thin lid of pastry and cut two or three slits in the lid. Bake in an oven, preheated to 375° F. [190° C.], for about 1 hour. Cover the top with aluminum foil if it darkens too much. Serve hot.

DOROTHY HARTLEY
FOOD IN ENGLAND

Onions with Garlic

Oignons à l'Ail

This dish was created in honor of the painter Toulouse-Lautrec, who preferred highly seasoned food. Alfred Edwards, the author of the recipe, relates that Lautrec almost made himself ill with overeating the day he sampled it. The technique for hollowing out onions is shown on page 70.

To serve 4

4	large, firm Spanish onions	4
8	large garlic cloves	8
	salt and pepper	
¼ cup	olive oil	50 ml.
2 tbsp.	butter	30 ml.

Parboil the onions for 30 minutes, adding the garlic for the last 5 minutes. Drain the onions and reserve the garlic.

Hollow out the onions and put the pulp with the garlic, salt, plenty of pepper and the oil into a mortar. Pound these ingredients with a pestle to make a smooth, firm paste, then use it to stuff the onions. Put the onions in a buttered baking dish and bake them in a moderate oven, preheated to 350° F. [180° C.], until they are cooked through and golden, in about 30 to 45 minutes. Serve hot.

GASTON DERYS
L'ART D'ÊTRE GOURMAND

Prince Edward Island Glazed Onions

	To serve 4	
12	small boiling onions, each about 1½ inches [4 cm.] in diameter	12
4 tbsp.	butter	60 ml.
2 tbsp.	honey	30 ml.
½ tsp.	salt	2 ml.

Preheat the oven to 400° F. [200° C.]. Drop the onions into enough boiling water to immerse them and cook briskly, uncovered, for about a minute. Drain the onions in a sieve or colander. With a small, sharp knife, trim the stem ends, slip off the white, parchment-like skins and cut the tops from the onions. Arrange the onions in a baking-serving dish just large enough to hold them in one layer.

In a small skillet, melt the butter over moderate heat. When the foam begins to subside, add the honey and salt, and stir until the mixture is hot and fluid. Pour it over the onions, turning them with a spoon to coat them evenly.

Basting the onions occasionally with the cooking liquid, bake them in the oven for about 45 minutes, or until they are golden brown and show no resistance when pierced deeply with the point of a small knife. Serve at once, directly from the baking dish.

FOODS OF THE WORLD/AMERICAN COOKING: NEW ENGLAND

Onions Stewed in Wine

Oignons à l'Etuvée

This is a dish to make when you have perhaps a glass of leftover wine—red, white, rosé, sweet, dry or aromatic (i.e., some sort of vermouth).

	To serve 4 to 8	
6 to 8	large, equal-sized onions, peeled	6 to 8
1 tbsp.	olive oil	15 ml.
½ cup	wine or vermouth	125 ml.
	water	
	salt and pepper	

Put the onions with the olive oil in a heavy ovenproof pan in which they just fit comfortably. Start them off over moderate heat and, when the oil is beginning to sizzle, pour in your wine. Let it boil fiercely for a few seconds. Add water to come halfway up the onions. Transfer to an oven, preheated to 325° F. [160° C.], and cook, uncovered, for about 1½ hours. Put back on top of the stove over high heat for 2 or 3 minutes, until the wine sauce is thick and syrupy. Season with salt and pepper. Serve as a separate vegetable, or around a roast.

ELIZABETH DAVID
FRENCH PROVINCIAL COOKING

Stuffed Onions

Gevulde Uien

The technique for hollowing out onions is demonstrated on page 70. If the chanterelles called for in this recipe are not obtainable, cultivated mushrooms may be substituted.

	To serve 4	
4	medium-sized onions	4
4 tbsp.	butter	60 ml.
6 oz.	fresh chanterelles, chopped (about 1½ cups [375 ml.])	175 g.
¾ cup	fresh bread crumbs, soaked in 2 tbsp. [30 ml.] light cream	175 ml.
2 tbsp.	chopped fresh parsley	30 ml.
⅛ tsp.	thyme	½ ml.
	salt and pepper	
½ cup	vegetable stock, seasoned with soy sauce	125 ml.
¼ cup	dry white wine	50 ml.
1 tbsp.	finely cut fresh chives	15 ml.

Cut off a thin slice from the bottom of each onion so it can stand steady. Scoop out the inside of each onion, leaving a shell about ¼ inch [6 mm.] thick all round. Chop the scooped-out onion—you will need ½ cup [125 ml.]. Parboil the onion shells for 5 minutes and drain them upside down on a wire rack.

Melt 2 tablespoons [30 ml.] of the butter and sauté the chopped onion to a golden brown, then add the chanterelles. Fry rapidly until nearly done. Squeeze out the soaked bread crumbs a little. Add the crumbs to the pan and simmer for 5 minutes, stirring all the time. Season with parsley, thyme, salt and pepper.

Sprinkle some salt and pepper into the onion shells and stuff them with the sautéed chanterelle mixture. Place them in a buttered fireproof casserole just large enough to hold them. Pour the vegetable stock and the wine around the onions. Top the onions with the remaining butter. Bring the liquid to a boil on top of the stove, then put the casserole in a moderate oven, preheated to 350° F. [180° C.], and cook for 45 minutes, basting two or three times.

Remove the onions and place them on a warmed serving platter. Reduce the liquid remaining in the casserole to half its volume, pour it over the onions and sprinkle them with the chives. Serve the stuffed onions with fried rice that has been mixed with sautéed, chopped peppers and garlic.

HUGH JANS
VRIJ NEDERLANDS KOOKBOEK

Onions in Madeira Cream

To serve 4 to 6

4	large, mild onions, thickly sliced	4
8 tbsp.	butter	120 ml.
½ cup	Madeira	125 ml.
	salt and freshly ground black pepper	
¼ cup	heavy cream	50 ml.
¼ cup	finely chopped fresh parsley	50 ml.

Melt the butter in a wide, heavy pan. Add the onion slices and turn them in the butter to coat them thoroughly. Cover the pan and cook over very low heat for 10 minutes, shaking the pan occasionally.

Uncover the pan, increase the heat slightly and stir in the Madeira. Cook, stirring frequently, until the Madeira evaporates and the onions are soft and lightly caramelized.

Season to taste with salt and pepper, and stir in the cream and parsley. Bring to a boil, then reduce the heat and simmer for 1 minute.

Serve hot. The onions are marvelous with steak, liver or any grilled meat.

GEORGE SEDDON AND HELENA RADECKA
YOUR KITCHEN GARDEN

Artichokes

Baked Stuffed Artichokes

Artichauts à la Niçarde

For instructions on stuffing artichokes see page 79.

To serve 4

4	young artichokes, trimmed	4
4	thick slices French or Italian bread, crusts removed	4
1 or 2	garlic cloves, chopped	1 or 2
¼ cup	chopped fresh parsley	50 ml.
	salt and pepper	
⅓ cup	olive oil	75 ml.

Soak the bread in a little water, squeeze out the excess liquid, then crumble the bread into a mixing bowl. Add the garlic and parsley and season with salt and pepper, mix thoroughly. Open up the leaves of the artichokes and place a little stuffing between them. Put the artichokes in an earthenware casserole, pour the oil over them and bake in a mod-

erate oven, preheated to 350° F. [180° C.], for about 40 minutes or until tender. Serve hot, straight from the casserole.

C. CHANOT-BULLIER
VIEILLES RECETTES DE CUISINE PROVENÇALE

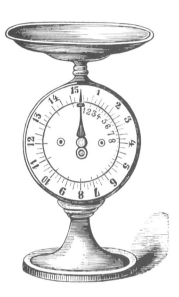

Artichoke and Onion Gratin

Artichaux la Fagit

For instructions on how to prepare artichoke bottoms, see the demonstration on page 25.

To serve 4

4	artichoke bottoms	4
	fresh lemon juice or white wine vinegar	
4 tbsp.	butter	60 ml.
3	medium-sized onions, coarsely chopped	3
	salt and pepper	
2 tbsp.	dry bread crumbs or freshly grated Parmesan cheese	30 ml.

Simmer the artichoke bottoms in water acidulated with lemon juice or white wine vinegar. When they are tender, after about 20 minutes, drain the artichoke bottoms and remove the chokes with a teaspoon.

Melt the butter in a saucepan and cook the onions until lightly colored. Season with salt and pepper, then leave the onions to cool in the butter. When it has cooled, use the onion and butter mixture to fill the artichoke bottoms, then sprinkle the bread crumbs or Parmesan cheese on top. Place the artichoke bottoms in a buttered, shallow baking dish, and bake them in a hot oven, preheated to 400° F. [200° C.], until they are lightly browned. Serve without a sauce.

LE CUISINIER GASCON

Artichokes Braised in White Wine

Artichauts à la Barigoule

	To serve 4 to 6	
4 to 6	artichokes, trimmed	4 to 6
⅓ cup	oil	75 ml.
1	medium-sized onion, chopped	1
2	carrots, finely diced	2
	salt and pepper	
1 cup	dry white wine	¼ liter
2	garlic cloves, crushed	2

Put half of the oil in a large, deep saucepan with the onion and carrots. Place the artichokes on top, upright, season them with salt and pepper, sprinkle with the remaining oil, cover the pan and place it over low heat. Gently shake the pan from time to time. When the onion and carrots begin to brown, moisten them with the white wine and cook, uncovered, until the wine has reduced by half. Add the garlic and a few tablespoons of water, cover and simmer over low heat for about 45 minutes, or until the artichokes are tender. Serve the artichokes with the juices poured over them.

J. B. REBOUL
LA CUISINIÈRE PROVENÇALE

Grilled Artichokes

Artichauts à la Bérigoule sur le Gril

This mid-19th Century recipe uses the old-fashioned method of grilling over hot embers, but the artichokes may also be cooked under a modern broiler, if placed 4 or 5 inches [10 or 13 cm.] from the heat. For instructions on trimming artichokes, see page 24.

	To serve 4	
8	small artichokes, stems and leaf tips removed	8
	salt and pepper	
⅓ cup	oil	75 ml.

Splay apart the leaves of the artichokes and put the artichokes, splayed sides facing the heat source, over coals or under a broiler for 10 to 12 minutes. Then turn them over, season with salt and pepper, and sprinkle with half the oil. After another 10 to 12 minutes, when the artichokes are cooked, transfer them to a plate and sprinkle the remainder of the oil over them.

CHARLES DURAND
LE CUISINIER DURAND

Artichoke Gratin

Gratin d'Artichauts

For instructions on trimming artichokes and turning artichoke bottoms, see pages 24-25.

	To serve 4	
4	young artichokes, each trimmed and cut lengthwise into 3 or 4 slices (or substitute 4 artichoke bottoms, thickly sliced)	4
4	thick slices French bread, crusts removed	4
1 cup	milk	¼ liter
1	medium-sized onion, chopped	1
2	garlic cloves, chopped	2
¼ cup	chopped fresh parsley	50 ml.
½ lb.	salt pork without the rind, blanched in boiling water for 5 minutes, drained and finely diced	¼ kg.
	salt and pepper	
2 to 3 tbsp.	olive oil	30 to 45 ml.

Soak the bread in the milk, squeeze out the excess liquid and roughly crumble the bread. Set it aside. Mix together the onion, garlic, parsley and salt pork. Spread the mixture in a smooth layer over the bottom of an earthenware baking dish. Put in the pieces of artichoke and season with salt and pepper. Cover the artichokes with the crumbled bread, sprinkle the top with the oil and bake in an oven, preheated to 325° F. [160° C.], for 1 to 1½ hours or until the artichokes are tender and the bread is brown.

C. CHANOT-BULLIER
VIEILLES RECETTES DE CUISINE PROVENÇALE

Braised Artichokes

Artichaux à la Galerienne

For this recipe, trim the artichokes in the usual way (page 24). Cut the artichokes in quarters and remove the chokes. Trim the inner leaves but leave the outside leaf on each quarter intact, to allow the diner to lift the artichoke by it. Dry white wine may be substituted for the Champagne.

	To serve 4	
4	medium-sized artichokes, trimmed, quartered and chokes removed	4
2 tbsp.	chopped fresh parsley	30 ml.
4	scallions, white parts only, chopped	4
1½ cups	fresh chopped mushrooms (about 4 oz. [125 g.])	375 ml.
2	shallots, chopped	2
2	garlic cloves, crushed	2
1	slice lemon	1
¼ cup	olive oil	50 ml.
½ cup	Champagne	125 ml.
½ cup	veal stock	125 ml.
1 tbsp.	fresh lemon juice	15 ml.

In a fireproof casserole, assemble the artichoke quarters, parsley, scallions, mushrooms, shallots, garlic, lemon slice and oil, and cook for a few minutes over low heat. Pour in the Champagne. Add veal stock to barely cover the artichokes and cook gently, covered, for about 45 minutes. Arrange the artichokes on a warmed serving platter, with the leaves pointing upward. Degrease the cooking juices, add the lemon juice, pour the sauce over the artichokes and serve.

LE CUISINIER GASCON

Mafalda's Stuffed Artichokes

Carciofi Ripieni Alla Mafalda

	To serve 6	
6	large artichokes	6
2 tbsp.	fresh bread crumbs	30 ml.
4	anchovy fillets soaked in cold water for 10 minutes, patted dry and finely chopped	4
2	garlic cloves, chopped	2
	olive oil	
⅔ cup	dry white wine	150 ml.

Prepare the artichokes by removing the outside leaves, cutting off the tops of the remaining leaves and scooping out the chokes. Make a stuffing with the bread crumbs, anchovy fillets and garlic, and fill the centers of the artichokes. Cover the bottom of a small deep pan with olive oil and, when it is warm, put in the stuffed artichokes. Add the white wine. Cover and simmer very gently for about an hour. Serve hot.

ELIZABETH DAVID
ITALIAN FOOD

Braised Artichoke Bottoms with Chervil

Émincé d'Artichaut au Cerfeuil

The crème fraîche called for in this recipe may be available at French food markets. If not, make it from the heavy —but not ultra-pasturized —cream usually sold in health food stores. Add about 1 teaspoon [5 ml.] of buttermilk to 1 cup [¼ liter] of cream. Cover the mixture, and let it rest in a warm place for 12 to 24 hours, or until it thickens. Refrigerate until ready to use.

The technique of trimming artichoke bottoms is demonstrated on page 25.

	To serve 4	
6	medium-sized artichokes	6
1	lemon, halved crosswise	1
½ cup	distilled white vinegar	125 ml.
2 tbsp.	butter	30 ml.
1	shallot, chopped	1
3 tbsp.	dry white wine	45 ml.
	salt and freshly ground pepper	
¾ cup	crème fraîche	175 ml.
1 tsp.	Dijon-style prepared mustard	5 ml.
2 tbsp.	chopped fresh chervil	30 ml.

Break the stems off the artichokes and strip off the hard outer leaves; using a very sharp knife, trim the artichoke bottoms. As you do, rub each artichoke well with half a lemon and plunge it into a bowl of cold water, to which the vinegar has been added, to prevent it from blackening.

Take the artichokes from the water one at a time, cut them into quarters and pull out the chokes. Rub each one again with lemon and return it to the acidulated water.

Melt the butter over low heat in a heavy saucepan just large enough to hold the artichokes side by side. Add the shallot and cook, covered, over low heat until soft. Do not allow the shallot to brown.

Deglaze the pan with the wine, drain the artichoke bottoms and arrange them in the pan. Add enough water to half-cover the artichokes, season with salt and pepper, and bring the liquid to a boil. Cover the saucepan tightly, reduce the heat and simmer the artichokes for 35 minutes.

Remove the cover and boil over high heat to reduce the liquid until only about 2 tablespoons [30 ml.] remain. Remove the artichokes and keep them warm. Add the *crème fraîche* to the saucepan, bring the sauce back to a boil, reduce the heat slightly and simmer the sauce for a few minutes.

Stir in the mustard, taste for seasoning, and return the artichokes to the saucepan. Simmer for 5 minutes, basting the artichokes continually with the sauce. Serve the artichokes liberally sprinkled with the chervil.

JEAN AND PIERRE TROISGROS
THE NOUVELLE CUISINE OF JEAN & PIERRE TROISGROS

Mixed Vegetables

Stir-fried Vegetables

Oseng-Oseng Campur

The *terasi* called for in this recipe is a dark-colored paste made from shrimps; it is used in very small amounts as a flavoring in a wide variety of Indonesian dishes.

To serve 2		
2	shallots, coarsely chopped	2
1 tsp.	*terasi*	5 ml.
2 tbsp.	vegetable oil	30 ml.
⅛ tsp.	cayenne pepper	½ ml.
1	carrot, cut lengthwise into thin sticks, then crosswise into 3 or 4 short pieces	1
⅓ cup	small cauliflower florets	75 ml.
⅓ cup	green beans, cut the same length as the carrot sticks	75 ml.
1 tsp.	sweet soy sauce	5 ml.
⅓ cup	water	75 ml.
¾ cup	fresh bean sprouts	175 ml.
	salt and pepper	

Crush the shallots and the *terasi* together in a mortar, then fry them in the oil in a large skillet over medium heat for about 30 seconds. Add the cayenne pepper, carrot sticks, cauliflower and beans. Stir continuously for 2 minutes while frying, then add the soy sauce and the water. Cover the pan and cook over medium heat for 10 minutes, then take the lid off and cook for 2 minutes. Add the bean sprouts and a little salt and pepper. Stir for 3 minutes. Serve immediately.

SRI OWEN
THE HOME BOOK OF INDONESIAN COOKERY

Sautéed Vegetables with Persillade

For general instructions on pan frying vegetables, see page 50. The technique for preparing persillade is on page 33.

The following vegetable selection and amounts are not mandatory. Sliced, tender asparagus, zucchini, broccoli and carrots could also be used. There should, however, be no more than five or six component parts to the dish, so that individual flavors are not lost in an anonymous hodgepodge.

To serve 4		
1 cup	young green beans, trimmed, parboiled for 5 minutes in lightly salted water and drained well	¼ liter
5	artichoke hearts, thinly sliced	5
4	tender ribs celery, trimmed and thinly sliced	4
6	scallions, white and pale green parts only, thinly sliced	6
12	button mushrooms, sliced	12
¼ cup	olive oil	50 ml.
	salt and pepper	
2 tbsp.	fresh lemon juice	30 ml.

Persillade

1	large garlic clove	1
2 tbsp.	chopped fresh parsley	30 ml.

Heat the oil in a sauté pan. Add the beans first and toss them for 3 or 4 minutes over brisk heat. Add the artichoke hearts, celery, scallions and, lastly, the mushrooms. Shake and toss the vegetables for 3 or 4 minutes until all are tender but crisp. Immediately stir in the *persillade* and seasoning, and toss the vegetable mixture for another minute. Add the lemon juice and serve at once.

JUDITH OLNEY
SUMMER FOOD

Potatoes Mashed with Cabbage

Kailkenny

The original name of this recipe from northeast Scotland is probably a corruption of colcanon, the name of the Irish version of the same dish.

To serve 4		
3 or 4	medium-sized potatoes, boiled and drained	3 or 4
1	small cabbage, cored, boiled and drained	1
1 cup	light cream	¼ liter
	salt and pepper	

In a bowl, mash the cabbage and potatoes together with a potato-masher instrument. Stir in the cream, season with salt and pepper and mix thoroughly. Serve very hot.

F. MARIAN MC NEILL
THE SCOTS KITCHEN

Irish Potato and Scallion Mash

Stelk

To serve 4

4 or 5	medium-sized potatoes (about 1 ½ lb. [¾ kg.])	4 or 5
½ lb.	scallions (about 20), trimmed and cut into ½-inch [1-cm.] lengths	¼ kg.
1 cup	milk	¼ liter
10 tbsp.	butter	150 ml.
	salt and pepper	

Set the scallions to simmer in a pan of milk. Meanwhile, boil the potatoes, drain and set them to keep warm on the stove.

When the scallions are tender, strain them. Use the flavored milk in mashing the potatoes, beating them until light. Add the scallion pieces and 6 tablespoons [90 ml.] of the butter, and season rather highly with salt and pepper. The mixture should be a creamy green fluff when done.

Make a well in the top of each serving, and put a lump of the remaining butter to melt in each one. You eat *stelk* from the outside of your serving, dipping into the pool.

DOROTHY HARTLEY
FOOD IN ENGLAND

Spiced Vegetables, Indian-Style

Subzi Patiala

To serve 4 to 6

3 cups	mixed diced carrots, cauliflower and green pepper	¾ liter
2 cups	freshly shelled peas	½ liter
1 tbsp.	chopped garlic	15 ml.
½ cup	water	125 ml.
⅓ cup	clarified butter	75 ml.
⅓ cup	chopped onion	75 ml.
½ tsp.	turmeric	2 ml.
2 tsp.	salt	10 ml.
1 tbsp.	thinly sliced fresh ginger root	15 ml.
1 tbsp.	finely chopped, seeded, fresh green chilies	15 ml.
3½ cups	milk	875 ml.
2 tbsp.	chopped coriander or fresh parsley	30 ml.
⅛ tsp.	ground cloves	½ ml.
⅛ tsp.	black pepper	½ ml.
⅛ tsp.	ground cardamom	½ ml.

In a blender, purée the garlic with the water. Keep this garlic water next to the stove. Heat the butter and onion together in a medium-sized saucepan. Cook over low heat, gradually adding the garlic water, until the onions are tender and the raw smell of the garlic has disappeared.

Take the pan off the heat, stir in the turmeric, and add the mixed vegetables (not the peas) and the salt. Return the pan to medium heat and stir the mixture until just tender. Add the remaining ingredients and stir over high heat until the peas are tender and the milk is reduced by about half.

Garnish and serve immediately in small, individual bowls or poured over rice.

SHIVAJI RAO AND SHALINI DEVI HOLKAR
THE COOKING OF THE MAHARAJAS

Meat-stuffed Vegetables

Etli Dolma

To serve 6

6	large tomatoes or peppers, or small eggplants or medium-sized zucchini	6
1 lb.	ground beef or lamb	½ kg.
2 tbsp.	butter	30 ml.
½ cup	raw, unprocessed long-grain rice	125 ml.
½ cup	water, or beef or veal stock	125 ml.
2	medium-sized onions, grated	2
2 to 3 tbsp.	roughly chopped, mixed fresh dill and parsley	30 to 45 ml.
	salt and pepper	
	beef or veal stock	
	butter, cut into small pieces	

Choose large, regularly formed vegetables for stuffing as these will stand up better and hold more. Cut off the tops of tomatoes or green peppers and keep them for lids. Halve eggplants or zucchini lengthwise; scoop out the insides and reserve for another use; sprinkle the shells with salt. (Eggplant or zucchini shells may be heavily salted and then rinsed off after 20 minutes.)

To make the stuffing, melt the butter in a saucepan and put in the washed rice, fry it for a few minutes and then cover it with water or stock to come just over the top of the rice. Boil off the water quite fast so that the grains are fairly dry. Allow the rice to cool. Put the ground meat into a bowl, add the onions and half of the chopped herbs. Add the rice to the meat mixture and knead until smooth. Season well.

Stuff the vegetables with the mixture, arrange them in a flat roasting pan; cover each vegetable with its lid and pour enough water or stock around the vegetables to come halfway up their sides. Dot with butter and bake in a moderate oven, preheated to 350° F. [180° C.], for 45 minutes, or until the vegetables are cooked through and soft, but have not lost their shape. Serve hot, sprinkled with the rest of the herbs.

VENICE LAMB
THE HOME BOOK OF TURKISH COOKERY

Rice Stuffing for Vegetables

Dolma Içi Zeytinyagli

The techniques of preparing vegetable shells for stuffing appear on pages 71 and 78.

To serve 6

6	large tomatoes or peppers, or small eggplants, or 10 medium-sized zucchini	6
	Rice stuffing	
1 cup	raw unprocessed rice	¼ liter
½ cup	olive oil	125 ml.
1	medium-sized onion, very thinly sliced	1
1	large tomato, peeled and coarsely chopped	1
2 tbsp.	pine nuts	30 ml.
2 tbsp.	dried currants, soaked in cold water for 30 minutes	30 ml.
½ tbsp.	sugar	7 ml.
	thyme	
	salt and pepper	
2 tbsp.	chopped fresh parsley	30 ml.
2 tbsp.	chopped fresh dill	30 ml.

Wash the rice in a colander until the water runs clear. In a deep pan, heat the olive oil and fry the onion until soft. Add the chopped tomato, nuts, currants, sugar and a pinch of thyme. Season with salt and pepper. Stir in the drained rice and fry for 2 or 3 minutes. Cover with just enough water to come ½ inch [1 cm.] above the level of the rice. Boil, covered, for 20 minutes or until the water has been absorbed. Remove the pan from the heat, cover and allow the rice mixture to steam for a few minutes. Uncover and cool the mixture, then use it to stuff the prepared vegetables.

Arrange the stuffed vegetables in a shallow baking dish, pour in enough water to come halfway up their sides, and bake in a moderate oven, preheated to 350° F. [180° C.], for 45 minutes or until the vegetables are cooked through but have not lost their shapes. Allow them to cool in the baking dish and serve them cold, sprinkled with the parsley and dill.

VENICE LAMB
THE HOME BOOK OF TURKISH COOKERY

Ohio Pudding

To serve 2 or 3

½ cup	puréed, boiled carrot (made from 2 medium-sized carrots)	125 ml.
½ cup	puréed, boiled sweet potato (made from 1 medium-sized sweet potato)	125 ml.
¼ tsp.	salt	1 ml.
2 tbsp.	brown sugar	30 ml.
½ cup	fine, dry white bread crumbs	125 ml.
1¼ cups	milk	300 ml.
1	large egg, lightly beaten	1
1 tbsp.	butter	15 ml.

In a bowl, combine the carrot, sweet potato, salt and sugar. Add the bread crumbs. Last, add the milk and beaten egg. Mix thoroughly, and pour the mixture into a buttered 1-quart [1-liter] casserole or baking dish. Bake, uncovered, for 1 hour in a moderate oven, preheated to 350° F. [180° C.]. This delicious pudding resembles yellow spoon bread and is excellent with chicken, ham or turkey.

ESTHER B. ARESTY
THE DELECTABLE PAST

Vegetable Stew, California-Style

Colache

To serve 4 to 6

2 lb.	zucchini or yellow straightneck squash, unpeeled and cut crosswise into ¼-inch [6-mm.] slices	1 kg.
1 lb.	green beans, cut into 1½-inch [4-cm.] lengths	½ kg.
4	medium-sized tomatoes, peeled, seeded and coarsely chopped	4
1 cup	fresh corn kernels, cut from 2 or 3 large ears of corn	¼ liter
2 tbsp.	vegetable oil	30 ml.
1 cup	finely chopped onion	¼ liter
1 tsp.	finely chopped garlic	5 ml.
1 tsp.	finely chopped fresh green chili	5 ml.
2 tsp.	salt	10 ml.
¼ tsp.	freshly ground black pepper	1 ml.

In a heavy 7-quart [7-liter] fireproof casserole, heat the oil over moderate heat until a light haze forms above it. Add the onion and garlic. Then, stirring frequently, cook for about 5 minutes, or until they are soft and translucent but not brown. Add the squash, green beans and chili, and stir for 2 to 3 minutes. Stir in the tomatoes, salt and pepper.

Reduce the heat to low, partially cover the casserole and simmer for 15 minutes. Add the corn, mix well and continue to simmer, partially covered, until the squash and green beans are tender but still somewhat crisp to the bite. Taste for seasoning and serve at once directly from the casserole.

If you like, you may cut the ears of corn crosswise into 2-inch [5-cm.] chunks instead of removing the kernels. Drop the corn chunks into enough lightly salted boiling water to cover them by at least 1 inch [2½ cm.]. At once, cover the pot and remove it from the heat. Let the corn stand for 5 minutes, then drain it in a colander or sieve. Add the chunks to the stew as described above, and simmer them with the other vegetables for about 5 minutes before serving.

FOODS OF THE WORLD/AMERICAN COOKING: THE GREAT WEST

Meatless Stuffing for Vegetables

Yemissis Horis Kreas

For instructions about preparing, filling and braising stuffed vegetables, see the demonstrations on pages 70-71.

To serve 6

12	medium-sized tomatoes, cored or 6 small eggplants, halved lengthwise or 12 medium-sized zucchini, halved lengthwise	12
1 cup	olive oil	¼ liter
2	onions, finely chopped	2
3 tbsp.	pine nuts	45 ml.
½ cup	raw unprocessed rice	125 ml.
¼ cup	finely chopped fresh parsley	50 ml.
1 tbsp.	finely chopped dill	15 ml.
	salt and pepper	

First scoop out the pulp from whatever vegetable you have chosen to stuff and chop the pulp finely. Heat the olive oil, then lightly fry the onions. When they begin to change color, add the vegetable pulp. Stir this mixture for 5 minutes. Add the nuts, rice, parsley, dill, salt and pepper, and cook gently for 10 minutes. The stuffing is now ready to be used in the vegetable shells.

ROBIN HOWE
GREEK COOKING

Rich Vegetable Pie

Torta tal-haxix

To serve 4

1	large onion, sliced	1
2 tbsp.	olive oil	30 ml.
2 tsp.	puréed tomato	10 ml.
1 lb.	shelled peas (about 2 cups [½ liter])	½ kg.
2 lb.	shelled and peeled broad beans (or substitute shelled but unpeeled lima beans)	1 kg.
2 lb.	spinach or chicory, chopped	1 kg.
3	carrots, thinly sliced	3
4	large artichoke hearts, quartered (optional)	4
½ cup	water	125 ml.
10	anchovy fillets, soaked in cold water for 10 minutes, patted dry and finely chopped	10
	pitted olives, chopped	
	salt and pepper	
	short-crust or rough puff pastry (recipe, page 167, but double the quantities called for)	

In a large saucepan, fry the onion in the olive oil until the slices are translucent but not browned. Add the puréed tomato and continue cooking over moderate heat for a few minutes. Now add all the other vegetables together with the water. Cover and cook for about 10 minutes, or until the vegetables are tender. (The amount of water is purposely small so as to avoid a watery stew, but if you think the vegetables are going to stick, you may add a little more water.) Remove the pan from the heat and mix in the anchovies and olives. Season well.

Line a deep 10-inch [25-cm.] pie dish, or 1½-quart [1½-liter] soufflé dish, with pastry. Pour in the vegetable mixture. Cover with a pastry lid and cut two or three slits in the top. Bake the pie in a hot oven, preheated to 400° F. [200° C.], for 25 minutes, then lower the heat to 350° F. [180° C.] and cook for 30 to 45 minutes.

ANNE AND HELEN CARUANA GALIZIA
RECIPES FROM MALTA

Okra, Corn and Tomato Mélange

To serve 6

½ lb.	okra (about 2 cups [½ liter]), cut into ¼-inch [6-mm.] slices	¼ kg.
4	ears corn, scraped (about 2 cups [½ liter] kernels)	4
3	large tomatoes, peeled and diced	3
4	slices bacon	4
1	onion, finely chopped	1
1	small green pepper, chopped	1
1 tsp.	sugar	5 ml.
	salt and pepper	
	Tabasco	

In a large skillet, fry the bacon until crisp. Remove the bacon, drain and crumble it. Set the bacon aside. Discard all but 4 tablespoons [60 ml.] of the bacon fat from the pan.

Stir the okra and onion into the bacon fat, add the corn kernels and cook over medium heat for 10 minutes, stirring constantly. Add the tomatoes, green pepper and sugar, and season with salt, pepper and a dash of Tabasco. Cover and simmer for about 25 minutes, or until all the vegetables are tender, stirring occasionally.

Correct the seasoning, pour into a serving dish and sprinkle with the crumbled bacon.

THE JUNIOR LEAGUE OF PINE BLUFF, ARKANSAS
SOUTHERN ACCENT

Baked Zucchini, Eggplant and Tomatoes

Confit Bayaldi

To serve 4

2 or 3	medium-sized zucchini (about ½ lb. [¼ kg.])	2 or 3
1	small eggplant (about ½ lb. [¼ kg.])	1
4	mushrooms, thinly sliced	4
2	medium-sized tomatoes (about ¾ lb. [⅓ kg.]), peeled and thinly sliced	2
1 or 2	small onions, thinly sliced	1 or 2
2 tsp.	olive oil	10 ml.
½ tsp.	thyme flowers (or substitute a pinch of dried thyme)	2 ml.
1	garlic clove, finely chopped	1
	salt and pepper	

Preheat the oven to 400° F. [200° C.]. Using a potato peeler, peel the zucchini and eggplant lengthwise, leaving a strip of

skin about ½ inch [1 cm.] wide between each peeled segment to give a striped effect. Cut these vegetables into slices less than ¼ inch [6 mm.] thick. In each of four small ovenproof dishes, about 5½ inches [14 cm.] across, arrange a quarter of the vegetables, overlapping them and alternating the colors. Mix together the olive oil, thyme and garlic, and spoon a quarter of this mixture over each dish. Season with salt and pepper. Cover the dishes with aluminum foil and bake them in the oven for 20 minutes. Then remove the foil, lower the heat to 300° F. [150° C.] and cook for 25 to 30 minutes, or until the mixture has reduced to a vegetable "marmalade."

MICHEL GUÉRARD
MICHEL GUÉRARD'S CUISINE MINCEUR

Mixed Vegetable Stew

Ragoût de Légumes

The artichokes called for in this recipe are best pared at the last moment and added immediately to the pan. They should then, at once, be turned around in the butter to coat all surfaces as protection from contact with air, which rapidly blackens them. However, if you are not accustomed to working this rapidly, prepare the artichokes just ahead of time, but place the quarters immediately in olive oil. Subsequently, when you place the quarters in the saucepan, cut down on the amount of butter used in the cooking.

To serve 4 to 6

1 lb.	large scallions, white parts only, or very small boiling onions, peeled	½ kg.
1	garlic bulb, with the loose husk removed, but unpeeled	1
6	medium-sized artichokes, pared, quartered and chokes removed	6
1	medium-sized head Boston or Bibb lettuce, coarsely shredded	1
1 lb.	small firm zucchini, thinly sliced	½ kg.
8 tbsp.	butter	120 ml.
1	bouquet garni made of a celery rib, fresh parsley, bay leaf and thyme	1
	salt and pepper	
2 tbsp.	chopped fresh parsley	30 ml.
½ tbsp.	finely chopped marjoram (optional)	7 ml.

In a large, shallow copper saucepan or fireproof earthenware casserole, melt about 3 tablespoons [45 ml.] of butter, and add the onions, the garlic cloves and the artichoke quarters.

Embed the bouquet garni at the heart of things, scatter over the lettuce, sprinkle with salt and cover the pan tightly. Allow the vegetables to sweat by cooking them very gently, tossing from time to time (or stirring with a wooden spoon), for about 30 minutes. At intervals, note the moisture in the pan: there should be just the suggestion of a slightly syrupy juice. If the heat is low enough, the lettuce will provide enough liquid. But if the vegetables are cooking in fat only and in danger of coloring, add a couple of tablespoons of water while gently shaking the contents of the pan.

When the onions and the artichokes are tender, melt 2 tablespoons [30 ml.] of butter in a large omelet pan and sauté the zucchini over high heat, tossing very often, for 5 to 6 minutes—or until all are just tender and only lightly colored. Add the zucchini to the other vegetables, cover the pan and allow the flavors to mingle for 5 to 10 minutes. Taste and season with salt; pepper generously and, away from the heat, add the remaining butter cut into small pieces. Swirl or gently stir the vegetables until the butter is absorbed into the juices. Discard the bouquet garni. Sprinkle the stew with parsley—adding the marjoram, if you like—and serve.

RICHARD OLNEY
SIMPLE FRENCH FOOD

Ratatouille Niçoise

To serve 4 to 6

3 cups	chopped onions (about 4 medium-sized)	¾ liter
2 or 3	tomatoes, peeled, seeded and chopped	2 or 3
3 or 4	medium-sized zucchini, peeled and sliced	3 or 4
1	medium-sized eggplant, peeled and sliced	1
3	red peppers, halved, seeded, deribbed and cut into strips	3
½ cup	olive oil	125 ml.
1	garlic clove, crushed	1
1	bouquet garni	1
	salt and pepper	

First cook the onions in the olive oil over low heat in a large covered pan for about 10 minutes, or until they are softened and yellowed. Add the tomatoes and cook for a few more minutes. Now add the zucchini, eggplant, red pepper, garlic, bouquet garni, salt and pepper. Cover and simmer over low heat for 1 hour, or until the vegetables have released their liquid and softened and blended with one another. To reduce the liquid, remove the lid and continue cooking over low heat for another 20 to 30 minutes.

LOUIS GINIÉS
LA CUISINE PROVENÇALE

Standard Preparations

Basic White Sauce

Use this recipe whenever béchamel sauce is called for.

To make about 1 ½ cups [375 ml.] sauce

2 tbsp.	butter	30 ml.
2 tbsp.	flour	30 ml.
2 cups	milk	½ liter
	salt	
	white pepper	
	grated nutmeg (optional)	
	heavy cream (optional)	

Melt the butter in a heavy saucepan. Stir in the flour and cook, stirring, over low heat for 2 to 5 minutes. Pour in all the milk at once, whisking constantly to blend the mixture smoothly. Raise the heat and continue whisking while the sauce comes to a boil. Season with a little salt. Reduce the heat to very low, and simmer for about 40 minutes, stirring every so often to prevent the sauce from sticking to the bottom of the pan. When the sauce thickens to the desired consistency, add white pepper and a pinch of nutmeg, if you like; taste for seasoning. Whisk again until the sauce is perfectly smooth, and add cream if you prefer a richer, whiter sauce.

Tomato Sauce

When fresh ripe tomatoes are not available, use 3 cups [¾ liter] of drained, canned Italian plum tomatoes.

To make about 1 cup [¼ liter] sauce

6	medium-sized ripe tomatoes, chopped	6
1	onion, diced	1
1 tbsp.	olive oil	15 ml.
1	garlic clove (optional)	1
1 tsp.	chopped fresh parsley	5 ml.
1 tsp.	mixed dried basil, marjoram and thyme	5 ml.
1 to 2 tbsp.	sugar (optional)	15 to 30 ml.
	salt and freshly ground pepper	

In a large enameled or stainless-steel saucepan, gently fry the diced onion in the oil until soft, but not brown. Add the other ingredients and simmer for 20 to 30 minutes, or until the tomatoes have been reduced to a thick pulp. Sieve the mixture, using a wooden pestle or spoon. Reduce the sauce further, if necessary, to reach the desired consistency.

Butter Sauce
Sauce Bâtarde

To make about 2 cups [½ liter] sauce

2	egg yolks	2
1 tbsp.	cold water	15 ml.
16 tbsp.	unsalted butter, diced	240 ml.
3 tbsp.	flour	45 ml.
2 cups	warm water, lightly salted	½ liter
1 tbsp.	strained fresh lemon juice	15 ml.

Put the egg yolks into a bowl with the cold water; beat the mixture until it is smooth, then set it aside.

In a heavy saucepan over low heat, melt 4 tablespoons [60 ml.] of the butter. Add the flour and stir until the mixture begins to bubble. Take the pan from the heat and add the lightly salted warm water, whisking rapidly. Return the pan to the heat and continue whisking until the mixture boils. Again remove the pan from the heat, allow the mixture to cool for at least a minute, then add the beaten egg yolks. Return the pan to the heat and continue to whisk until the sauce thickens slightly. Do not allow the sauce to boil.

Off the heat, pour in the lemon juice, then add the rest of the butter and whisk steadily until it is amalgamated with the sauce. Adjust the seasoning and serve immediately.

Hollandaise Sauce

To make about 1 cup [¼ liter] sauce

3	egg yolks	3
1 tbsp.	cold water	15 ml.
16 tbsp.	unsalted butter, chilled and finely diced	240 ml.
	salt and white pepper	
	cayenne pepper	
1 tsp.	strained fresh lemon juice	5 ml.

Pour water to a depth of about 1 inch [2½ cm.] into the bottom of a double boiler—or a large saucepan or fireproof casserole if you are making a bain-marie. Heat the water until it simmers, then reduce the heat to low. Place the top of the double boiler over the bottom; or set a rack or trivet into the bain-marie and place the saucepan on the rack or trivet. Be sure the pan in which you are making the hollandaise does not touch the water. Put the egg yolks and the cold water in the double boiler or saucepan, and beat them until the yolks are smooth. Whisk a handful of the butter into the yolks and, when the butter has been absorbed, continue adding the diced butter in this way until all of it has been used. Beat until the sauce becomes thick and creamy. Season the sauce with salt, white pepper and cayenne to taste, and add the lemon juice.

Chicken Stock

To make about 2 quarts [2 liters] stock

4 lb.	raw or cooked chicken carcasses, but raw trimmings, necks, gizzards and hearts	2 kg.
3 to 4 quarts	water	3 to 4 liters
	salt	
4	medium-sized carrots	4
2	large onions, 1 stuck with 2 whole cloves	2
1	large leek, halved lengthwise and washed	1
1	rib celery	1
1	large bouquet garni, made of parsley, thyme sprigs and a bay leaf	1

Put all the chicken pieces in a heavy stockpot, and cover by 2 inches [5 cm.] with water. Bring to a boil over low heat, skimming to remove the scum as it rises to the surface. Occasionally add a little cold water to help precipitate the scum. Add the salt, vegetables and bouquet garni, pushing them down into the liquid to make sure they are all submerged. Return the liquid to a boil and simmer gently for 2 hours, skimming and degreasing as necessary. Strain the stock through a colander into a large bowl or clean pot. Discard the chicken pieces, vegetables and bouquet garni. Cool the stock and remove every trace of fat that rises to the top.

Veal Stock

To make 2 to 3 quarts [2 to 3 liters] stock

1	veal knucklebone, sawed into 2-inch [5-cm.] pieces	1
4 lb.	meaty veal trimmings (neck, shank or rib tips)	2 kg.
3 to 5 quarts	water	3 to 5 liters
4	carrots	4
2	large onions, 1 stuck with 2 or 3 whole cloves	2
1	whole garlic bulb, unpeeled	1
1	rib celery	1
1	leek, halved lengthwise and washed	1
1	large bouquet garni, made of parsley, thyme sprigs and a bay leaf	1
	salt	

Put the bones into a heavy stockpot and place the meat on top of them. Add cold water to cover by 2 inches [5 cm.].

Bring to a boil over low heat, starting to skim before the liquid begins to boil. Keep skimming, occasionally adding a glass of cold water, until no more scum rises. Do not stir the bones and meat lest you cloud the stock.

Add a dash of salt, the vegetables and a bouquet garni to the pot, pushing them down into the liquid so that everything is submerged. Continue skimming until a boil is reached. Reduce the heat to very low and cook, partially covered, at a bare simmer for 4 hours, skimming off the surface fat three or four times.

Strain the stock by pouring the contents of the pot through a colander into a large bowl or clean pot. Discard the bones, veal pieces, vegetables and bouquet garni. Cool the strained stock and skim the last traces of fat from the surface. If there is any residue at the bottom of the container after the stock cools, decant the clear liquid carefully into another bowl or pot and discard the sediment.

Beef Stock

Beef stock can be prepared in the same way as veal stock. Substitute 4 pounds [2 kg.] of oxtail or beef shank or chuck for the meaty veal trimmings, but use the veal shank bone—omitting the bone only if a less gelatinous stock is desired. Simmer the stock for at least 5 hours.

Vegetable Stock

Boil aromatic vegetables—equal amounts of chopped carrot, leek and celery combined with half those amounts of chopped onion and turnip—with a bouquet garni and a crushed garlic clove for 30 minutes in enough lightly salted water to cover the vegetables. Strain the stock and discard the vegetables and bouquet garni. Alternatively, use the water in which any vegetables have been boiled as a stock or as the cooking liquid for producing a vegetable stock.

Batter for Deep Frying

The technique of making batter for deep frying is demonstrated on page 58.

To make about 1 ½ cups [375 ml.] batter

1 cup	flour	¼ liter
¼ tsp.	salt	1 ml.
3 tbsp.	olive oil or cooled, melted butter	45 ml.
1 cup	beer or water	¼ liter
2	eggs, yolks separated from whites	2

Mix together the flour, salt and oil or butter in a bowl. Gradually add the beer or water, and whisk for only as long as it takes to produce a smooth batter. Whisk in the egg yolks, but do not overwork the mixture. Leave the batter to rest for at least 1 hour at room temperature, otherwise it will shrink away from the vegetable pieces and provide an uneven coating. Beat the egg whites until they form soft peaks and fold them into the batter just before using it.

Short-Crust and Rough Puff Pastry

One simple formula produces dough for both plain short-crust pastry and for rough puff pastry. The difference is in how you roll it out.

To line an 8-inch [20-cm.] piepan

1 cup	flour	¼ liter
¼ tsp.	salt	1 ml.
8 tbsp.	cold unsalted butter, cut into small pieces	120 ml.
3 to 4 tbsp.	cold water	45 to 60 ml.

Mix the flour and salt in a mixing bowl. Add the butter and cut it into the flour rapidly, using two table knives, until the butter is in tiny pieces. Do not work for more than a few minutes. Add half the water and, with a fork, quickly blend it into the flour-and-butter mixture. Add just enough of the rest of the water to enable you to gather the dough together with your hands into a firm ball. Wrap the dough in plastic wrap or wax paper and refrigerate it for 2 to 3 hours, or put it in the freezer for 20 minutes until the outside surface is slightly frozen.

To roll out short-crust pastry: Remove the ball of pastry dough from the refrigerator or freezer and put it on a cool, floured surface (a marble slab is ideal). Press the dough out partially with your hand, then give it a few gentle smacks with the rolling pin to flatten it and render it more supple. Roll out the dough from the center until the pastry forms a circle about ½ inch [1 cm.] thick. Turn the pastry over so that both sides are floured and continue rolling until the circle is about ⅛ inch [3 mm.] thick. Roll the pastry onto the rolling pin, lift it up and unroll it over the piepan. If you are using the pastry to line a piepan, press the pastry firmly against all surfaces and trim the edges. If you are using the pastry to cover a pie, trim the pastry to within ½ inch of the rim, turn under the edges of the pastry around the rim to form a double layer, and press the pastry firmly to the rim with thumb and forefinger to crimp the edges.

To roll out rough puff pastry: Place the dough on a cool, floured surface and smack it flat with the rolling pin. Turn the dough over to make sure that both sides are well floured. Roll out the pastry rapidly into a rectangle about 1 foot [30 cm.] long and 5 to 6 inches [13 to 15 cm.] wide. Fold the two short ends to meet each other in the center, then fold again to align the folded edges with each other. Following the direction of the fold lines, roll the pastry into a rectangle again, fold again in the same way and refrigerate for at least 30 minutes. Repeat this process two or three more times before using the pastry. Always let the pastry dough rest in the refrigerator in between rollings.

Recipe Index

All recipes in the index that follows are listed by their English titles except in cases where a dish of foreign origin, such as ratatouille Niçoise, is universally recognized by its source name. Entries are organized by the types of vegetables and also by the major ingredients specified in recipe titles. Sauces and stuffings are listed separately. Foreign recipes are listed by country or region of origin. Recipe credits appear on pages 174-176.

General Index/ Glossary

Included in this index to the cooking demonstrations are definitions, in italics, of special culinary terms not explained elsewhere in this volume. The Recipe Index begins on page 168.

Acidulated water, 13; use of, 13, 24, 25, 41. *See also Blanc*
Acorn squash, 18, 19; splitting and seeding, 18, 19
Al dente: *an Italian term, literally translated as "to the tooth." Used to describe the texture of cooked pasta or vegetables when they are firm to the bite: not too soft on the outside and barely cooked through.*
Alfalfa sprouts, 14
Aromatic mixtures, how to prepare, 33; *duxelles, 33; mirepoix, 33; persillade, 33; sofrito, 33*
Aromatics: *all substances —such as vegetables, herbs and spices —that add aroma and flavor to food when used in cooking.*
Artichoke(s), 5, 6, 24-25; availability, 24, *chart* 34-35; baked, stuffed, 79; boiling instructions, *chart* 41; cooking methods, *chart* 34-35; herbs used with, 26; preparing whole, 24; preventing discoloration, 24, 83; removing choke before cooking, 24; whole stuffed, 79; wine for braising, 66. *See also Jerusalem artichokes*
Artichoke bottoms, 52; baked with eggplant fans, 80, 81; deep fried in batter, 5, 58; in pan-fried vegetable mixture, 50; preparing, 25; sliced and gratinéed, 82, 83; in stew, 60, 61, 72
Asparagus, 6, 20; availability, 20, *chart* 34-35; boiling, 39; boiling and steaming, *chart* 41; cooking methods, *chart* 34-35; draining, 39, 42; herbs with, 26; in pan-fried vegetable mixture, 50; peeling, 20, 21, 39; stir frying, 51; testing for doneness, 39; trimming ends, 39; tying bundles, 39
Availability of vegetables, 6, 7, *chart* 34-35
Bacon, in stuffing, 46
Bain-marie, 88-89, 91; how to make, 43
Baking, 74-75, 76-91; artichokes, stuffed, 79; beets in skin, 76, 77; cauliflower pudding, 88-89; garlic bulbs, 77; gratinéing, 75, 82-87; mixed vegetables in covered baking dish, 80-81; onions in skin, 76, 77; potatoes, stuffed, 76; potatoes in skin, 76; sweet potatoes in skin, 76; tomatoes, stuffed, 78; vegetables for, *chart* 34-35; zucchini soufflé, 90-91
Basil, 26-27, 86, 87
Basting: *pouring or spooning oil, fat or liquid over food to prevent it from drying up during cooking;* 92, 93, 94
Batter: for fritters, 58, 59; for potato

pancakes, 52; vegetables for deep frying in, *chart* 34-35
Bay leaves, 26, 28, 33
Bean sprouts, 14; availability and cooking methods, *chart* 34-35; boiling and steaming times, *chart* 41
Beans, broad, 14; availability and cooking methods, *chart* 34-35; boiling and steaming, *chart* 41; braised with thickened sauce, 67; shelling and peeling, 15; in stew, 61, 73
Beans, green, 5, 6, 14-15; availability and cooking methods, *chart* 34-35; boiling, 36; boiling and steaming, *chart* 41; in croquettes, 54; as decoration, 89; deep fried in batter, 58; pan frying, 50; puréed, 44; removing strings, 15; steamed in lettuce leaves, 40
Beans, lima, 5, 14-15; availability and cooking methods, *chart* 34-35; boiling and steaming, *chart* 41
Beans, wax, 14-15; availability and cooking methods, *chart* 34-35; boiling and steaming, *chart* 41
Beer, in fritter batter, 59
Beet(s), 5, 12-13; availability and cooking methods, *chart* 34-35; baked in skin, 76, 77; boiling, *chart* 41; glazed, 64; gratinéed, 84
Beet greens, 8, 9; availability and cooking methods, *chart* 34-35; boiling and steaming instructions, *chart* 41
Belgian endive. *See Endive, Belgian*
Beurre manié: *an uncooked sauce-thickener made by kneading together equal amounts of flour and butter.*
Blanc, *chart* 41
Blanching: *plunging food into boiling water for a short period. Done for a number of reasons: to remove strong flavors, such as the excess saltiness of some salt pork; to soften vegetables before further cooking; to facilitate the removal of skins or shells. Another meaning is "to whiten";* 6
Boiling, 36-47; asparagus, 38; broccoli, 38; cabbage, stuffed whole, 46-47; cooking times for, *chart* 41; covered-pan, shallow-water method, 38, *chart* 41; cutting vegetables for, 32, 41; drying vegetables after, 36, 38, 42; green beans, 36; instructions for individual vegetables, *chart* 41; open-pan, deep-water method, 38, *chart* 41; vegetables for, *chart* 34-35; *See also Puréeing cooked vegetables; Sauces for boiled vegetables; Steaming*
Bok choy, 20-21; availability, 20, *chart* 34-35; boiling and steaming, *chart* 41; cooking methods, *chart* 34-35
Bouquet garni: *a bunch of mixed herbs —the classic three being parsley, thyme and bay leaf —tied together or wrapped in cheesecloth and used for flavoring stocks, sauces, braises and stews;* 26, 28, 72

Braise (braising), 60-73; broad beans in thickened sauce, 67; carrots, glazed, 64-65; celery in stock, 62-63; cutting vegetables for, 32; fennel in water, 62-63; flavorings in, 62; herbs used, 26, 28; liquids for, 61, 62, 66, 67, 68, 70; preparing vegetables for, 62; red cabbage in wine, 66; stuffed leaves, 68-69; thickened with egg yolks and cream, 67; vs. stewing, 61; vegetables for, *chart* 34-35; white onions, glazed, 64-65; with wine, 66, 70. *See also Stew(ing); Stuffed vegetables*
Bread crumbs: as coating for fragile vegetables, 51; in croquette mixture, 54; for crust of gratin, 82, 84, 86, 87; with pan-fried vegetables, 50; with stuffed onions, 69
Broccoli, 5, 10-11; availability and cooking methods, *chart* 34-35; boiling, 38; boiling and steaming, *chart* 41; in croquettes, 54; deep fried in batter, 5, 58; draining and serving, 38; peeling and slicing stems, 10, 11; stir frying, 51; testing for doneness, 38
Broiling, 75, 92-93; adding garnish, 93; adding topping, 92; basting during, 92, 93; butter coating for slow-cooking vegetables, 92, 93; oiling vegetable slices, 92; skewered vegetables, 92, 93; testing for doneness, 92; vegetables for, *chart* 34-35
Brousse: *a soft, smooth-textured, white cheese, similar to ricotta, made from sheep's milk.*
Brussels sprouts, 5, 10; availability and cooking methods, *chart* 34-35; boiling and steaming, *chart* 41; cooking, 10; parboiled for braise, 62; trimming, 11
Butter, 57; as binder in croquettes, 54; as binder for puréed vegetables, 44, 45; clarified for frying, 50; coating for broiled vegetables, 92, 93; in glaze, 64; in gratins, 84, 85, 87; herbs blended with, 27; as a sauce, 42; in sauce, 42, 43; in stew, 72
Butter sauce *(sauce bâtarde),* 42
Butternut squash, 18, 19
Cabbage(s), head, 5, 10-11; availability and cooking methods, *chart* 34-35; boiling and steaming, *chart,* 41; Chinese, 10; coring, 66; green, 10, 11; herbs used with, 26, 28; red, 10-11; red, braised in wine, 66; Savoy, 10, 11; shredded with knife, 30; stuffed, boiled whole, 46-47; stuffed leaves of, 68-69. *See also Brussels sprouts*
Cabbage family, 5, 10-11; cooking, 10
Calvados: *French apple brandy.*
Caramelizing: *heating sugar until it turns brown and syrupy. Also, evaporating meat or vegetable juices to leave a brown "caramel" residue on the bottom of the pan;* 64-65
Carbon steel knives, chemical reaction with, 10, 24

Carrots, 12-13; availability and cooking methods, *chart* 34-35; boiling and steaming, *chart* 41; in celery braise, 62; in croquettes, 54; cut for steaming, 40; cutting out core, 13; as decoration for pudding, 89; glazed, 64-65; gratinéed, 84; herbs used with, 26; in *mirepoix,* 33; parboiled before frying, 50; paring, 13; prepared for broiling, 92, 93; puréed, 45; roll-cut, 31; shaped for garnish, 32; shredded, 52; in sliced potato gratin, 84
Cauliflower, 10,11; availability and cooking methods, baked, 88-89; *chart* 34-35; boiling and steaming, *chart* 41; croquettes, 54; deep fried in batter, 5, 58; gratinéed with cheese sauce, 86; preparing, 11; pudding, 88-89; puréed, 45, 88
Celeriac, 12-13; availability and cooking methods, *chart* 34-35; boiling, *chart* 41; in mixed vegetable purée, 44-45; parboiled for braise, 62; paring technique, 13
Celery, 5, 20-21; availability, 20, *chart* 34-35; baking, 80; boiling and steaming, *chart* 41; braised in stock, 62-63; cooking methods, *chart* 34-35; cut on the diagonal, 31; gratinéed with cheese sauce, 86; leaves, 20; in *mirepoix,* 33; parboiled for braise, 62; puréed, 45; use of, when cooking cabbage, 10
Celery root. *See Celeriac*
Chard, Swiss, 20-21; availability, 20, *chart* 34-35; cooking methods, *chart* 34-35; deep fried in batter, 58; gratinéed, 82; leaves, in stuffing, 46; removing leaves and skin, 21; ribs, gratinéed with white sauce, 86, 87; stuffing leaves of, 68
Chayotes, 18, 19; availability and cooking methods, *chart* 34-35; boiling and steaming, *chart* 41; glazed, 64
Cheese, grated: for broiled vegetables, 92; for gratin crust, 82, 83, 84, 86, 87
Cheese, shredded, 52
Cheese custard, for gratin, 86, 87
Cherry tomatoes, 16; broiling, 93
Chervil, 26
Chestnuts, in cabbage braise, 66
Chiffonade: *a French term for any green leafy herb or vegetable that has been sliced into fine ribbons;* 30
Chives, 26
Chopping. *See Cutting techniques*
Cilantro. *See Coriander*
Clarified butter: *butter with its easily burned milk solids removed. To make, melt butter over low heat; spoon off the foam; let stand off the heat until the milk solids settle; then decant the clear yellow liquid on top, discarding the milk solids;* 50
Collard greens, 8-9; availability and cooking methods, *chart* 34-35; boiling and steaming, *chart* 41
Coriander, 26, 27
Corn, 5, 14-15; availability and cooking methods, *chart* 34-35; boiling

and steaming, *chart* 41; cooking, 15; grilled in husks, 94

Cornhusks: corn grilled in, 94; stuffed, 68

Cornmeal, as coating for fragile vegetables, 51

Cream: egg yolks and, added to braising liquid, 67; gratin topped with, 84, 85

Croquettes: leftover meat in, 54; potato, 54; vegetables in, 54

Croutons: *small cubes of bread fried in butter and used as garnish.*

Cucumber(s), 5, 6; availability and cooking methods, *chart* 34-35; boiling and steaming, *chart* 41; herbs used with, 26; sliced and coated for frying, 51

Cutting techniques, 29-32; chopping leafy herbs, 30; chopping onions, 29; and cooking time, 29; for deep frying, 58; diagonal slicing, 29, 31; for different types of cooking, 32, 40; forming cylinders, 32; French names for simple shapes, 32; for frying, 49, 50, 51; keeping rounded vegetables from rolling, 30; for *olivettes* or *noisettes,* 32; roll-cut, 29, 31; shaping fans, 80; shaping garnish vegetables, 32; shredding individual leaves of lettuce and spinach, 30; shredding with rotary shredder, 52; shredding tight heads of leaves with knife, 30; slices, strips and dice, 30; for steaming, 40

Deep frying, 49, 54-59; amount of oil for, 57, 59; choosing oil for, 57; croquettes, 54; French-fried potatoes, 55; marinating vegetables before, 58; mixed vegetables, 58-59; onion rings, 48; pan for, 57; parboiling before, 58; preparing vegetables, 58; removing vegetables from oil, 57, 59; shapes of potatoes for, 56-57; testing heat of oil, 54, 55, 59; vegetable fritters, 58-59; vegetables for, *chart* 34-35

Dill, 26-27, 93

Dittany of Crete, 28

Duxelles, 33, 54; how to make, 33

Egg(s): as binder in potato pancakes, 52; in gratin, 86

Egg whites: folding vegetables and, together, 90; in fritter batter, 59; in zucchini soufflé, 90

Egg yolks: as binder in croquettes, 54; as emulsifier in braising liquid, 67; as emulsifier in sauce, 42, 43; in fritter batter, 59

Eggplant(s), 5, 6, 16; availability and cooking methods, *chart* 34-35; baked, 80; baked in skin, 76; boiling and steaming, *chart* 41; browned for braise, 62; fans made from, 80; gratinéed, 82; gratinéed with cheese custard, 86, 87; herbs used with, 26; paring, 17; prepared for broiling, 92; prepared for stuffing, 71; in *ratatouille,* 61, 72; removing excess moisture from, 17; seeding, 17; sliced and broiled, 92; slicing, stripping and

dicing, 30; stuffed, baked, 78; stuffed, braised, 70

Endive, Belgian, 6, 8, 9; availability and cooking methods, *chart* 34-35; boiling and steaming, *chart* 41; coring, 9; in a gratin, 74

Fava beans. See Beans, broad

Fennel, 20; availability, 20, *chart* 34-35; boiling and steaming, *chart* 41; braised in water, 62-63; cooking methods, *chart* 34-35; leaves, 20, 26; prepared for broiling, 92, 93; stringing the base, 21; in veal stock, 62

Fillings. See Stuffings and fillings

Fines herbes: *a mixture of finely chopped fresh herbs —the classic herbs being parsley, chives, tarragon and chervil;* 26

Finocchio. See Fennel

Flour: as binder in potato pancakes, 52; as coating for fragile vegetables, 51; in fritter batter, 59; preventing taste of, in sauce, 67; in sauce, 42, 67

Foil: garlic baked in, 77; vegetables grilled in, 94

French-fried potatoes, 55

Fritters, 5, 58-59; batter for, 58, 59; vegetables for, 58

Frying, 48-59; cutting techniques for, 32, 49, 50, 51; parboiling before, 49, 50, 51. *See also* Deep frying; Pan frying; Stir frying in wok

Garlic, 5, 22-23; availability and cooking methods, *chart* 34-35; baked with mixed vegetables, 80, 81; in braise, 61, 62; bulbs, baked, 77; cooking, 23; in gratin crust, 83; oven-baked bulbs for a purée, 77; with pan-fried vegetables, 50; peeling a clove, 23; in *persillade,* 33; in *ratatouille,* 72; in stew, 72; for stir frying, 51

Ginger root, sliced, fried with vegetables, 50

Glaze (glazing): caramelized, 64-65; carrots, 64-65; clear, 64-65; vegetables for, 64; white onions, small, 64-65. *See also* Caramelizing

Grapevine leaves, 8, 9; availability, 8; stuffed, 68; stuffing for, 46

Gratin(s), 82-87; with added liquid, 82, 83; artichoke bottoms, sliced, 82, 83; baking dish for, 82; Belgian endive, braised, 74; with bread to conserve moisture, 83; bread crumbs for crust of, 82, 84, 86, 87; cauliflower with cheese sauce, 86; cheese custard sauce for, 86, 87; cream for crust of, 84, 85; eggplant, 82; eggplant with cheese custard, 86, 87; grated cheese for crust of, 82, 83, 84, 86; moistened with cream, 84-85; with moisture-rendering vegetables, 82; potatoes, sliced, 5, 84, 85; spinach, 82; Swiss chard, 82; Swiss chard ribs with white sauce, 86, 87; tomato, 82; turnips, grated, 84; vegetables for, *chart* 34-35; white sauce for, 86, 87; winter squash or pumpkin, 82, 83; zucchini, 82

Gratinéing, 74, 82

Greens, 9-10; availability and cooking methods, *chart* 34-35; boiling and steaming, *chart* 41. See also Leaf vegetables

Grilling, 75, 94; basting during, 94; preparing vegetables for, 94; vegetables for, *chart* 34-35; vegetables sealed in packages, 94

Herbs: blended with butter and frozen, 27; in braise, 61; dried, storage of, 28; for drying, 27-28; fresh, 26-27; fresh, preservation of, 27; frozen, 27; how to dry, 27; how to keep in refrigerator, 27; leafy, chopping of, 30; uses of, 26, 28. *See also* Bouquet garni; Fines herbes

Hollandaise, 42, 43

Hubbard squash, 18, 19; gratinéed, 83

Hyssop, 26

Jerusalem artichokes, 12, 13; availability and cooking methods, *chart* 34-35; boiling and steaming, *chart* 41; cleaning, 13; kept white after peeling, 13

Kale, 8, 9; availability and cooking methods, *chart* 34-35; boiling and steaming, *chart* 41

Kebabs, 93; vegetables for, 93

Kohlrabi, 5, 10; availability and cooking methods, *chart* 34-35; boiling, *chart* 41; cooking, 10

Lard, 57

Leaf vegetables, 8-9; availability, 8; preserving color, flavor and texture during cooking, 9

Leeks, 5, 22-23; availability and cooking methods, *chart* 34-35; boiling and steaming, *chart* 41; cooking, 23; gratinéed with cheese sauce, 86; parboiling, 72; splitting and washing, 23; wine for braising, 66

Lemon juice: in braise, 61; in marinade, 58; in pan-fried mixture of vegetables, 50; in sauce, 42, 43

Lettuce, 5, 8, 9; availability and cooking methods, *chart* 34-35; boiling and steaming, *chart* 41; butterhead, 8, *chart* 41; chiffonade, 30; steaming vegetables in leaves, 40; in stew, 60, 61, 72

Lovage, 26, 27

Marinade: *a seasoning mixture, usually liquid, in which food is steeped or with which food is coated before cooking. Most marinades are based on oil and a tenderizing but flavorful acid liquid such as vinegar, lemon juice or wine;* 26

Marinating: before deep frying, 58; for broiling, 92, 93

Marjoram: pot, 28; sweet, 28

Milk, in creamy gratins, 84, 85

Mint, 26, 27

Mirepoix, 33; in braise, 61, 62; how to cook, 33

Mirliton. See Chayotes

Mixed spices: *a mixture of spices and herbs —classically, equal proportions of nutmeg, mace,*

cinnamon, cayenne pepper, white pepper, cloves, ground bay leaf, thyme, marjoram and savory.

Morel: *an edible, wild mushroom, available dried at specialty markets.*

Mornay sauce, 86

Mung bean sprouts, 14. *See also* Bean sprouts

Mushroom(s), 6, 15; availability, 15, *chart* 34-35; with baked mixed vegetables, 80; broiled, 92; cooking methods, *chart* 34-35; deep fried in batter, 5, 58; extracting liquid from, 15; in fillings, 70, 71; frying, 50; how to make *duxelles,* 33; in pan-fried vegetable mixture, 50; soufflé, 90; steaming, *chart* 41; stuffed and baked, 78

Mustard greens, 8, 9; availability and cooking methods, *chart* 34-35; boiling and steaming, *chart* 41

Noisettes: how to make, 32

Oil(s): amount to use for deep frying, 57, 59; choice of, for deep frying, 57; for pan frying, 50; removing vegetables from, 57; in sauce, 42, 43; storage of, 57; testing heat of, for frying, 54, 55, 59

Okra, 16-17; availability and cooking methods, *chart* 34-35; boiling and steaming, *chart* 41; trimming, 17

Olive(s), black, 80, 81

Olive oil, 57; for baked artichokes, 79; with baked mixed vegetables, 80, 81; blended with puréed baked garlic, 77; for frying, 50; in gratins, 82, 83; in marinade, 58; as a sauce, 42; in sauce, 42

Olivettes: how to make, 32

Onion family, 22-23; availability, 22; cooking, 23

Onions, 6, 22-23, 52: availability and cooking methods, *chart* 34-35; with baked mixed vegetables, 80, 81; baked in skin, 76, 77; for boiling, 22; boiling and steaming, *chart* 41; brown-glazed, 64-65; in celery braise, 62; cooking, 23; in *duxelles,* 33; in gratin crust, 83; herbs used with, 26, 28; how to chop, 29; in *mirepoix,* 33; in mixed vegetable purée, 44-45; peeling without tears, 23; in *ratatouille,* 61, 72; scooping out, 70; rings, deep fried, 48; in sliced potato gratin, 84; small white, gratinéed, 84; small white, in stew, 60, 61, 72; in *sofrito,* 33; Spanish, 22; stuffed, baked, 78; stuffed, braised, 71; in stuffing, 46; in veal stock, 62; white-glazed, 64; yellow, 22

Oregano, 28

Paillasson (straw cake), 52-53

Pan frying, 49, 50-53; coated vegetable slices, 50, 51; combining quick frying with steaming, 52-53; cutting vegetables for, 50; garlic in, 50; green beans, 50; mixture of vegetables, 50; oils for, 50; parboiling before, 49, 50; potato pancakes, 52-53; potato straw cake *(paillasson),* 52-53; seasoned with *persillade,* 50; a

cities, *but usually found canned.*
Tuber(s), 12-13. *See also* Roots and tubers
Turnip(s), 5, 12-13; availability and cooking methods, *chart* 34-35; boiling and steaming, *chart* 41; gratinéed, 84; in mixed vegetable purée, 44-45; parboiled for braise, 62; removing moisture from, 84; shaped for garnish, 32; soufflé, 90; stir frying, 51
Turnip greens, 8, 9; availability and cooking methods, *chart* 34-35; boiling and steaming, *chart* 41
Veal, in stuffing, 46

Veal stock: in braise, 61, 62, 66; celery braised in, 62-63; for glazed onions, 64
Vegetable fruits, 16-17; availability, 16; shopping for, storing and preparing, 16-17
Velouté, 86
Vinaigrette, 42, 43; with puréed garlic, 77
Vine leaves. *See* Grapevine leaves
Vinegar: red wine, 43; in sauce, 42, 43
Water: acidulated, 13, 24, 25; amount of, for boiling and

steaming, 41
White sauce, 86; in cauliflower pudding, 88; in zucchini soufflé, 90
Wine(s): for baked artichokes, 79; in braise, 61, 70; red, in braised red cabbage, 66; types of, for braising, 66
Winter squashes, 18, 19; availability and cooking methods, *chart* 34-35; baked in skin, 76; boiling and steaming, *chart* 41; gratinéed, 82, 83; seeds of, sautéed for snack, 19
Wok, 51; stir frying in, 50, 51
Yams. *See* Sweet potatoes

Yellow crookneck(s), 18, 19
Zucchini, 5, 18, 19; availability and cooking methods, *chart* 34-35; baked, cut up, 80; boiling and steaming, *chart* 41; browned for braise, 62; cut for steaming, 40; deep fried in batter, 58; gratinéed, 82, 84; gratinéed with cheese custard, 86; grilled, 94; prepared for stuffing, 71; pudding, 88; in ratatouille, 61, 73; soufflé, 90; squeezing liquids from, 90; in stew, 72; stuffed, baked, 78; stuffed, braised, 70; wine for braising, 66. *See also* Summer squashes

Recipe Credits

The sources for the recipes in this volume are shown below. Page references in parentheses indicate where the recipes appear in the anthology.

Acton, Eliza, *Modern Cookery.* Published by Longman, Green, Longman, and Roberts, 1865(126).
Ainé, Offray, *Le Cuisinier Méridional.* Imprimeur-Libraire, 1855(117, 126).
Ali-Bab, *Encyclopedia of Practical Gastronomy.* Translated by Elizabeth Benson. English Translation. Copyright © 1974 by McGraw-Hill, Inc. Published by McGraw-Hill Book Company, New York. With permission of McGraw-Hill Book Co.(112, 126).
Anderson, Jean, *The Grass Roots Cookbook.* Copyright © 1977 by Jean Anderson. Published by Times Books. Reprinted by permission of Times Books, a Division of Quadrangle/The New York Times Book Co., Inc.(141).
Anderson, Jean, and Elaine Hanna, *The Doubleday Cookbook.* Copyright © 1975 by Doubleday & Company, Inc. Reprinted by permission of the publisher(140).
Aresty, Esther B., *The Delectable Past.* Copyright © 1964 by Esther B. Aresty. Published by Simon & Schuster, a Division of Gulf & Western Corporation. Reprinted by permission of Simon & Schuster, a Division of Gulf & Western Corporation(115, 162).
Bautte, A., *239 Manières d'Accommoder les Pommes de Terre.* Published by Librairie Bernardin-Bechet, Paris, 1932(120).
Beard, James, *James Beard's American Cookery.* Copyright © 1972 by James Beard. Published by Little, Brown and Company, Boston. By permission of Little, Brown and Company(119, 148).
Besson, Joséphine, *La Mère Besson "Ma cuisine provençale."* © Éditions Albin Michel, 1977. Published by Éditions Albin Michel, Paris. Translated by permission of Éditions Albin Michel(149).
Blanchard, Marjorie Page, *The Home Gardener's Cookbook.* Copyright 1974 by Garden Way Publishing Company, Charlotte, Vermont. Reprinted by permission of Writers House Inc.(132, 144).
Boni, Ada, *Italian Regional Cooking.* Copyright © 1969 s.c. by Arnoldo Mondadori. Published by Bonanza Books. By permission of Arnoldo Mondadori(133).
Boni, Ada, *The Talisman Italian Cook Book.* Copyright 1950, 1978 by Crown Publishers, Inc. Published by Crown Publishers, Inc., New York. Used by permission of Crown Publishers, Inc.(152).
Boxer, Arabella, *Nature's Harvest: The Vegetable Cook Book.* © 1974 by Arabella Boxer. Published by Contemporary Books, Inc., Chicago. By permission of Contemporary Books, Inc.(118).

Boyd, Lizzie, (Editor), *British Cookery.* Copyright © British Farm Produce Council and British Tourist Authority. Published by Croom Helm (London). By permission of British Farm Produce Council and British Tourist Authority(117, 118).
Breteuil, Jules, *Le Cuisinier Européen.* Published by Garnier Frères c. 1860(114, 136).
Buc'hoz, *Manuel Alimentaire des Plantes.* Published in 1771(135).
The Buckeye Cookbook. As published by the Buckeye Publishing Co. 1883. Published by Dover Publications Inc., New York 1975(108, 119, 132, 149).
Burros, Marian, *Pure and Simple.* Copyright © 1978 by Marian Fox Burros. Published by William Morrow & Company, Inc. Reprinted by permission of William Morrow & Company, Inc.(146).
Byron, May, *May Byron's Vegetable Book.* Published by Hodder & Stoughton Limited, London 1916. By permission of Hodder & Stoughton, Limited(122, 154).
Carlos, Don, *Spanish-Mexican Cookbook.* Published by Charles Parnell Leahy, 1951, Los Angeles, California(124).
Carnacina, Luigi, and Luigi Veronelli, *La Buona Vera Cucina Italiana.* © 1966 by Rizzoli Editore. Published by Rizzoli Editore, Milan. Translated by permission of Rizzoli Editore(98, 105, 141).
Caruana Galizia, Anne and Helen, *Recipes from Malta.* Copyright © Anne and Helen Caruana Galizia, 1972. Published by Progress Press Co. Ltd., Valetta. By permission of Anne and Helen Caruana Galizia(116, 128, 163).
Cavalera, Giovanni, and Odilla Marchesini, *La Cucina delle Stagioni.* © 1975, Longanesi & C. Published by Longanesi & C., Milan. Translated by permission of Longanesi & C.(101).
Chanot-Bullier, C., *Vieilles Recettes de Cuisine Provençale.* Published by Tacussel, Marseilles. Translated by permission of Tacussel, Éditeur(115, 157, 158).
Clarisse ou la Vieille Cuisinière. Copyright © 1922 by Éditions de l'Abeille d'Or. Published by Éditions de l'Abeille d'Or, Paris. Translated by permission of Éditions Rombaldi, Paris(130).
Conran, Terence, and Maria Kroll, *The Vegetable Book.* © Conran Ink 1976. Published by William Collins Sons & Co. Ltd., Glasgow and Crescent, New York (an imprint of Crown Publishers, Inc.). By permission of William Collins Sons & Co. Ltd.(154).
Cook to a Florentine Family, The, *Not Only Spaghetti!* Published by Libreria Editrice Fiorentina, Florence, Italy. By permission of Libreria Editrice Fiorentina(102, 111, 147).
Costa, Margaret, *Margaret Costa's Four Seasons Cookery Book.* Copyright © Margaret Costa. First published in Great Britain by Thomas Nelson & Sons Ltd., 1970, also by Sphere Books Ltd., London 1976. By permission of Margaret Costa(142).
Le Cuisinier Gascon—1740. Reprinted by Éditions Daniel Morcrette, B.P. 26,95270, Luzarches, France. Translated by permission of Éditions Daniel Morcrette(106,

157, 159).
Curnonsky, *Cuisine et Vins de France.* Copyright © 1953 by Augé Gillon, Hollier-Larousse, Moreau et Cie. (Librairie Larousse), Paris. Published by Librairie Larousse, Paris. Translated by permission of Société Encyclopédique Universelle(104, 110, 121, 154).
Cutler, Carol, *The Six-Minute Soufflé and Other Culinary Delights.* Copyright © 1976 by Carol Cutler. Published by Clarkson N. Potter, Inc. By permission of Clarkson N. Potter, Inc.(100, 129, 150).
Dannenbaum, Julie, *Julie Dannenbaum's Creative Cooking School.* Copyright © 1971 by Julie Dannenbaum. Published by E.P. Dutton, New York. By permission of E.P. Dutton(106, 141).
Dannenbaum, Julie, *Menus for All Occasions.* Copyright © 1974 by Julie Dannenbaum. Published by E.P. Dutton, New York. Reprinted by permission of E.P. Dutton(143).
David, Elizabeth, *French Country Cooking.* Copyright © Elizabeth David, 1951, 1958, 1966. Published by Penguin Books Ltd., London. By permission of Penguin Books Ltd.(138).
David, Elizabeth, *French Provincial Cooking.* Copyright © Elizabeth David, 1960, 1962, 1967, 1970. Published by Penguin Books Ltd., London. By permission of Elizabeth David(156).
David, Elizabeth, *Italian Food.* Copyright © Elizabeth David, 1954, 1963, 1969. Published by Penguin Books Ltd., London. By permission of Penguin Books Ltd.(159).
David, Elizabeth, *Spices, Salt and Aromatics in the English Kitchen.* Copyright © Elizabeth David, 1970. Published by Penguin Books Ltd., London. By permission of Penguin Books Ltd.(121).
Day, Irene F., *The Moroccan Cookbook.* Copyright © 1975 by Irene F. Day. Published by Quick Fox, a division of Music Sales Corporation. Reprinted by permission of Quick Fox(137).
de Aquino, Josefina Velilla, *Tembi'u Paraguai Comida Paraguaya.* Ediciones Primer Instituto de Arte Culinario, Asunción. Fourth Edition, published 1977(131).
de Croze, Austin, *Les Plats Régionaux de France.* Published by Éditions Daniel Morcrette, B.P. 26,95270, Luzarches, France. Translated by permission of Éditions Daniel Morcrette(107, 108, 118, 128).
De Gouy, Louis P., *The Gold Cook Book* (revised edition). Copyright 1948, 1964 by the author. Published by Chilton Book Company, Radnor, Pennsylvania. Reprinted with the permission of the publisher, Chilton Book Company(97, 105, 112, 127).
Derys, Gaston, *L'Art d'Être Gourmand.* Copyright by Albin Michel, 1929. Published by Éditions Albin Michel, Paris. Translated by permission of Éditions Albin Michel(153, 155).
Duff, Gail, *Fresh All The Year.* © Gail Duff, 1976. Published by Macmillan London Ltd., 1976. By permission of Macmillan London Ltd.(127).
Durand, Charles, *Le Cuisinier Durand.* Privately published by the author, 1843(151, 158).

Elkon, Juliette, *A Belgian Cookbook.* Copyright © 1958 by Farrar, Straus & Cudahy, Inc. (now Farrar, Straus & Giroux, Inc.). Reprinted with the permission of Farrar, Straus & Giroux, Inc.(124).

Eren, Neset, *The Art of Turkish Cooking.* Copyright © 1969 by Neset Eren. Published by Doubleday & Company, Inc., New York. Reprinted by permission of Neset Eren(147).

Escoffier, Auguste, *Ma Cuisine.* © English text 1965 by The Hamlyn Publishing Group Limited. Published by The Hamlyn Publishing Group Limited, London. By permission of The Hamlyn Publishing Group Limited(109, 142).

Evelyn, John, *Acetaria.* Privately published 1699(99).

Farmer, Fannie Merritt, *The Boston Cooking-School Cookbook,* (1924 Edition). Copyright 1896, 1900, 1901, 1902, 1903, 1904, 1905, 1906, 1912, 1914 by Fannie Farmer. Copyright 1915, 1918, 1923, 1924, 1928, 1929 by Cora D. Perkins. Copyright 1930, 1931, 1932, 1933, 1934, 1936, 1940, 1941, 1942, 1943, 1946, 1951, © 1959, 1964, 1965 by Dexter Perkins Corporation. Published by Little, Brown and Company, Boston. By permission of Little, Brown and Company(140).

Fitzgibbon, Theodora, *A Taste of Ireland.* Copyright © 1968 by Theodora Fitzgibbon. Published by Houghton Mifflin Company, Boston. Reprinted by permission of Houghton Mifflin Company(155).

Foods of the World, *American Cooking: The Great West, American Cooking: New England, The Cooking of Germany, The Cooking of Provincial France, The Cooking of Scandinavia.* Copyright © 1971 Time Inc., Copyright © 1970 Time Inc., Copyright © 1969 Time-Life Books Inc., Copyright © 1968 Time Inc., Copyright © 1968 Time-Life Books Inc.(162; 156; 96, 100, 120, 136; 110; 102, 122).

Fried, Barbara R., *The Four-Season Cookbook.* Copyright © Macmillan Publishing Co., Inc., 1961. Reprinted with permission of Macmillan Publishing Co., Inc.(133).

Garlin, *Le Cuisinier Modern.* Published in 1887(104).

Giniés, Louis, *La Cuisine Provençale.* Published by UNIDE, Paris, 1976. Translated by permission of UNIDE(138, 165).

Gould-Marks, Beryl, *The Home Book of Italian Cookery.* © Beryl Gould-Marks, 1969. Published by Faber & Faber, London. By permission of Faber & Faber(105, 137).

Grigson, Jane, *Good Things.* Copyright © 1968, 1969, 1970, 1971 by Jane Grigson, Copyright © 1971 by Alfred A. Knopf. Reprinted by permission of Alfred A. Knopf(116, 149).

Grossinger, Jennie, *The Art of Jewish Cooking.* Copyright © 1958 by Random House, Inc. Published by Random House, Inc. Reprinted by permission of Random House, Inc.(122).

Guérard, Michel, *Michel Guérard's Cuisine Minceur.* English translation copyright © 1976 by Éditions Robert Laffont S.A. By permission of William Morrow & Company, Inc.(164).

Guillot, André, *La Grande Cuisine Bourgeoise.* © 1976, Flammarion, Paris. Published by Flammarion et Cie. Translated by permission of Flammarion et Cie.(100).

Harrington, Geri, *Summer Garden, Winter Kitchen.* Copyright © 1976 Geri Harrington. Published by Atheneum Publishers. Used by permission of Atheneum Publishers(99).

Hartley, Dorothy, *Food in England.* Published by Macdonald & Jane's, London, 1975. By permission of Macdonald & Jane's(155, 161).

Harwood, Jim, and Ed Callahan, *Soul Food Cookbook.* Copyright © 1969 by Nitty Gritty Productions, Concord, California. All rights reserved. Published by Nitty Gritty Productions. Used by permission of Nitty Gritty Productions(124).

Hawkes, Alex D., *Cooking With Vegetables.* Copyright © 1968 by Alex D. Hawkes. Published by Simon & Schuster, a Division of Gulf & Western Corporation. Reprinted by permission of Simon & Schuster, a Division of Gulf & Western Corporation(134, 145).

Hazelton, Nika, *The Unabridged Vegetable Cookbook.* Copyright © 1976 by Nika Hazelton. Published by M. Evans and Company, Inc., New York. Reprinted by permission of M. Evans and Company, Inc., New York(125, 144, 146).

Hazelton, Nika Standen, *The Regional Italian Kitchen.* Copyright © 1978 by Nika Standen Hazelton. Published by M. Evans and Company, Inc., New York. Translated by permission of M. Evans and Company, Inc.(114).

Hewitt, Jean, *The New York Times Natural Foods Cookbook.* Copyright © 1974 by Jean Hewitt. Published by Avon Books. By permission of Quadrangle/The New York Times Book Co., Inc.(123, 128, 143).

Heyraud, H., *La Cuisine à Nice.* Published by Imprimerie-Librairie-Papeterie, Nice, 1922(142).

Hibben, Sheila, *American Regional Cookery.* Copyright © 1932, 1946, by Sheila Hibben. Published by Little, Brown and Company, Boston. By permission of McIntosh and Otis, Inc.(150).

Holkar, Shivaji Rao and Shalini Devi, *The Cooking of the Maharajas.* Copyright © 1975 by Shivaji Rao and Shalini Devi Holkar. Published by The Viking Press, New York. By permission of The Viking Press, Inc.(111, 161).

Housewright, Mrs. L. V., *The Great Green Chili Cooking Classic.* Edited by Lynn B. Villella and Patricia Gins © The Albuquerque Tribune. Reprinted by permission of The Albuquerque Tribune(98).

Howe, Robin, *Greek Cooking.* © Robin Howe 1960. Published by André Deutsch Limited, London. By permission of André Deutsch Limited(163).

Jans, Hugh, *Vrij Nederlands Kookboek.* © Unieboek/C. A. J. van Dishoeck, Bussum. Published by Unieboek/C. A. J. van Dishoeck, Bussum. Translated by permission of Unieboek B.V.(116, 156).

Jouveau, René, *La Cuisine Provençale.* Copyright © Bouquet & Baumgartner, Flamatt, Switzerland. Published by Éditions du Message, 1962, Berne. Translated by permission of Bouquet & Baumgartner(103, 145).

Junior League of Dallas, The, *The Dallas Junior League Cookbook.* Copyright © 1976 The Junior League of Dallas, Inc. Published by The Junior League of Dallas, Inc. By permission of The Junior League of Dallas(155).

Junior League of New Orleans, The, *The Plantation Cookbook.* Copyright © 1972 by The Junior League of New Orleans, Inc. Published by Doubleday & Company, Inc., New York. Reprinted by permission of Doubleday & Company, Inc.(132).

Junior League of Pasadena, The, *The California Heritage Cookbook.* Copyright © 1976 by The Junior League of Pasadena, Inc. Published by Doubleday & Company, Inc. Used by permission of Doubleday & Company, Inc.(104).

Junior League of Pine Bluff, The, *Southern Accent.* Copyright © 1976 by The Junior League of Pine Bluff, Inc. Published by The Junior League of Pine Bluff, Inc. By permission of The Junior League of Pine Bluff, Arkansas, Inc.(164).

Junior League of Winston-Salem, The, *Winston-Salem's Heritage of Hospitality.* Copyright © 1975 by The Junior League of Winston-Salem. Published by The Junior League of Winston-Salem. Translated by permission of The Junior League of Winston-Salem(150).

Kamman, Madeleine M., *When French Women Cook.* Copyright © 1976 by Madeleine M. Kamman. Published by Atheneum Publishers, New York. Reprinted by permission of Atheneum Publishers(113).

Kennedy, Diana, *The Cuisines of Mexico.* Copyright © 1972 by Diana Kennedy. Published by Harper & Row, Publishers, Inc. Reprinted by permission of Harper & Row, Publishers, Inc.(146).

Kiehnle, Hermine, and Maria Hädecke, *Das neue Kiehnle Kochbuch.* © Walter Hädecke Verlag. Published by Walter Hädecke Verlag. (D-7252 Weil der Stadt.) Translated by permission of Walter Hädecke Verlag(115, 125).

Krapotkin, Alexandra, *The Best of Russian Cooking.* Copyright © 1964 by Alexandra Krapotkin. Published by Charles Scribner's Sons. Reprinted by permission of Charles Scribner's Sons(113, 120).

Labarre, Irene, *La Cuisine des Trois B.* © Solar, 1976. Published by Solar, Paris. Translated by permission of Solar(153).

Lamb, Venice, *The Home Book of Turkish Cookery.* © Venice Lamb 1969, 1973. Published by Faber & Faber, Ltd., London. By permission of Faber & Faber Ltd.(114, 154, 162).

Larousse Treasury of Country Cooking. © Copyright Librairie Larousse, 1968, 1975. English Translation © Vineyard Books, Inc., 1975. Published by Crown Publishers, Inc., New York. By permission of Crown Publishers, Inc., New York(131).

L'Escole Parfaites des Officiers de Bouche. Anonymous. Published by Jean Ribou, 1662(149).

Lin, Florence, *Florence Lin's Chinese Regional Cookbook.* Copyright © 1975 by Florence Lin. Published by Hawthorn Books, Inc. Used by permission of Hawthorn Books, Inc.(105).

McNeill, F. Marian, *The Scots Kitchen.* Published by Blackie & Son Limited, London. Reprinted by permission of Blackie & Son Limited(160).

Magyar, Elek, *Kochbuch für Feinschmecker.* Printed in Hungary, 1967. Published by Corvina Kiado, Budapest. Translated by permission of Dr. Balint Magyar and Dr. Pal Magyar(113, 119).

Marton, Beryl M., *Out of the Garden into the Kitchen.* Copyright © 1977 Beryl M. Marton. Published by David McKay Co., Inc. By permission of David McKay Co., Inc.(112, 131, 132, 144).

Mathiot, Ginette, *A Table avec Edouard de Pomiane.* © Éditions Albin Michel, 1975. Published by Éditions Albin Michel, Paris. Translated by permission of Éditions Albin Michel(119).

Médecin, Jacques, *La Cuisine du Comté de Nice.* © Juillard, 1972. Published by Penguin Books Ltd., London. Translated by permission of Penguin Books Ltd.(102, 130, 150).

Menon, *La Cuisinière Bourgeoise.* 1745(134).

Mercier, Jean, and Irene Labarre, *La Cuisine du Poitou et de la Vendée.* © Solar. Published by Solar, Paris. Translated by permission of Solar(101, 113, 134).

Merigot, *La Cuisinière Républicaine.* 1782(117).

Montagné, Prosper, *The New Larousse Gastronomique.* English translation © 1977 by Hamlyn Publishing Group Limited. Published by Crown Publishers, Inc. By permission of Crown Publishers, Inc.(107).

Montagné, Prosper, and A. Gottschalk, *Mon Menu — Guide d'Hygiène Alimentaire.* Published by Société d'Applications Scientifiques, Paris(115, 122).

Moore-Betty, Maurice, *Cooking for Occasions.* Copyright © 1970 by Maurice Moore-Betty. Published by David White, Inc. Reprinted by permission of David White, Inc.(102, 143).

Moyer, Anne, *The Green Thumb Cookbook.* © 1977 by Rodale Press. Published by Rodale Press. Used by permission of Rodale Press, Inc., Emmaus, Pennsylvania(99).

Muffoletto, Anna, *The Art of Sicilian Cooking.* Copyright © 1971 by Anna Muffoletto. Published by Doubleday & Company, Inc., New York. By permission of Doubleday & Company, Inc.(135, 139).

Nignon, Edouard, *Les Plaisirs de la Table.* Published by author c. 1920. Translated by permission of Daniel Morcrette, B.P. 26,95270, Luzarches, France(103).

Oliver, Raymond, *La Cuisine — sa technique, ses secrets.* Published by Éditions Bordas, Paris. Translated by permission of Leon Amiel Publishers, New York(118).

Olney, Judith, *Summer Food.* Copyright © 1978 by Judith Olney. Published by Atheneum Publishers, New York. By permission of Atheneum Publishers(97, 127, 160).

Olney, Richard, *Simple French Food.* Copyright © 1974 by Richard Olney. Published by Atheneum Publishers, New York. By permission of Atheneum and A. M. Heath & Company, Author's Agents(137, 148, 152, 164).

Orga, Irfan, *Cooking with Yogurt.* First published 1956 by André Deutsch Limited, London. By permission of André Deutsch Limited(106, 139, 151).

Ortiz, Elisabeth Lambert, *The Complete Book of Caribbean Cooking.* Copyright © Elisabeth Lambert Ortiz, 1973, 1975. Published by M. Evans and Company, Inc. By permission of John Farquharson Limited(140, 144).

Owen, Sri, *The Home Book of Indonesian Cookery.* © Sri Owen, 1976. Published by Faber & Faber Ltd., London. By permission of Faber & Faber Ltd.(160).

Paddleford, Clementine, *The Best in American Cook-*

ing. Copyright © 1970 Chase Manhattan Bank, executors of the Estate of Clementine Paddleford. Published by Charles Scribner's Sons. Reprinted by permission of Charles Scribner's Sons(123, 125).
Palay, Simin, *La Cuisine du Pays.* © 1970 Marrimpouey Jeune-Pau. Published by Éditions Marrimpouey Jeune et Cie. Translated by permission of Éditions Marrimpouey Jeune et Cie.(123).
Pearl, Mary, *Vermont Maple Recipes.* Published by Mary Pearl. Used by permission of Mary Pearl(124).
Peck, Paula, *Paula Peck's Art of Good Cooking.* © 1966 by Paula Peck. Published by Simon & Schuster, a Division of Gulf & Western Corporation. By permission of Simon & Schuster(135).
Penton, Anne-Marie, *Customs and Cookery in the Périgord and Quercy.* © Anne-Marie Penton 1973. Published by David and Charles (Holdings) Limited, Newton Abbot. By permission of Anne-Marie Penton(129, 146).
Petits Propos Culinaires, © 1979 by Prospect Books. Published by Prospect Books, Washington, D.C. By permission of Prospect Books(138).
Philippon, Henri, *Cuisine de Provence.* © Éditions Albin Michel, 1977. Published by Éditions Albin Michel, Paris. Translated by permission of Éditions Albin Michel(152).
Point, Fernard, *Ma Gastronomie.* © Flammarion. English Language edition © 1974, Lyceum Books, Inc. Published by Lyceum Books, Inc., Wilton, Connecticut. By permission of Lyceum Books(121).
Quillet, Aristide, *La Cuisine Moderne.* Copyright Libraire Aristide Quillet, 1946. Published by Libraire Aristide Quillet. Translated by permission of Libraire Aristide Quillet(128).
Reboul, J. B., *La Cuisinière Provençale.* Published by Tacussel, Marseilles. Translated by permission of Tacussel, Éditeur(158).
Ross, Janet, and Michael Waterfield, *Leaves from our Tuscan Kitchen.* © Michael Waterfield, 1973. Published by Atheneum Publishers, New York. By permission of Atheneum Publishers(96, 134, 147, 153).

Rundell, Mrs. Maria, *Domestic Cookery.* 1837 Edition(103).
Saint-Ange, Madame, *La Bonne Cuisine de Madame Saint-Ange.* Copyright 1929 by Augé, Gillon, Hollier-Larousse, Moreau et Cie. (Librairie Larousse), Paris. Published by Librairie Larousse, Paris. Translated by permission of Éditions Chaix(96, 114).
Schwartz, Florence, (Editor), *Vegetable Cooking of All Nations.* © 1973 by Crown Publishers, Inc. Published by Crown Publishers, Inc. Used by permission of Crown Publishers, Inc.(133).
Seddon, George, and Helena Radecka, *Your Kitchen Garden.* © Michael Beazley Publishers Limited, 1975. Published by Doubleday & Company, Inc., New York. By permission of Michael Beazley Publishers, Limited(108, 151, 157).
Serra, Victoria, translated by Elizabeth Gili, *Tia Victoria's Spanish Kitchen.* Text Copyright © Elizabeth Gili, 1963. Published by Kaye & Ward Ltd., London. By permission of Kaye & Ward Ltd. and Elizabeth Gili(111, 123).
Singh, Dharamjit, *Indian Cookery.* © Dharamjit Singh, 1970. Published by Penguin Books Ltd., London. By permission of Penguin Books Ltd.(109, 130).
Stone, Marie, *The Covent Garden Cookbook.* Copyright © 1974 by Marie Stone. Published by Allison & Busby, Limited, London. Reprinted by permission of Allison & Busby Limited(96, 133).
Stubbs, Joyce M., *The Home Book of Greek Cookery.* © 1963 Joyce M. Stubbs. Published by Faber & Faber, London. By permission of Faber & Faber(101).
Taber, Gladys, *My Own Cook Book: From Stillmeadow and Cape Cod.* Copyright © 1972 by Gladys Taber. Published by J. B. Lippincott Company. Reprinted by permission of J. B. Lippincott Company(121).
Troisgros, Jean and Pierre, *The Nouvelle Cuisine of Jean & Pierre Troisgros.* Copyright © 1978 in the English translation by William Morrow & Company, Inc. Originally published under the title of *Cuisiniers à Roanne,* copyright © 1977 by Éditions Robert Laffont S. A. By permission of William Morrow & Company, Inc.(159).

Turgeon, Charlotte, *Of Cabbages and Kings Cookbook.* © 1977 The Curtis Publishing Company. Published by The Curtis Publishing Company. Reprinted by permission of The Curtis Publishing Company(98).
Ungerer, Miriam, *Good Cheap Food.* Copyright © 1966 by Miriam Ungerer. Published by The Viking Press, Inc. By permission of The Viking Press(107, 141).
Uvezian, Sonia, *The Best Foods of Russia.* Copyright © 1976 by Sonia Uvezian. Published by Harcourt Brace Jovanovich, Inc., New York. Reprinted by permission of Harcourt Brace Jovanovich, Inc.(117, 129).
Uvezian, Sonia, *The Book of Yogurt.* Copyright © 1978 by Sonia Uvezian. Published by 101 Productions. Reprinted by permission of 101 Productions(145).
Voltz, Jeanne A., *The Flavor of the South.* Copyright © 1977 by Jeanne A. Voltz. Reprinted by permission of Doubleday & Company, Inc.(131).
Wason, Betty, *The Art of German Cooking.* © 1967 by Elizabeth Wason Hall. Published by Doubleday & Company, Inc., New York. Used by permission of Doubleday & Company, Inc.(130).
White, Mrs. Peter A., *The Kentucky Housewife.* 1885, Bellford, Clarke and Company, Chicago and New York(116, 124).
Widenfelt, Sam, (Editor), *Swedish Food.* Published by Wezäta Förlag, Sweden. Translated by permission of Wezäta Förlag(109).
Willinsky, Grete, *Kochbuch der Büchergilde.* © Büchergilde Gutenberg, Frankfurt am Main. Published by Büchergilde Gutenberg. Translated by permission of Büchergilde Gutenberg(136).
Wilson, Mrs. W. H., and Miss Mollie Huggins, *Good Things to Eat.* Published by the Publishing House of the M. E. Church, South, Nashville, Tennessee, 1909(135).
Wolfert, Paula, *Mediterranean Cooking.* Copyright © 1977 by Paula Wolfert. Published by Quadrangle/The New York Times Book Co., Inc., New York. By permission of Paula Wolfert and Quadrangle/The New York Times Book Co., Inc.(142).

Acknowledgments

The indexes for this book were prepared by Anita R. Beckerman. The editors are particularly indebted to Pat Alburey, Hertfordshire, England; Elaine Asp, Department of Food Science and Nutrition, University of Minnesota, St. Paul; Jeremiah Tower, Berkeley, California; and Dr. Ronald Smith, Aberdeen, Scotland.

The editors also wish to thank: Dr. Victor R. Boswell, Hyattsville, Maryland; California Table Grape Commission, Fresno; Karen Caplan, Frieda's Finest Produce Specialties, Inc., Los Angeles, California; Dr. Clyde M. Christianson, Department of Horticulture, University of Minnesota, St. Paul; R. C. Coates, London; Dr. O. B. Combs, Department of Horticulture, University of Wisconsin, Madison; Sue Crowther, London; Audrey Ellison, London; Mary S. Goddard, Nutrient Data Research Group, Hyattsville, Maryland; Diana Grant, London; Victoria Hainworth, Dumfriesshire, Scotland; Maggie Heinz, London; Les Hubbard, Western Growers Association, Newport Beach, California; Marion Hunter, Surrey, England; Brenda Jayes, London; Dr. Janet Johnson, Department of Horticulture, Virginia Polytechnic Institute and State University, Blacksburg; Dr. W. Raymond Kays, Department of Horticulture, University of Oklahoma, Stillwater; Dr. Stanley Kays, Department of Horticulture, University of Georgia, Athens; John Leslie, London; Frank J. McNeil, Standardization Branch, U.S. Department of Agriculture, Washington, D.C.; National Vegetable Research Station, London; Professor Jean A. Phillips, Department of Human Nutrition and Foods, Virginia Polytechnic Institute and State University, Blacksburg; José Sanchez, Manuel Rodriguez, Ivano Greengrocers, London; Nicole Segré, London; Mr. Lloyd Stolich, California Artichoke Advisory Board, Castroville; Marguerite Tarrant, London; Liz Timothy, London; J. M. Turnell & Co., New Covent Garden, England; Eileen Turner, London; United Fresh Fruits and Vegetable Association, Alexandria, Virginia; Hilary Walden, London; Robert A. Wearne, Eugene, Oregon; Dr. Raymond E. Webb, Dr. James P. San Antonio, Vegetable Laboratory, Beltsville Agricultural Research Center, U.S. Department of Agriculture, Beltsville, Maryland.

Picture Credits

The sources for the pictures in this book are listed below. Credits for each of the photographers and illustrators are listed by page number in sequence with successive pages indicated by hyphens; where necessary, the locations of pictures within pages are also indicated — separated from page numbers by dashes.

Photographs by Alan Duns: cover, 4, 9—left and center, 13—top right, bottom left and center, 15—bottom left, 17—bottom, 21—bottom, 23—top right and bottom, 25—center and bottom, 36, 43—top and center, 46-47, 50, 52—top, 53—top and right, 55-60, 62-63—bottom, 64-65—top, 68—top and bottom center, 69—top, 70-74, 77—top, 79-82, 83—bottom, 84-89.
Photographs by Aldo Tutino: 11—bottom, 13—bottom right, 17—top center and right, 19—top, 24, 29-33, 39-40, 51, 52—bottom, 53—bottom left, 66, 76, 78, 83—top, 92-94.
Photographs by Tom Belshaw: 9—right, 13—top left and center, 17—top left, 21—top and center, 27—bottom, 38, 42, 43—bottom, 44-45, 48, 54, 64-65—bottom, bottom left, 69—bottom, 77—bottom.
Other photographs (alphabetically): Bob Cramp, 62-63—top, 68—bottom right, 90-91. Paul Kemp, 23—top left and center. Roger Phillips, 15—bottom center and right, 67.
Illustrations (alphabetically): Mary Evans Picture Library and private sources, 97-164. Basil Smith, 26-27—top, 28. Whole Hog Studios, Atlanta, Georgia, 8, 10-11—top, 12, 14, 15—top, 16, 18-19—bottom, 20, 22, 25—top.

Library of Congress Cataloguing in Publication Data
Time-Life Books.
Vegetables.
(The Good cook, techniques and recipes)
Includes index.
1. Cookery (Vegetables) I. Title. II. Series.
TX801.T55   1979   641.6′5   78-26177
ISBN 0-8094-2860-1
ISBN 0-8094-2859-8 lib. bdg.
ISBN 0-8094-2858-X retail ed.